THE BOOK OF RUBY

THE BOOK OF™ RUBY

A Hands-On Guide for the Adventurous

by Huw Collingbourne

no starch press

San Francisco

THE BOOK OF RUBY. Copyright © 2011 by Huw Collingbourne

Printed in Canada

15 14 13 12 11   1 2 3 4 5 6 7 8 9

ISBN-10: 1-59327-294-4
ISBN-13: 978-1-59327-294-4

Publisher: William Pollock
Production Editor: Serena Yang
Developmental Editor: Keith Fancher
Technical Reviewer: Pat Eyler
Copyeditor: Kim Wimpsett
Compositors: Serena Yang and Alison Law
Proofreader: Ward Webber

For information on book distributors or translations, please contact No Starch Press, Inc. directly:

No Starch Press, Inc.
38 Ringold Street, San Francisco, CA 94103
phone: 415.863.9900; fax: 415.863.9950; info@nostarch.com; www.nostarch.com

Library of Congress Cataloging-in-Publication Data

Collingbourne, Huw.
  The book of Ruby : a hands-on guide for the adventurous / Huw Collingbourne.
       p. cm.
  Includes index.
  ISBN-13: 978-1-59327-294-4
  ISBN-10: 1-59327-294-4
  1. Ruby (Computer program language) 2. Object-oriented programming (Computer science) I. Title.
  QA76.73.R83C65 2011
  005.1'17--dc23

                                    2011014782

BRIEF CONTENTS

CONTENTS IN DETAIL

3
STRINGS AND RANGES

33

4
ARRAYS AND HASHES

47

5
LOOPS AND ITERATORS

67

6
CONDITIONAL STATEMENTS   83

7
METHODS   97

8
PASSING ARGUMENTS AND RETURNING VALUES   121

9
EXCEPTION HANDLING
139

10
BLOCKS, PROCS, AND LAMBDAS
155

19
RUBY ON RAILS   299

20
DYNAMIC PROGRAMMING   325

A
DOCUMENTING RUBY WITH RDOC   345

ACKNOWLEDGMENTS

I'd like to express my appreciation of all the hard work that's gone into the preparation of this book by the people at No Starch Press, especially Keith Fancher, Serena Yang, and Bill Pollock. Thanks also to the copyeditor, Kim Wimpsett, and to the technical reviewer, Pat Eyler. For keeping me on the right side of sanity, I owe a debt of gratitude to my two dogs, Beryl and Seven, and to their beautiful mother, Bethan, who, to my enormous sadness, died while I was writing this book.

INTRODUCTION

As you are now reading a book on Ruby, I think it is safe to assume you don't need me to persuade you of the merits of the Ruby language. Instead, I'll take the somewhat unconventional step of starting with a warning: Many people are attracted to Ruby by its simple syntax and its ease of use. They are wrong. Ruby's syntax may *look* simple at first sight, but the more you get to know the language, the more you will realize that it is, on the contrary, extremely complex. The plain fact of the matter is that Ruby has a number of pitfalls just waiting for unwary programmers to drop into.

In this book, it is my aim to guide you safely over the pitfalls and lead you through the choppy waters of Ruby's syntax and class libraries. In the process, I'll be exploring both the smooth, well-paved highways and the gnarlier, bumpy little byways of Ruby. By the end of the journey, you should be able to use Ruby safely and effectively without getting caught by unexpected hazards along the way.

The Book of Ruby describes versions 1.8.*x* and 1.9.*x* of the Ruby language. In most respects, Ruby 1.8 and 1.9 are very similar, and most programs written for one version will run unmodified in the other. There are important exceptions to this rule, however, and these are noted in the text. Ruby 1.9 may be regarded as a stepping stone toward Ruby 2.0. At the time of writing, a release date for Ruby 2.0 has not been announced. Even so, on the basis of currently available information, I anticipate that most (or all) of the information on Ruby 1.9 in this book should also apply to Ruby 2.0.

What Is Ruby?

Ruby is a cross-platform interpreted language that has many features in common with other "scripting" languages such as Perl and Python. It has an easily readable type of syntax that looks somewhat Pascal-like at first sight. It is thoroughly object-oriented and has a good deal in common with the great-granddaddy of "pure" object-oriented languages, Smalltalk. It has been said that the languages that most influenced the development of Ruby were Perl, Smalltalk, Eiffel, Ada, and Lisp. The Ruby language was created by Yukihiro Matsumoto (commonly known as Matz), and it was first released in 1995.

What Is Rails?

Over the past few years, much of the excitement surrounding Ruby can be attributed to a web development framework called Rails—popularly known as *Ruby on Rails*. Rails is an impressive framework, but it is not the be-all, end-all of Ruby. Indeed, if you were to leap right into Rails development without first mastering Ruby, you might find that you end up creating applications that you don't even understand. (This is all too common among Ruby on Rails novices.) Understanding Ruby is a necessary prerequisite for understanding Rails. You'll look at Rails in Chapter 19.

Matters of Ruby Style

Some Ruby programmers have very fixed—or even obsessive—views on what constitutes a "Ruby style" of programming. Some, for example, are passionately wedded to the idea that `method_names_use_underscores` while `variableNamesDoNot`. The style of naming in which separate words are indicated by capital letters `likeThis` is called *camel case*—and that is the last time it will be mentioned in this book.

I have never understood why people get so worked up about naming conventions. You like underscores, I can't stand them; you say po_ta_toes, I say poTaToes. As far as I am concerned, the way in which you choose to write the names of identifiers in Ruby is of no interest to anyone but you or your programming colleagues.

That is not to say that I have no opinions on programming style. On the contrary, I have very strong opinions. In my view, good programming style has nothing to do with naming conventions and everything to do with good code structure and clarity. Language elements such as parentheses, for instance, are important. Parentheses clarify code and avoid ambiguity that, in a highly dynamic language such as Ruby, can mean the difference between a program that works as you expect and one that is full of surprises (also known as *bugs*). For more on this, refer to the index entries on "ambiguity" and "parentheses."

In more than two decades of programming, one thing I have learned through bitter experience is that the most important characteristics of well-written code are clarity and lack of ambiguity. Code that is easy to understand and easy to debug is also likely to be easier to *maintain*. If adopting certain naming conventions helps you achieve that goal, that's fine. If not, that's fine too. *The Book of Ruby* does not preach on matters of style.

How to Read This Book

The book is divided into bite-sized chunks. Each chapter introduces a theme that is subdivided into subtopics. Each programming topic is accompanied by one or more small, self-contained, ready-to-run Ruby programs.

If you want to follow a well-structured "course," read each chapter in sequence. If you prefer a more hands-on approach, you can run the programs first and refer to the text when you need an explanation. If you already have some experience with Ruby, feel free to cherry-pick topics in any order you find useful. There are no monolithic applications in this book, so you don't have to worry you might lose the plot if you read the chapters out of order!

Digging Deeper

Every chapter, apart from the first one, includes a section called "Digging Deeper." This is where you will explore specific aspects of Ruby (including a few of those gnarly byways I mentioned a moment ago) in greater depth. In many cases, you could skip the "Digging Deeper" sections and still learn all the Ruby you will ever need. On the other hand, it is in these sections that you will often get closest to the inner workings of Ruby, so if you skip them, you are going to miss out on some pretty interesting stuff.

Making Sense of the Text

In *The Book of Ruby*, Ruby source code is written like this:

```
def saysomething
    puts( "Hello" )
end
```

Often the code will be annotated with *comments*. Ruby comments are any text following a hash mark (#) on a single line. The comments are ignored by the Ruby interpreter. When I want to draw attention to some output that Ruby displays or to a value returned by a piece of code (even if that value is not displayed), I indicate this with this type of comment: # =>. Occasionally, when I want to draw attention to some input that the user should enter, I use this type of comment: # <=. Here is an example to illustrate these commenting conventions:

```
puts("Enter a calculation:" ) # Prompt user        this is a simple comment
exp = gets().chomp()          # <= Enter 2*4     comment shows data to enter
puts( eval( exp ))            # => 8      comment shows result of evaluation
```

When a piece of code returns or displays too much data to be shown in a single-line comment, the output may be shown like this:

```
This is the data returned from method #1
This is the data returned from method #2
This is the data returned from method #3
```

helloname.rb   When a sample program accompanies the code, the program name is shown in the margin as it is here.

Explanatory notes that provide hints or extra information are shown like this:

NOTE   *This is an explanatory note.*

More in-depth explanation of points mentioned in the text may be shown in a box like this:

FURTHER EXPLANATION

This is some additional information. You can skip it if you like—but if you do, you may miss something interesting!

Downloading Ruby

You can download the latest version of Ruby at *http://www.ruby-lang.org/en/ downloads/*. Be sure to download the binaries (not merely the source code). Windows users have the option of installing Ruby using the Ruby Installer, available at *http://www.rubyinstaller.org/*. There are also several alternative implementations of Ruby, the most established of which is JRuby. You can find information on where to download these implementations in Appendix D.

Getting the Source Code of the Sample Programs

All the programs in every chapter in this book are available for download as a *.zip* archive at *http://www.nostarch.com/boruby.htm*.

When you unzip the programs, you will find that they are grouped into a set of directories—one for each chapter.

Running Ruby Programs

It is often useful to keep a command window open in the source directory containing your Ruby program files. Assuming that the Ruby interpreter is correctly pathed on your system, you will then be able to run programs by entering ruby *programname*. For example, this is the command you would enter in order to run the *helloworld.rb* program:

```
ruby helloworld.rb
```

If you use a Ruby IDE, you may be able to load the Ruby programs into the IDE and run them using the integrated tools of that IDE.

The Ruby Library Documentation

The Book of Ruby covers many of the classes and methods in the standard Ruby library—but by no means all of them! At some stage, therefore, you will need to refer to documentation on the full range of classes used by Ruby. Fortunately, the Ruby class library contains embedded documentation that has been extracted and compiled into an easily browsable reference, which is available in several formats. For example, you can find the online documentation for Ruby 1.9 at *http://www.ruby-doc.org/ruby-1.9/index.html*. For Ruby 1.8, go to *http://www.ruby-doc.org/ruby-1.8/index.html*.

Okay, that's enough of the preamble—let's get down to work.

1

STRINGS, NUMBERS, CLASSES, AND OBJECTS

The first thing to know about Ruby is that it's easy to use. To prove this, let's look at the code of the traditional "Hello world" program:

```
puts 'hello world'
```

That's it in its entirety. The program contains one method, puts, and one string, "hello world." It doesn't have any headers or class definitions, and it doesn't have any import sections or "main" functions. This really is as simple as it gets. Load the code, *1helloworld.rb*, and try it.

Getting and Putting Input

Having "put" a string to the output (here, a command window), the obvious next step is to "get" a string. As you might guess, the Ruby method for this is gets. The *2helloname.rb* program prompts the user for his or her name—let's suppose it's Fred—and then displays a greeting: "Hello Fred." Here is the code:

2helloname.rb

```
print( 'Enter your name: ' )
name = gets()
puts( "Hello #{name}" )
```

Although this is still very simple, a few important details need to be explained. First, notice that I've used print rather than puts to display the prompt. This is because puts adds a line feed at the end of the printed string, whereas print does not; in this case, I want the cursor to remain on the same line as the prompt.

On the next line, I use gets() to read in a string when the user presses ENTER. This string is assigned to the variable name. I have not predeclared this variable, nor have I specified its type. In Ruby, you can create variables as and when you need them, and the interpreter "infers" their types. In the example, I have assigned a string to name so Ruby knows that the type of the name variable must be a string.

NOTE   *Ruby is case sensitive. A variable called myvar is different from one called myVar. A variable such as name in the sample project must begin with a lowercase character. If it begins with an uppercase character, Ruby will treat it as a constant. I'll have more to say on constants in Chapter 6.*

Incidentally, the parentheses following gets() are optional, as are the parentheses enclosing the strings after print and puts; the code would run just the same if you removed them. However, parentheses can help resolve ambiguities, and in some cases, the interpreter will warn you if you omit them.

Strings and Embedded Evaluation

The last line in the sample code is rather interesting:

```
puts( "Hello #{name}" )
```

Here the name variable is embedded into the string. You do this by placing the variable between two curly brackets preceded by a *hash mark* (or "number" or "pound" character), as in #{}. This kind of *embedded* evaluation works only with strings delimited by double quotes. If you were to try this with a string delimited by single quotes, the variable would not be evaluated, and the string 'Hello #{name}' would be displayed exactly as entered.

You can also embed nonprinting characters such as newlines ("\n") and tabs ("\t"), and you can even embed bits of program code and mathematical expressions. For instance, let's assume you have a method called showname that returns the string "Fred." The following string would, in the process of evaluation, call the showname method and display "Hello Fred":

```
puts "Hello #{showname}"
```

See whether you can figure out what would be displayed by the following:

3string_eval.rb

```
puts( "\n\t#{(1 + 2) * 3}\nGoodbye" )
```

Now run the *3string_eval.rb* program to see whether you are right.

Numbers

Numbers are just as easy to use as strings. For example, let's suppose you want to calculate the selling price or grand total of some item based on its pretax value or subtotal. To do this, you would need to multiply the subtotal by the applicable tax rate and add the result to the value of the subtotal. Assuming the subtotal to be $100 and the tax rate to be 17.5 percent, this Ruby program does the calculation and displays the result:

4calctax.rb

```
subtotal = 100.00
taxrate = 0.175
tax = subtotal * taxrate
puts "Tax on $#{subtotal} is $#{tax}, so grand total is $#{subtotal+tax}"
```

Obviously, this program would be more useful if it could perform calculations on a variety of subtotals rather than calculating the same value time after time! Here is a simple calculator that prompts the user to enter a subtotal:

```
taxrate = 0.175
print "Enter price (ex tax): "
s = gets
subtotal = s.to_f
tax = subtotal * taxrate
puts "Tax on $#{subtotal} is $#{tax}, so grand total is $#{subtotal+tax}"
```

Here s.to_f is a method of the String class. It attempts to convert the string to a floating-point number. For example, the string "145.45" would be converted to the floating-point number 145.45. If the string cannot be converted, 0.0 is returned. For instance, "Hello world".to_f would return 0.0.

Comments

Many of the source code examples that come with this book are documented with comments that are ignored by the Ruby interpreter. You can place a comment after the hash mark (#). The text on a line following this character is all treated as a comment:

```
# this is a comment
puts( "hello" ) # this is also a comment
```

If you want to comment out multiple lines of text, you can place =begin at the start and =end at the end (both =begin and =end must be flush with the left margin):

```
=begin
 This is a
 multiline
 comment
=end
```

Testing a Condition: if..then

The problem with the simple tax calculator code shown earlier is that it accepts negative subtotals and calculates negative tax on them—a situation upon which the government is unlikely to look favorably! I therefore need to check for negative numbers and, when found, set them to zero. This is my new version of the code:

5taxcalculator.rb

```
taxrate = 0.175
print "Enter price (ex tax): "
s = gets
subtotal = s.to_f

if (subtotal < 0.0)   then
   subtotal = 0.0
end

tax = subtotal * taxrate
puts "Tax on $#{subtotal} is $#{tax}, so grand total is $#{subtotal+tax}"
```

The Ruby if test is similar to an if test in other programming languages. Note, however, that the parentheses are once again optional, as is the keyword then. However, if you were to write the following, with no line break after the test condition, the then would be obligatory:

```
if (subtotal < 0.0) then subtotal = 0.0 end
```

Putting everything on one line like this adds nothing to the clarity of the code, which is why I tend to avoid it. My long familiarity with Pascal instinctively makes me want to add a then after the if condition, but because this really is not required, you may look upon this as a willful eccentricity of mine. The end keyword that terminates the if block is *not* optional. If you forget to add it, your code will not run.

Local and Global Variables

In the previous example, I assigned values to variables such as subtotal, tax, and taxrate. Variables such as these that begin with a lowercase character are called *local variables*. This means they exist only within a specific part of a program—in other words, they are restricted to a well-defined scope. Here is an example:

variables.rb

```
localvar = "hello"
$globalvar = "goodbye"

def amethod
    localvar = 10
    puts( localvar )
    puts( $globalvar )
end

def anotherMethod
    localvar = 500
    $globalvar = "bonjour"
    puts( localvar )
    puts( $globalvar )
end
```

In the previous code, there are two functions (or *methods*), amethod and anotherMethod, each of which is declared using the keyword def and contains code up to the keyword end. There are three local variables called localvar. One is assigned the value "hello" within the "main scope" of the program; two others are assigned integers within the scope of two separate methods. Since each local variable has a different scope, the assignments have no effect on the other local variables with the same name in different scopes. You can verify this by calling the methods in turn. The following examples show output in comments followed by the => characters. In this book, output or returned values will often be indicated in this way:

```
amethod            #=> localvar = 10
anotherMethod      #=> localvar = 500
amethod            #=> localvar = 10
puts( localvar )   #=> localvar = "hello"
```

On the other hand, a *global variable*—one that begins with the dollar sign character (\$)—has global scope. When an assignment is made to a global variable inside a method, that affects the value of that variable elsewhere in the program too:

```
amethod           #=>  $globalvar = "goodbye"
anotherMethod     #=>  $globalvar = "bonjour"
amethod           #=>  $globalvar = "bonjour"
puts( $globalvar ) #=>  $globalvar = "bonjour"
```

Classes and Objects

Instead of going through all the rest of Ruby's syntax—its types, loops, modules, and so on—let's move rapidly on and look at how to create classes and objects. (But fear not, we'll return to those other topics soon.)

> **BASIC TERMINOLOGY: CLASSES, OBJECTS, AND METHODS**
>
> A class is the blueprint for an object. It defines the data an object contains and the way it behaves. Many different objects can be created from a single class. So, you might have one Cat *class* but three cat *objects*: tiddles, cuddles, and flossy. A *method* is like a function or subroutine that is defined inside the class.

It may seem like no big deal to say that Ruby is object-oriented. Aren't all languages these days? Well, up to a point. Most modern "object-oriented" languages (Java, C++, C#, Object Pascal, and so on) have a greater or lesser degree of object-oriented programming (OOP) features. Ruby, on the other hand, is obsessively object-oriented. In fact, unless you have programmed in Smalltalk or Eiffel (languages that are even more obsessive than Ruby about objects), it is likely to be the most object-oriented language you have ever used. Every chunk of data—from a simple number or string to something more complicated like a file or a module—is treated as an object. And almost everything you do with an object is done by a method. Even operators such as plus (+) and minus (-) are methods. Consider the following:

```
x = 1 + 2
```

Here + is a method of the Fixnum (Integer) object 1. The value 2 is sent to this method; the result, 3, is returned, and this is assigned to the object x. Incidentally, the assignment operator (=) is one of the rare exceptions to the rule that "everything you do with an object is done by a method." The assignment operator is a special built-in "thingummy" (this is not the formal terminology, I hasten to add), and it is not a method of anything.

Now you'll see how to create objects of your own. As in most other OOP languages, a Ruby object is defined by a class. The class is like a blueprint from which individual objects are constructed. For example, this class defines a dog:

6dogs.rb

```ruby
class Dog
    def set_name( aName )
        @myname = aName
    end
end
```

Note that the class definition begins with the keyword class (all lowercase) and the name of the class itself, which must begin with an uppercase letter. The class contains a method called set_name. This takes an incoming argument, aName. The body of the method assigns the value of aName to a variable called @myname.

Instance Variables

Variables beginning with the at sign (@) are *instance variables*, which means they belong to individual objects (or *instances*) of the class. It is not necessary to predeclare instance variables. I can create instances of the Dog class (that is, "dog objects") by calling the new method. Here I am creating two dog objects (note that although class names begin with uppercase letters, object names begin with lowercase letters):

```ruby
mydog = Dog.new
yourdog = Dog.new
```

At the moment, these two dogs have no names. So, the next thing I do is call the set_name method to give them names:

```ruby
mydog.set_name( 'Fido' )
yourdog.set_name( 'Bonzo' )
```

Retrieving Data from an Object

Having given each dog a name, I need to have some way to find out their names later. How should I do this? I can't poke around inside an object to get at the @name variable, since the internal details of each object are known only to the object itself. This is a fundamental principle of "pure" object orientation: The data inside each object is private. There are precisely defined ways into each object (for example, the method set_name) and precisely defined ways out. Only the object itself can mess around with its internal state; the outside world cannot. This is called *data hiding*, and it is part of the principle of *encapsulation*.

Since you need each dog to know its own name, let's provide the Dog class with a get_name method:

```
def get_name
    return @myname
end
```

The return keyword here is optional. When it is omitted, Ruby methods will return the last expression evaluated. However, for the sake of clarity—and to avoid unexpected results from methods more complex than this one—I will make a habit of explicitly returning any values that I plan to use.

Finally, let's give the dog some behavior by asking it to talk. Here is the finished class definition:

```
class Dog
    def set_name( aName )
        @myname = aName
    end

    def get_name
        return @myname
    end

    def talk
        return 'woof!'
    end
end
```

Now, you can create a dog, name it, display its name, and ask it to talk:

```
mydog = Dog.new
mydog.set_name( 'Fido' )
puts(mydog.get_name)
puts(mydog.talk)
```

I've written an expanded version of this code in the *6dogs.rb* program. This also contains a Cat class that is similar to the Dog class except that its talk method, naturally enough, returns a *meow* instead of a *woof.*

Messages, Methods, and Polymorphism

This cats and dogs example, incidentally, is based on a classic Smalltalk demo program that illustrates how the same "message" (such as talk) can be sent to different objects (such as cats and dogs), and each different object responds differently to the same message with its own special method (here the talk method). The ability to have different classes containing methods with the same name goes by the fancy object-oriented name of *polymorphism*.

When you run a program such as *6dogs.rb*, the code is executed in sequence. The code of the classes themselves is not executed until instances of those classes (that is, objects) are created by the code at the bottom of the program. You will see that I frequently mix class definitions with "free-standing" bits of code that execute when the program is run. This may not be the way you would want to write a major application, but for just trying things, it is extremely convenient.

One obvious defect of this program is that the two classes, Cat and Dog, are highly repetitive. It would make more sense to have one class, Animal, that has get_name and set_name methods and two descendant classes, Cat and Dog, that contain only the behavior specific to that species of animal (woofing or meowing). We'll find out how to do this in the next chapter.

Constructors: new and initialize

Let's take a look at another example of a user-defined class. Load *7treasure.rb*. This is an adventure game in the making. It contains two classes, Thing and Treasure. The Thing class is similar to the Cat and Dog classes from the previous program—except that it doesn't woof or meow, that is.

7treasure.rb

```
class Thing
    def set_name( aName )
        @name = aName
    end

    def get_name
        return @name
    end
end

class Treasure
    def initialize( aName, aDescription )
        @name       = aName
        @description = aDescription
    end

    def to_s # override default to_s method
      "The #{@name} Treasure is #{@description}\n"
    end
end

thing1 = Thing.new
thing1.set_name( "A lovely Thing" )
puts thing1.get_name

t1 = Treasure.new("Sword", "an Elvish weapon forged of gold")
t2 = Treasure.new("Ring", "a magic ring of great power")
puts t1.to_s
puts t2.to_s
# The inspect method lets you look inside an object
puts "Inspecting 1st treasure: #{t1.inspect}"
```

The Treasure class doesn't have get_name and set_name methods. Instead, it contains a method named initialize, which takes two arguments. Those two values are then assigned to the @name and @description variables. When a class contains a method named initialize, it will be called automatically when an object is created using the new method. This makes it a convenient place to set the values of an object's instance variables.

This has two clear benefits over setting each instance variable using methods such set_name. First, a complex class may contain numerous instance variables, and you can set the values of all of them with the single `initialize` method rather than with many separate "set" methods; second, if the variables are all automatically initialized at the time of object creation, you will never end up with an "empty" variable (like the "nil" value returned when you tried to display the name of someotherdog in the previous program).

Finally, I have created a method called to_s, which returns a string representation of a Treasure object. The method name, to_s, is not arbitrary—the same method name is used throughout the standard Ruby object hierarchy. In fact, the to_s method is defined for the Object class itself, which is the ultimate ancestor of all other classes in Ruby (with the exception of the BasicObject class, which you'll look at more closely in the next chapter). By redefining the to_s method, I have added new behavior that is more appropriate to the Treasure class than the default method. In other words, I have *overridden* its to_s method.

Since the new method creates an object, it can be thought of as the object's *constructor*. A constructor is a method that allocates memory for an object and then executes the initialize method, if it exists, to assign any specified values to the new object's internal variables. You should not normally implement your own version of the new method. Instead, when you want to perform any "setup" actions, do so in the initialize method.

GARBAGE COLLECTION

In many languages (such as C++ and Delphi for Win32), it is the programmer's responsibility to destroy any object that has been created when it is no longer required. In other words, objects are given *destructors* as well as constructors. This isn't necessary in Ruby, since a built-in *garbage collector* automatically destroys objects and reclaims the memory they used when they are no longer referenced in your program.

Inspecting Objects

Notice that in the *7treasure.rb* program I "looked inside" the Treasure object t1 using the inspect method:

```
puts "Inspecting 1st treasure: #{t1.inspect}"
```

The inspect method is defined for all Ruby objects. It returns a string containing a human-readable representation of the object. In the present case, it displays something like this:

```
#<Treasure:0x28962f8 @description="an Elvish weapon forged of gold", @name="Sword">
```

This begins with the class name, Treasure. This is followed by a number, which may be different from the number shown earlier—this is Ruby's internal identification code for this particular object. Next the names and values of the object's variables are shown.

Ruby also provides the p method as a shortcut to inspect objects and print their details, like this:

```
p( anobject )
```

where anobject can be any type of Ruby object. For example, let's suppose you create the following three objects: a string, a number, and a Treasure object:

p.rb

```
class Treasure
    def initialize( aName, aDescription )
      @name        = aName
      @description = aDescription
    end

    def to_s # override default to_s method
        "The #{@name} Treasure is #{@description}\n"
    end
end

a = "hello"
b = 123
c = Treasure.new( "ring", "a glittery gold thing" )
```

Now you can use p to display those objects:

```
p( a )
p( b )
p( c )
```

This is what Ruby displays:

```
"hello"
123
#<Treasure:0x3489c4 @name="ring", @description="a glittery gold thing">
```

To see how you can use to_s with a variety of objects and test how a Treasure object would be converted to a string in the absence of an overridden to_s method, try the *8to_s.rb* program.

8to_s.rb

```
puts(Class.to_s)        #=> Class
puts(Object.to_s)       #=> Object
puts(String.to_s)       #=> String
puts(100.to_s)          #=> 100
puts(Treasure.to_s)     #=> Treasure
```

As you will see, classes such as Class, Object, String, and Treasure simply return their names when the to_s method is called. An object, such as the Treasure object t, returns its identifier—which is the same identifier returned by the inspect method:

```
t = Treasure.new( "Sword", "A lovely Elvish weapon" )
puts(t.to_s)
    #=> #<Treasure:0x3308100>
puts(t.inspect)
    #=> #<Treasure:0x3308100 @name="Sword", @description="A lovely Elvish
weapon">
```

Although the *7treasure.rb* program may lay the foundations for a game containing a variety of different object types, its code is still repetitive. After all, why have a Thing class that contains a name and a Treasure class that also contains a name? It would make more sense to regard a Treasure as a "type of" Thing. In a complete game, other objects such as Rooms and Weapons might be yet other types of Thing. It is clearly time to start working on a proper class hierarchy, which is what you will do in the next chapter.

2

CLASS HIERARCHIES, ATTRIBUTES, AND CLASS VARIABLES

We ended the previous chapter by creating two new classes: a Thing and a Treasure. Despite the fact that these two classes shared some features (notably both had a "name"), there was no connection between them.

These two classes are so trivial that this tiny bit of repetition doesn't really matter much. However, when you start writing real programs of some complexity, your classes will frequently contain numerous variables and methods, and you really don't want to keep coding the same things over and over again.

It makes sense to create a class hierarchy in which one class may be a "special type" of some other (ancestor) class, in which case it will automatically inherit the features of its ancestor. In our simple adventure game, for instance, a Treasure is a special type of Thing, so the Treasure class should inherit the features of the Thing class.

NOTE *In this book, I will often talk about descendant classes inheriting features from their ancestor classes. These terms deliberately suggest a kind a family relationship between "related" classes. Each class in Ruby has only one parent. It may, however, descend from a long and distinguished family tree with many generations of parents, grandparents, great-grandparents, and so on.*

The behavior of Things in general will be coded in the Thing class. The Treasure class will automatically "inherit" all the features of the Thing class, so we won't need to code them all over again; it will then add some additional features, specific to Treasures.

As a general rule, when creating a class hierarchy, the classes with the most generalized behavior are higher up the hierarchy than classes with more specialist behavior. So, a Thing class with just a name and a description would be the ancestor of a Treasure class that has a name, a description, and, additionally, a value; the Thing class might also be the ancestor of some other specialist class such as a Room that has a name, a description, and exits . . . and so on.

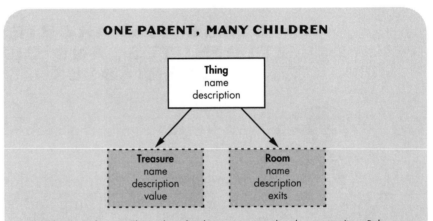

This diagram shows a Thing class that has a *name* and a *description* (in a Ruby program, these might be internal variables such as @name and @description plus some methods to access them). The Treasure and Room classes both descend from the Thing class, so they automatically "inherit" a *name* and a *description*. The Treasure class adds one new item, *value*, so it now has *name*, *description*, and *value*. The Room class adds *exits*—so it has *name*, *description*, and *exits*.

Let's see how to create a descendant class in Ruby. Load the *1adventure.rb* program. This starts simply enough with the definition of a Thing class, which has two instance variables, @name and @description.

1adventure.rb

```
class Thing
    def initialize( aName, aDescription )
      @name        = aName
      @description = aDescription
    end
```

```
    def get_name
        return @name
    end

    def set_name( aName )
        @name = aName
    end

    def get_description
        return @description
    end

    def set_description( aDescription )
        @description = aDescription
    end
end
```

The @name and @description variables are assigned values in the initialize method when a new Thing object is created. Instance variables generally cannot (and should not) be directly accessed from the world outside the class itself, because of the principle of encapsulation (as explained in the previous chapter). To obtain the value of each variable, you need a *get* accessor method such as get_name; in order to assign a new value, you need a *set* accessor method such as set_name.

Superclasses and Subclasses

Now look at the Treasure class, which is also defined in the following program:

1adventure.rb

```
class Treasure < Thing
    def initialize( aName, aDescription, aValue )
        super( aName, aDescription )
        @value = aValue
    end

    def get_value
        return @value
    end

    def set_value( aValue )
        @value = aValue
    end
end
```

Notice how the Treasure class is declared:

```
class Treasure < Thing
```

The left angle bracket (<) indicates that Treasure is a *subclass*, or descendant, of Thing, and therefore it inherits the data (variables) and behavior (methods) from the Thing class. Since the methods get_name, set_name, get_description, and set_description already exist in the ancestor class (Thing), these methods don't need to be recoded in the descendant class (Treasure).

The Treasure class has one additional piece of data, its value (@value), and I have written *get* and *set* accessors for this. When a new Treasure object is created, its initialize method is automatically called. A Treasure has three variables to initialize (@name, @description, and @value), so its initialize method takes three arguments. The first two arguments are passed, using the super keyword, to the initialize method of the superclass (Thing) so that the Thing class's initialize method can deal with them:

```
super( aName, aDescription )
```

When used inside a method, the super keyword calls a method with the same name as the current method in the ancestor or *super*class. If the super keyword is used on its own, without any arguments being specified, all the arguments sent to the current method are passed to the ancestor method. If, as in the present case, a specific list of arguments (here aName and aDescription) is supplied, then only these are passed to the method of the ancestor class.

Passing Arguments to the Superclass

Parentheses matter when calling the superclass! If the argument list is empty and no parentheses are used, *all* arguments are passed to the superclass. But if the argument list is empty and parentheses are used, *no* arguments are passed to the superclass:

super_args.rb
```
# This passes a, b, c to the superclass
def initialize( a, b, c, d, e, f )
   super( a, b, c )
end

# This passes a, b, c to the superclass
def initialize( a, b, c )
   super
end

# This passes no arguments to the superclass
def initialize( a, b, c)
   super()
end
```

NOTE   *To gain a better understanding of the use of super, see "Digging Deeper" on page 25.*

Accessor Methods

Although the classes in this would-be adventure game work well enough, they are still fairly verbose because of all those *get* and *set* accessors. Let's see what you can do to remedy this.

Instead of accessing the value of the @description instance variable with two different methods, get_description and set_description, like this:

```
puts( t1.get_description )
t1.set_description("Some description" )
```

it would be so much nicer to retrieve and assign values just as you would retrieve and assign values to and from a simple variable, like this:

```
puts( t1.description )
t1.description = "Some description"
```

To be able to do this, you need to modify the Treasure class definition. One way of accomplishing this would be to rewrite the accessor methods for @description as follows:

accessors1.rb

```
def description
    return @description
end

def description=( aDescription )
    @description = aDescription
end
```

I have added accessors similar to these in the *accessors1.rb* program. Here, the *get* accessor is called description, and the *set* accessor is called description= (that is, it appends an equals sign to the method name used by the corresponding *get* accessor). It is now possible to assign a new string like this:

```
t.description = "a bit faded and worn around the edges"
```

And you can retrieve the value like this:

```
puts( t.description )
```

Note that when you write a *set* accessor in this way, you must append the = character to the method name, not merely place it somewhere between the method name and the arguments. In other words, this is correct:

```
def name=( aName )
```

but this results in an error:

```
def name   = ( aName )
```

Attribute Readers and Writers

In fact, there is a simpler and shorter way of creating a pair of *get* and *set* accessors simultaneously. All you have to do is use two special methods, attr_reader and attr_writer, followed by a *symbol* (a name preceded by a colon):

```
attr_reader :description
attr_writer :description
```

You should add this code inside your class definition like this:

```
class Thing
    attr_reader :description
    attr_writer :description
    # maybe some more methods here...
end
```

Calling attr_reader with a symbol has the effect of creating a *get* accessor (here named description) for an instance variable (@description) with a name matching the symbol (:description).

Calling attr_writer similarly creates a *set* accessor for an instance variable. Instance variables are considered to be the "attributes" of an object, which is why the attr_reader and attr_writer methods are so named.

WHAT IS A SYMBOL?

In Ruby, a *symbol* is a name preceded by a colon (for example, :description). The Symbol class is defined in the Ruby class library to represent names inside the Ruby interpreter. When you pass one or more symbols as arguments to attr_reader (which is a method of the Module class), Ruby creates an instance variable and a *get* accessor method. This accessor method returns the value of the corresponding variable; both the instance variable and the accessor method will take the name that was specified by the symbol. So, attr_reader(:description) creates an instance variable with the name, @description, and an accessor method named description(). Symbols are discussed in detail in Chapter 11.

The *accessors2.rb* program contains some examples of attribute readers and writers in action. This is its version of the Thing class:

accessors2.rb

```
class Thing

❶    attr_reader :description
     attr_writer :description
❷    attr_writer :name

     def initialize( aName, aDescription )
         @name        = aName
         @description = aDescription
     end
```

```
        # get accessor for @name
❸   def name
        return @name.capitalize
    end

end
```

Here the Thing class explicitly defines a *get* method accessor for the `@name` attribute. The advantage of writing a complete method like this is that it gives you the opportunity to do some extra processing rather than simply reading and writing an attribute value. The *get* accessor, `name` ❸, uses the `String.capitalize` method to return the string value of `@name` with its initial letter in uppercase.

When assigning a value to the `@name` attribute, I don't need to do any special processing, so I have given it an attribute writer instead of a `set` accessor method ❷.

The `@description` attribute needs no special processing at all, so I use `attr_reader` and `attr_writer` instead of accessor methods in order to get and set the value of the `@description` variable ❶.

NOTE   *Are they attributes or properties? Don't be confused by the terminology. In Ruby, an* attribute *is the equivalent of what many programming languages call a* property.

When you want both to read and to write a variable, the `attr_accessor` method provides a shorter alternative than using both `attr_reader` and `attr_writer`. I have used this to access the value attribute in the Treasure class:

```
attr_accessor :value
```

This is equivalent to the following:

```
attr_reader :value
attr_writer :value
```

Earlier I said that calling `attr_reader` with a symbol actually creates a variable with the same name as the symbol. The `attr_accessor` method also does this.

In the code for the Thing class, this behavior is not obvious since the class has an `initialize` method that explicitly creates the variables. The Treasure class, however, makes no reference to the `@value` variable in its `initialize` method:

```
class Treasure < Thing
    attr_accessor :value

    def initialize( aName, aDescription )
        super( aName, aDescription )
    end
end
```

The only indication that @value exists at all is this accessor definition:

```
attr_accessor :value
```

My code at the bottom of the *accessors2.rb* source file sets the value of each Treasure object as a separate operation, following the creation of the object itself, like this:

```
t1.value = 800
```

Even though it has never been formally declared, the @value variable really does exist, and you are able to retrieve its numerical value using the *get* accessor: t1.value. To be absolutely certain that the attribute accessor really has created @value, you can always look inside the object using the inspect method. I have done so in the final two code lines in this program:

```
puts "This is treasure1: #{t1.inspect}"
puts "This is treasure2: #{t2.inspect}"
```

This displays the data inside the t1 and t2 objects, including the @value variables:

```
This is treasure1: #<Treasure:0x33a6c88 @value=100, @name="sword",
@description="an Elvish weapon forged of gold (now somewhat tarnished)">
This is treasure2: #<Treasure:0x33a6c4c @value=500, @name="dragon horde",
@description="a huge pile of jewels">
```

Attribute accessors can initialize more than one attribute at a time if you send them a list of symbols separated by commas, like this:

accessors3.rb
```
attr_reader :name, :description
attr_writer(:name, :description)
attr_accessor(:value, :id, :owner)
```

As always, parentheses around the arguments are optional but, in my view (for reasons of clarity), are to be preferred.

Now let's see how to put attribute readers and writers to use in my adventure game. Load the *2adventure.rb* program. You will see that I have created two readable attributes in the Thing class: name and description. I have also made description writeable; however, because I don't plan to change the names of any Thing objects, the name attribute is not writeable:

2adventure.rb
```
attr_reader( :name, :description )
attr_writer( :description )
```

I have created a method called to_s, which returns a string describing the Treasure object. Recall that all Ruby classes have a to_s method as standard. The Thing.to_s method overrides (and replaces) the default one.

```
def to_s # override default to_s method
    return "(Thing.to_s):: The #{@name} Thing is #{@description}"
end
```

You can override existing methods when you want to implement new behavior appropriate to the specific class type.

Calling Methods of a Superclass

The game in *2adventure.rb* will have two classes descending from Thing: the Treasure class and the Room class. The Treasure class adds a value attribute, which can be both read and written. Note that its initialize method calls its superclass in order to initialize the name and description attributes before initializing the new @value variable:

```
super( aName, aDescription )
@value = aValue
```

Here, if I had omitted the call to the superclass, the name and description attributes would never be initialized. This is because Treasure.initialize overrides Thing.initialize, so when a Treasure object is created, the code in Thing.initialize will *not* automatically be executed.

On the other hand, the Room class, which also descends from Thing, currently has no initialize method, so when a new Room object is created, Ruby goes scrambling back up the class hierarchy in search of one. The first initialize method it finds is in Thing, so a Room object's name and description attributes are initialized there.

Class Variables

A few other interesting things are going on in this program. Right at the top of the Thing class you will see this:

```
@@num_things = 0
```

The two @ characters at the start of this variable name, @@num_things, define this to be a *class variable*. The variables we've used inside classes up to now have been instance variables, preceded by a single @, like @name. Whereas each new object (or instance) of a class assigns its own values to its own instance variables, all objects derived from a specific class share the same class variables. I have assigned 0 to the @@num_things variable to ensure that it has a meaningful value at the outset.

Here, the @@num_things class variable is used to keep a running total of the number of Thing objects in the game. It does this simply by incrementing the class variable (by adding 1 to it: += 1) in its initialize method every time a new object is created:

```
@@num_things += 1
```

If you look later in the code, you will see that I have created a Map class to contain an array of rooms. This includes a version of the to_s method that prints information on each room in the array. Don't worry about the implementation of the Map class right now; we'll be looking at arrays and their methods in Chapter 4.

```ruby
class Map

    def initialize( someRooms )
        @rooms = someRooms
    end

    def to_s
        @rooms.each {
            |a_room|
            puts(a_room)
        }
    end

end
```

Scroll to the code at the bottom of the file, and run the program to see how I have created and initialized all the objects and used the class variable, @@num_things, to keep a tally of all the Thing objects that have been created.

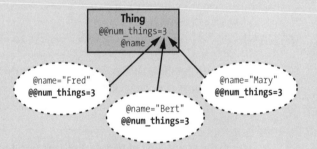

CLASS VARIABLES AND INSTANCE VARIABLES

This diagram shows a Thing class (the rectangle) that contains a class variable, @@num_things, and an instance variable, @name. The three oval shapes represent "Thing objects"—that is, instances of the Thing class. When one of these objects assigns a value to its instance variable, @name, that value affects only the @name variable in the object itself. So here, each object has a different value for @name. But when an object assigns a value to the class variable, @@num_things, that value "lives inside" the Thing class and is shared by all instances of that class. Here @@num_things equals 3, and that is true for all the Thing objects.

DIGGING DEEPER

Every class you create will descend from one or more other classes. Here I explain the fundamentals of the Ruby class hierarchy.

Superclasses

To understand how the super keyword works, take a look at the sample program *super.rb*. This contains five related classes. The Thing class is the ancestor of all the others, and from Thing descends Thing2, from Thing2 descends Thing3, from Thing3 descends Thing4, and from Thing4 descends Thing5.

super.rb

```
class Thing
    def initialize( aName, aDescription )
        @name = aName
        @description = aDescription
        puts("Thing.initialize: #{self.inspect}\n\n")
    end

    def aMethod( aNewName )
        @name = aNewName
        puts("Thing.aMethod: #{self.inspect}\n\n")
    end
end

class Thing2 < Thing
    def initialize( aName, aDescription )
        super
        @fulldescription = "This is #{@name}, which is #{@description}"
        puts("Thing2.initialize: #{self.inspect}\n\n")
    end

    def aMethod( aNewName, aNewDescription )
        super( aNewName )
        puts("Thing2.aMethod: #{self.inspect}\n\n")
    end
end

class Thing3 < Thing2
    def initialize( aName, aDescription, aValue )
        super( aName, aDescription )
        @value = aValue
        puts("Thing3.initialize: #{self.inspect}\n\n")
    end
```

```
        def aMethod( aNewName, aNewDescription, aNewValue )
            super( aNewName, aNewDescription )
            @value = aNewValue
            puts("Thing3.aMethod: #{self.inspect}\n\n")
        end
end

class Thing4 < Thing3
    def aMethod
        puts("Thing4.aMethod: #{self.inspect}\n\n")
    end
end

class Thing5 < Thing4
end
```

Let's take a closer look at the first three classes in this hierarchy: The Thing class has two instance variables, @name and @description. Thing2 also defines @fulldescription (a string that contains @name and @description); Thing3 adds yet another variable, @value.

These three classes each contain an initialize method that sets the values of the variables when a new object is created; they also each have a method named, rather inventively, aMethod, which changes the value of one or more variables. The descendant classes, Thing2 and Thing3, both use the super keyword in their methods.

At the bottom of this code unit I've written a "main" loop that executes when you run the program. Don't worry about the syntax of this; you'll be learning about loops in Chapter 5. I've added this loop so that you can easily run the different bits of code contained in the methods, test1 to test5. You can run the program in a command window and enter a number, 1 to 5, when prompted, or Q to quit. When you run it for the first time, type **1** at the prompt and press the ENTER key. This will run the test1 method containing these two lines of code:

```
t = Thing.new( "A Thing", "a lovely thing full of thinginess" )
t.aMethod( "A New Thing" )
```

The first line here creates and initializes a Thing object, and the second line calls its aMethod method. Because the Thing class doesn't descend from anything special, nothing very new or interesting happens here. In fact, as with all Ruby classes, Thing descends from the Object class, which is the ancestor of all other classes (with the sole exception of the BasicObject class in Ruby 1.9, as explained later in this chapter). The output uses the inspect method to display the internal structure of the object when the Thing.initialize and Thing.aMethod methods are called. This is the result:

```
Thing.initialize: #<Thing:0x28e0290 @name="A Thing", @description="a lovely
thing full of thinginess">
Thing.aMethod: #<Thing:0x28e0290 @name="A New Thing", @description="a lovely
thing full of thinginess">
```

The inspect method can be used with all objects and is an invaluable debugging aid. Here, it shows a hexadecimal number, which identifies this specific object followed by the string values of the @name and @description variables.

Now enter **2** at the prompt to run test2, which contains the following code:

```
t2 = Thing2.new( "A Thing2", "a Thing2 thing of great beauty" )
t2.aMethod( "A New Thing2", "a new Thing2 description" )
```

This creates a Thing2 object, t2, and calls t2.aMethod. Look carefully at the output. You will see that even though t2 is a Thing2 object, it is the Thing class's initialize method that is called first. And only then is the Thing2 class's initialize called.

```
Thing.initialize: #<Thing2:0x2a410a0 @name="A Thing2", @description="a Thing2
thing of great beauty">

Thing2.initialize: #<Thing2:0x2a410a0 @name="A Thing2", @description="a Thing2
thing of great beauty", @fulldescription="This is A Thing2, which is a Thing2
thing of great beauty">
```

To understand why this is so, look at the code of the Thing2 class's initialize method:

```
def initialize( aName, aDescription )
   super
   @fulldescription = "This is #{@name}, which is #{@description}"
   puts("Thing2.initialize: #{self.inspect}\n\n")
end
```

This uses the super keyword to call the initialize method of Thing2's ancestor, or *superclass*. The superclass of Thing2 is Thing, as you can see from its declaration:

```
class Thing2 < Thing
```

In Ruby, when the super keyword is used on its own (that is, without any arguments), it passes all the arguments from the current method (here Thing2.initialize) to a method with the same name in its superclass (here Thing.initialize). Alternatively, you can explicitly specify a list of arguments following super. So, in this case, the following code would have the same effect:

```
super( aName, aDescription )
```

Although it is permissible to use the super keyword all on its own, it is often preferable to explicitly specify the list of arguments to be passed to the super-class, for the sake of clarity. If you want to pass only a limited number of the arguments sent to the current method, an explicit argument list is necessary.

Thing2's aMethod, for example, passes only the aName argument to the initialize method of its superclass, Thing1:

```
super( aNewName )
```

This explains why the @description variable is not changed when Thing2.aMethod is called.

Now if you look at Thing3, you will see that this adds one more variable, @value. In its implementation of initialize, it passes the two arguments, aName and aDescription, to its superclass, Thing2. In its turn, as you've already seen, Thing2's initialize method passes these same arguments to the initialize method of its superclass, Thing.

With the program running, enter **3** at the prompt to view the output. The following code will execute:

```
t3 = Thing3.new("A Thing3", "a Thing3 full of Thing and Thing2iness",500)
t3.aMethod( "A New Thing3", "and a new Thing3 description",1000)
```

Note how the flow of execution goes right up the hierarchy so that code in the initialize and aMethod methods of Thing execute before code in the matching methods of Thing2 and Thing3.

It is not obligatory to override a superclass's methods as I have done in the examples so far. This is required only when you want to add some new behavior. Thing4 omits the initialize method but implements the aMethod method.

Enter **4** at the prompt to execute the following code:

```
t4 = Thing4.new( "A Thing4", "the nicest Thing4 you will ever see", 10 )
t4.aMethod
```

When you run it, notice that the first available initialize method is called when a Thing4 object is created. This happens to be Thing3.initialize, which, once again, also calls the initialize methods of its ancestor classes, Thing2 and Thing. However, the aMethod method implemented by Thing4 contains no call to its superclasses, so this executes right away, and the code in any other aMethod methods in the ancestor classes is ignored:

```
def aMethod
    puts("Thing4.aMethod: #{self.inspect}\n\n")
end
```

Finally, Thing5 inherits from Thing4 and doesn't introduce any new data or methods. Enter **5** at the prompt to execute the following:

```
t5 = Thing5.new( "A Thing5", "a very simple Thing5", 40 )
t5.aMethod
```

This time, you will see that the call to new causes Ruby to backtrack through the class hierarchy until it finds the first initialize method. This happens to belong to Thing3 (which also calls the initialize methods of Thing2 and Thing). The first implementation of aMethod, however, occurs in Thing4, and there are no calls to super, so that's where the trail ends.

The Root of All Classes

As I mentioned earlier, all our Ruby classes will ultimately descend from the Object class. You may think of Object as the "root" or "base" class of the Ruby hierarchy. In Ruby 1.8 this is literally true—there are no classes from which Object itself descends. In Ruby 1.9, however, Object is derived from a new class called BasicObject. This new class was created to provide programmers with a very lightweight class—one that supplies only the bare minimum of methods for creating objects, testing equality, and manipulating special methods called *singletons*. (I'll talk more about singletons in Chapter 7.)

The Ruby 1.9 Object class inherits the methods from BasicObject and adds a number of new methods of its own. BasicObject does not exist in Ruby 1.8, and the Object class supplies all the methods provided by the combination of BasicObject and Object in Ruby 1.9. Since all normal Ruby classes—both Ruby 1.8 and Ruby 1.9—descend from Object, you may generally think of Object as being the "root" of all other classes. Just bear in mind that in Ruby 1.9, the ultimate ancestor of all classes is BasicObject.

The root class itself has no superclass, and any attempt to locate its superclass will return nil. You can see this for yourself by running *superclasses.rb*. This calls the superclass method to climb up the class hierarchy from the Three class to the Object or BasicObject class. At each turn through the loop, the variable x is assigned the class of x's immediate parent until x equals nil. Here class and superclass are methods that return references to Ruby classes rather than to objects created from those classes. The begin..until block is one of Ruby's looping constructs, which you'll look at in more detail in Chapter 5.

superclasses.rb

```
class One
end

class Two < One
end

class Three < Two
end

# Create ob as instance of class Three
# and display the class name
ob = Three.new
x = ob.class
puts( x )
```

```
# now climb back through the hierarchy to
# display all ancestor classes of ob
begin
    x = x.superclass
    puts(x.inspect)
end until x == nil
```

The previous code displays the following output:

```
Three
Two
One
Object
BasicObject    # Ruby 1.9 only!
nil
```

Constants Inside Classes

There may be times when you need to access constants (identifiers beginning with a capital letter, which are used to store nonchanging values)
declared inside a class. Let's assume you have this class:

classconsts.rb
```
class X
  A = 10

  class Y
  end
end
```

To access the constant A, you would need to use the special scope resolution operator :: like this:

```
X::A
```

Class names are constants, so this same operator gives you access to
classes inside other classes. This makes it possible to create objects from
"nested" classes such as class Y inside class X:

```
ob = X::Y.new
```

Partial Classes

In Ruby it is not obligatory to define a class all in one place. If you want, you
can define a single class in separate parts of your program. When a class
descends from a specific superclass, each subsequent partial (or *open*) class
definition may optionally repeat the superclass in its definition using the <
operator.

```
```

Here I create one class, A, and another that descends from it, B:

partial_classes.rb

```ruby
class A
   def a
      puts( "a" )
   end
end

class B < A
   def ba1
      puts( "ba1" )
   end
end

class A
   def b
      puts( "b" )
   end
end

class B < A
   def ba2
      puts( "ba2" )
   end
end
```

Now, if I create a B object, all the methods of both A and B are available to it:

```ruby
ob = B.new
ob.a
ob.b
ob.ba1
ob.ba2
```

You can also use partial class definitions to add features to Ruby's standard classes such as Array:

```ruby
class Array
   def gribbit
      puts( "gribbit" )
   end
end
```

This adds the gribbit method to the Array class so that the following code can now be executed:

```ruby
[1,2,3].gribbit
```

3

STRINGS AND RANGES

I've made use of strings in many of my programs so far. In fact, a string was featured in the very first program in the book. Here it is again:

```
puts 'hello world'
```

Although that first program used a string enclosed within single quotes, my second program used a string in double quotes:

```
print('Enter your name: ' )
name = gets()
puts( "Hello #{name}" )
```

Double-quoted strings do more work than single-quoted strings. In particular, they have the ability to evaluate bits of themselves as though they were programming code. To have something evaluated, you need to place it between a pair of curly brackets preceded by a hash mark (#).

In the previous example, #{name} in a double-quoted string tells Ruby to get the value of the name variable and insert that value into the string itself. The second line of code calls the gets() method to get some user input, which is then assigned to the variable name. If the user entered **Fred**, the final line of code would evaluate the embedded variable, #{name}, and the string "Hello Fred" would be displayed. The *1strings.rb* sample program provides a few more examples of embedded evaluation in double-quoted strings. For example, here I have created an object, ob, from a custom class, MyClass, and used embedded evaluation to display the values of its name and number attributes:

1strings.rb

```ruby
class MyClass
    attr_accessor :name
    attr_accessor :number

    def initialize( aName, aNumber )
        @name   = aName
        @number = aNumber
    end

    def ten
        return 10
    end

end

ob = MyClass.new( "James Bond", "007" )
puts( "My name is #{ob.name} and my number is #{ob.number}" )
```

When the final line of code executes, this is displayed:

```
My name is James Bond and my number is 007
```

A double-quoted string can also evaluate expressions such as 2*3, bits of code such as the method-call ob.ten (where ten is a method name), and escape characters such as \n and \t (representing a newline and a tab). A single-quoted string does no such evaluation. A single-quoted string can, however, use a backslash to indicate that the next character should be used literally. This is useful when a single-quoted string contains a single-quote character, like this:

```
'It\'s my party'
```

Assuming that the method named ten returns the value 10, you might write the following code:

```ruby
puts( "A tab\t a new line\na calculation #{2*3} and method-call #{ob.ten}" )
```

Because this is a double-quoted string, the embedded elements are evaluated, and the following is displayed:

```
A tab        new line
calculation 6 and method-call 10
```

Now let's see what happens when a single-quoted string is used:

```
puts( 'A tab\tnew line\na calculation #{2*3} and method-call #{ob.ten}' )
```

This time, no embedded evaluation is done, so this is what is displayed:

```
A tab\tnew line\ncalculation #{2*3} and method-call #{ob.ten}
```

User-Defined String Delimiters

If, for some reason, single and double quotes aren't convenient—for example, if your strings contain lots of quote characters and you don't want to have to keep putting backslashes in front of them—you can also delimit strings in many other ways.

The standard alternative delimiters for double-quoted strings are %Q and / or %/ and /, while for single-quoted strings they are %q and /. Thus . . .

2strings.rb

```
%Q/This is the same as a double-quoted string./
%/This is also the same as a double-quoted string./
%q/And this is the same as a single-quoted string/
```

You can even define your own string delimiters. They must be non-alphanumeric characters, and they may include nonprinting characters such as newlines or tabs as well as various characters that normally have a special meaning in Ruby such as the hash mark (#). Your chosen character should be placed after %q or %Q, and you should be sure to terminate the string with the same character. If your delimiter is an opening square bracket, the corresponding closing bracket should be used at the end of the string, like this:

3strings.rb

```
%Q[This is a string]
```

You will find examples of a broad range of user-selected string delimiters in the sample program *3strings.rb*. Here are two examples using an asterisk (*) after %Q instead of a double-quoted string and using an exclamation point (!) after %q instead of a single-quoted string:

```
puts( %Q*a)Here's a tab\ta new line\na calculation using \* #{2*3} and a method-call #{ob.ten}* )
puts( %q!b)Here's a tab\ta new line\na calculation using \* #{2*3} and a method-call #{ob.ten}! )
```

Here, as in the previous program, ob is a user-defined object whose method named ten returns the integer, 10. The previous code produces the following output:

```
a)Here's a tab    a new line
a calculation using * 6 and a method-call 10
b)Here's a tab\ta new line\na calculation using \* #{2*3} and a method-call
#{ob.ten}
```

Although there may be times when it is useful to delimit a string by some esoteric character such as a newline or an asterisk, in many cases the disadvantages (not least the mental anguish and confusion) resulting from such arcane practices may significantly outweigh the advantages.

Backquotes

One other type of string deserves a special mention: a string enclosed by backquotes—that is, the inward-pointing quote character that is usually tucked away up toward the top-left corner of the keyboard: `.

Ruby considers anything enclosed by back-quotes to be a command that can be passed for execution by the operating system using a method such as print or puts. By now, you will probably already have guessed that Ruby provides more than one way of doing this. It turns out %x/some command/ has the same effect as `somecommand` and so does %x{some command}. On the Windows operating system, for example, each of the three lines shown next would pass the command dir to the operating system, causing a directory listing to be displayed:

4backquotes.rb

```
puts(`dir`)
puts(%x/dir/)
puts(%x{dir})
```

You can also embed commands inside double-quoted strings like this:

```
print( "Goodbye #{%x{calc}}" )
```

Be careful if you do this. The command itself is evaluated first. Your Ruby program then waits until the process that starts has terminated. In the present case, the calculator will pop up. You are now free to do some calculations, if you want. Only when you close the calculator will the string "Goodbye" be displayed.

String Handling

Before leaving the subject of strings, you'll take a quick look at a few common string operations.

Concatenation

You can concatenate strings using << or + or just by placing a space between them. Here are three examples of string concatenation; in each case, s is assigned the string "Hello world":

```
s = "Hello " << "world"
s = "Hello " + "world"
s = "Hello "   "world"
```

Note that when you use the << method, you can append Fixnum integers (in the range 0 to 255), in which case those integers are converted to the character with that character code. Character codes 65 to 90 are converted to the uppercase characters *A* to *Z*, 97 to 122 are converted to the lowercase *a* to *z*, and other codes are converted to punctuation, special characters, and non-printing characters. However, if you want to print the number itself, you must convert it to a string using the to_s method. The to_s method is obligatory when concatenating Fixnums using the + method or a space; attempting to concatenate a number without using to_s is an error. The following program prints out characters and numeric codes for values between 0 and 126, which include the standard Western alphanumeric and punctuation characters:

```
i = 0
begin
    s = "[" << i << ":" << i.to_s << "]"
    puts(s)
    i += 1
end until i == 126
```

For examples of concatenating using <<, +, or a space, see *string_contact.rb*:

```
s1 = "This " << "is" << " a string " << 36 # char 36 is '$'
s2 = "This "   + "is" + " a string "   + 36.to_s
s3 = "This "   "is"   " a string "   + 36.to_s

puts("(s1):" << s1)
puts("(s2):" << s2)
puts("(s3):" << s3)
```

The previous program produces this output:

```
(s1):This is a string $
(s2):This is a string 36
(s3):This is a string 36
```

What About Commas?

You may sometimes see Ruby code that uses commas to separate strings and other data types. In some circumstances, these commas appear to have the effect of concatenating strings. For example, the following code might, at first sight, seem to create and display a string from three substrings plus an integer:

```
s4 = "This " , "is" , " not a string!", 10
print("print (s4):" , s4, "\n")
```

In fact, a list separated by commas creates an array—an ordered list of the original strings. The *string_concat.rb* program contains examples that prove this to be the case:

```
x = "This " , "is" , " not a string!", 36
print("print (x):" , x, "\n")
puts("puts(x):", x)
puts("puts x.class is: " << (x.class).to_s )

print("print(x):" , x, "\n")
puts("puts(x):", x)
puts("puts x.class is: " << (x.class).to_s )
```

The previous code causes the following to be displayed:

```
print (x):This is not a string!36
puts(x):
This
is
 not a string!
36
puts x.class is: Array
```

The first print statement here looks as though it is displaying a single string. This is because each successive item in the array, x, is printed on the same line as the preceding item. When you use puts instead of print, you can see that each item is printed on a separate line. This is because puts prints each item in turn and appends a carriage return after it. The fact that you are dealing with an array rather than a string is confirmed when you ask Ruby to print the class of the x object. It displays Array. You'll learn about arrays in more depth in the next chapter.

String Assignment

The Ruby String class provides a number of useful string-handling methods. Most of these methods create new string objects. So, for example, in the following code, the s on the left side of the assignment on the second line is not the same object as the s on the right side:

```
s = "hello world"
s = s + "!"
```

A few string methods actually alter the string itself without creating a new object. These methods generally end with an exclamation mark (for example, the capitalize! method changes the original string, whereas the capitalize method does not). In addition, the string itself is also modified—and no new string is created—when you assign a character at an index of the string. For example, s[1] = 'A' would place the character *A* at index 1 (the second character) of the string s.

If in doubt, you can check an object's identity using the object_id method. I've provided a few examples of operations that do and do not create new strings in the *string_assign.rb* program. Run this, and check the object_id of s after each string operation is performed.

string_assign.rb
```
s = "hello world"
print( "1) s='#{s}' and s.object_id=#{s.object_id}\n" )
s = s + "!"              # this creates a new string object
print( "2) s='#{s}' and s.object_id=#{s.object_id}\n" )
s = s.capitalize        # this creates a new string object
print( "3) s='#{s}' and s.object_id=#{s.object_id}\n" )
s.capitalize!           # but this modifies the original string object
print( "4) s='#{s}' and s.object_id=#{s.object_id}\n" )
s[1] = 'A'              # this also modifies the original string object
print( "5) s='#{s}' and s.object_id=#{s.object_id}\n" )
```

This produces output similar to that shown next. The actual object ID values may differ, but the important thing to notice is when consecutive values remain the same, showing that the string object, s, remains the same and, when they change, showing that a new string object, s, has been created:

```
1) s='hello world' and s.object_id=29573230
2) s='hello world!' and s.object_id=29573190
3) s='Hello world!' and s.object_id=29573160
4) s='Hello world!' and s.object_id=29573160
5) s='HAllo world!' and s.object_id=29573160
```

Indexing into a String

In one of the previous examples, I treated a string as an array of characters and specified a character index with an integer inside square brackets: s[1]. Strings and arrays in Ruby are indexed from the first character at index 0. So, for instance, to replace the character *e* with *u* in the string s (which currently contains "Hello world"), you would assign a new character to index 1:

```
s[1] = 'u'
```

If you index into a string in order to find a character at a specific location, the behavior differs according to which version of Ruby you are using. Ruby 1.8 returns a numeric ASCII code of the character, whereas Ruby 1.9 returns the character itself.

```
s = "Hello world"
puts( s[1] )    #=> Ruby 1.8 displays 101; Ruby 1.9 displays 'e'
```

To obtain the actual character from the numeric value returned by
Ruby 1.8, you can use a double index to print a single character, starting
at index 1:

```
s = "Hello world"
puts( s[1,1] ) # prints out 'e'
```

If, on the other hand, you need the numeric value of the character
returned by Ruby 1.9, you can use the ord method like this:

```
puts( s[1].ord)
```

The ord method does not exist in Ruby 1.8, so the previous code causes
an "undefined method" error. To ensure compatibility between Ruby 1.8
and 1.9, you should use the double-index technique, with the first index indicating the starting position and the second index indicating the number of
characters. For example, this returns one character at position 1: s[1,1]. You
can see some more examples in the *char_in_string.rb* program:

char_in_string.rb
```
s = "Hello world"
puts( s[1] )
achar=s[1]
puts( achar )
puts( s[1,1] )
puts( achar.ord )
```

When you run this code, Ruby 1.9 displays this:

```
e
e
e
101
```

whereas Ruby 1.8 displays this:

```
101
101
e
undefined method `ord' for 101:Fixnum (NoMethodError)
```

You can also use double-indexes to return more than one character. If
you want to return three characters starting at position 1, you would enter this:

```
puts( s[1,3] )    # prints 'ell'
```

This tells Ruby to start at position 1 and return the next three characters. Alternatively, you could use the two-dot range notation:

```
puts( s[1..3] )      # also prints 'ell'
```

NOTE *Ranges are discussed in more detail later in this chapter.*

Strings can also be indexed using negative values, in which case -1 is the index of the last character, and, once again, you can specify the number of characters to be returned:

string_index.rb
```
puts( s[-1,1] )      # prints 'd'
puts( s[-5,5] )      # prints 'world'
```

When specifying ranges using a negative index, you must use negative values for both the start and end indexes:

string_methods.rb
```
puts( s[-5..5] )     # this prints an empty string!
puts( s[-5..-1] )    # prints 'world'
```

Finally, you may want to experiment with a few of the standard methods available for manipulating strings. These include methods to change the case of a string, reverse it, insert substrings, remove repeating characters, and so on. I've provided a few examples in *string_methods.rb*. The method names are generally descriptive of their functions. However, bear in mind that methods such as reverse (with no ! at the end) return a new string but do not modify the original string, whereas reverse! (with the !) modifies the original string. You saw similar behavior with the capitalize end capitalize! methods used earlier.

The insert method takes two arguments, an index and a string, and it inserts the string argument at the given index of the string, s. The squeeze method returns a string with any repeating character, such as the second adjacent *l* in "Hello" removed. The split method splits a string into an array. I'll have more to say on split when I discuss regular expressions in Chapter 6. The following examples assume that s is the string "Hello world" and the output is shown in the #=> comments. In the program supplied in this book's code archive, you may also experiment using much longer strings:

```
s.length              #=> 11
s.reverse!            #=> Hello world
s.reverse             #=> dlrow olleH
s.upcase              #=> HELLO WORLD
s.capitalize          #=> Hello world
s.swapcase            #=> hELLO WORLD
s.downcase            #=> hello world
s.insert(7,"NOT ")    #=> hello wNOT orld
s.squeeze             #=> helo wNOT orld
s.split               #=> ["helo", "wNOT", "orld"]
```

Removing Newline Characters: chop and chomp

A couple of handy string-processing methods deserve special mention. The chop and chomp methods can be used to remove characters from the end of a string. The chop method returns a string with the last character removed or with the carriage return and newline characters removed (\r\n) if these are found at the end of the string. The chomp method returns a string with the terminating carriage return or newline character removed (or both the carriage return *and* the newline character if both are found).

These methods are useful when you need to remove line feeds entered by the user or read from a file. For instance, when you use gets to read in a line of text, this returns the line including the terminating *record separator*, which, by default, is the newline character.

THE RECORD SEPARATOR: $/

Ruby predefines a variable, $/, as a record separator. This variable is used by methods such as gets and chomp. The gets method reads in a string up to and including the record separator. The chomp method returns a string with the record separator removed from the end (if present); otherwise, it returns the original string unmodified. You can redefine the record separator if you want, like this:

```
$/= "*"       # the "*" character is now the record separator
```

When you redefine the record separator, this new character (or string) will now be used by methods such as gets and chomp. Here's an example:

record_separator .rb

```
$/= "world"
s = gets()     # user enters "Had we but world enough and time..."
puts( s )      # displays "Had we but world"
```

You can remove the newline character using either chop or chomp. In most cases, chomp is preferable because it won't remove the final character unless it is the record separator (usually a newline), whereas chop will remove the last character no matter what it is. Here are some examples:

chop_chomp.rb

```
# NOTE: s1 includes a carriage return and linefeed
s1 = "Hello world
"
s2 = "Hello world"
s1.chop           # returns "Hello world"
s1.chomp          # returns "Hello world"
s2.chop           # returns "Hello worl" - note the missing 'd'!
s2.chomp          # returns "Hello world"
```

The chomp method also lets you specify a character or string to use as the separator:

```
s2.chomp('rld')   # returns "Hello wo"
```

Format Strings

Ruby provides the `printf` method to print "format strings" containing specifiers starting with a percent sign (%). The format string may be followed by one or more data items separated by commas; the list of data items should match the number and type of the format specifiers. The actual data items replace the matching specifiers in the string, and they are formatted accordingly. These are some common formatting specifiers:

```
%d - decimal number
%f - floating-point number
%o - octal number
%p - inspect object
%s - string
%x - hexadecimal number
```

You can control floating-point precision by putting a point-number before the floating-point formatting specifier, %f. For example, this would display the floating-point value to six digits (the default) followed by a carriage return ("\n"):

string_printf.rb
```
printf( "%f\n", 10.12945 )          #=> 10.129450
```

And the following would display the floating-point value to two digits ("%0.02f"). It is purely a matter of stylistic preference whether the floating-point specifier includes a preceding 0 or not and "%0.2f" is equivalent.

```
printf( "%0.02f\n", 10.12945 )      #=> 10.13
```

Here are a couple more examples:

```
printf("d=%d f=%f o=%o x=%x s=%s\n", 10, 10, 10, 10, 10)
```

That would output d=10 f=10.000000 o=12 x=a s=10.

```
printf("0.04f=%0.04f : 0.02f=%0.02f\n", 10.12945, 10.12945)
```

That would output 0.04f=10.1295 : 0.02f=10.13.

Ranges

In Ruby, a Range is a class that represents a set of values defined by a starting value and an ending value. Typically a range is defined using integers, but it may also be defined using other ordered values such as floating-point numbers or characters. Values can be negative, though you should be careful that your starting value is lower than your ending value!

Here are a few examples:

ranges.rb

```
a = (1..10)
b = (-10..-1)
c = (-10..10)
d = ('a'..'z')
```

You can also specify ranges using three dots instead of two; this creates a range that omits the final value:

```
d = ('a'..'z')      # this two-dot range = 'a'..'z'
e = ('a'...'z')     # this three-dot range = 'a'..'y'
```

You can create an array of the values defined by a range using the to_a method, like this:

```
(1..10).to_a
```

Note that to_a is not defined for floating-point numbers for the simple reason that the number of possible values between two floating-point numbers is not finite.

Ranges of Strings

You can even create ranges of strings—though you would need to take great care in so doing because you might end up with more than you bargain for. For example, see whether you can figure out which values are specified by this range:

str_range.rb

```
str_range = ('abc'..'def')
```

At first sight, the range from 'abc' to 'def' might not look like much. In fact, this defines a range of no less than 2,110 values! They are ordered like this: abc, abd, abe, and so on, until the end of the *a*s; then you start on the *b*s: baa, bab, bac, and so on. Suffice to say that ranges of this sort are probably rather a rare requirement and are best used with extreme caution or not at all.

Iterating with a Range

You may use a range to iterate from a start value to an end value. For example, here is one way of printing all the numbers from 1 to 10:

for_to.rb

```
for i in (1..10) do
    puts( i )
end
```

DIGGING DEEPER

Here you will learn how to create and iterate over ranges, write multiline strings with heredocs, and define your own string delimiters.

Heredocs

Although you can write long strings spanning multiple lines between single or double quotes, many Ruby programmers prefer to use an alternative type of string called a *heredoc*. A heredoc is a block of text that starts by specifying an end marker, which is simply an identifier of your choice. Here, I specify EODOC as the end marker:

heredoc.rb

```
hdoc1 = <<EODOC
```

This tells Ruby that everything following the previous line is a single string that terminates when the end marker is located. The string is assigned to the variable, hdoc1. Here is an example of a complete heredoc assignment:

```
hdoc1 = <<EODOC
I wandered lonely as a #{"cloud".upcase},
That floats on high o'er vale and hill...
EODOC
```

By default, heredocs are treated as double-quoted strings, so expressions such as #{"cloud".upcase} will be evaluated. If you want a heredoc to be treated as single-quoted string, specify its end marker between single quotes:

```
hdoc2 = <<'EODOC'
I wandered lonely as a #{"cloud".upcase},
That floats on high o'er vale and hill...
EODOC
```

The end marker of a heredoc must, by default, be placed flush with the left margin. If you want to indent it, you should use <<- rather than << when assigning the end marker:

```
hdoc3 = <<-EODOC
I wandered lonely as a #{"cloud".upcase},
That floats on high o'er vale and hill...
    EODOC
```

It is up to you to pick an appropriate end marker. It is even legitimate (though, perhaps, not particularly sensible!) to use a reserved word:

```
hdoc4 = <<def
I wandered lonely as a #{"cloud".upcase},
That floats on high o'er vale and hill...
def
```

A variable to which a heredoc is assigned can be used just like any other string variable:

```
puts( hdoc1 )
```

String Literals

As explained earlier in this chapter, you can optionally delimit strings by %q/ and / for single-quoted strings and either %Q/ and / or %/ and / for double-quoted strings.

Ruby provides similar means of delimiting back-quoted strings, regular expressions, symbols, and arrays of either single-quoted or double-quoted strings. The ability to define arrays of strings in this way is particularly useful since it avoids the necessity of entering string delimiters for each item. Here is a reference to these string literal delimiters:

```
%q/    /    # single-quoted
%Q/    /    # double-quoted
%/     /    # double-quoted
%w/    /    # array
%W/    /    # array double-quoted
%r|    |    # regular expression
%s/    /    # symbol
%x/    /    # operating system command
```

Note that you may choose which delimiters to use. I have used / except with the regular expression where I have used | (since / is the "normal" regular expression delimiter), but I could equally have used square brackets, asterisks, ampersands, or other symbols (for example, %W*dog cat #{1+2}* or %s&dog&). Here is an example of these literals in use:

literals.rb

```
p %q/dog cat #{1+2}/        #=> "dog cat \#{1+2}"
p %Q/dog cat #{1+2}/        #=> "dog cat 3"
p %/dog cat #{1+2}/         #=> "dog cat 3"
p %w/dog cat #{1+2}/        #=> ["dog", "cat", "\#{1+2}"]
p %W/dog cat #{1+2}/        #=> ["dog", "cat", "3"]
p %r|^[a-z]*$|              #=> /^[a-z]*$/
p %s/dog/                   #=> :dog
p %x/vol/                   #=> " Volume in drive C is OS [etc...]"
```

4

ARRAYS AND HASHES

Up to now, you've generally been using objects one at a time. In this chapter, you'll find out how to create a list of objects. You'll start by looking at the most common type of list structure: an array.

Arrays

An *array* is a sequential collection of items in which each item can be indexed. In Ruby (unlike many other languages), a single array can contain items of mixed data types such as strings, integers, and floats or even a method call that returns some value. For example, the final element in a1 shown here calls my method, array_length, which returns the length of the array, a0:

array0.rb

```
def array_length( anArray )
    return anArray.length
end
```

```
a0 = [1,2,3,4,5]
a1 = [1,'two', 3.0, array_length( a0 ) ]
p( a1 )          #=>[1, "two", 3.0, 5]
```

The first item in an array has the index 0, which means the final item has an index equal to the total number of items in the array minus 1. Given the array a1, shown previously, this is how to obtain the values of the first and last items:

```
a1[0]          # returns 1st item (at index 0)
a1[3]          # returns 4th item (at index 3)
```

You've already used arrays a few times—for example, in *2adventure.rb* you used an array to store a map of Room objects:

```
mymap = Map.new([room1,room2,room3])
```

Creating Arrays

Like many other programming languages, Ruby uses square brackets to delimit an array. You can easily create an array, fill it with some comma-delimited values, and assign it to a variable:

```
arr = ['one','two','three','four']
```

As with most other things in Ruby, arrays are objects. They are defined, as you might guess, by the Array class and, just like strings, they are indexed from 0. You can reference an item in an array by placing its index between square brackets. If the index is invalid, nil is returned:

array1.rb

```
arr = ['a', 'b', 'c']
puts(arr[0])       # shows 'a'
puts(arr[1])       # shows 'b'
puts(arr[2])       # shows 'c'
puts(arr[3])       # nil
```

DISPLAYING NIL

When you attempt to display a nil value using print or puts, Ruby 1.8 displays "nil," whereas Ruby 1.9 displays an empty string. If you want to be sure that the string representation of nil is displayed, use p or the inspect method instead of print. You may also display its class (nil is an instance of NilClass) or test whether it is nil using the nil? method:

array1.rb

```
puts(arr[3].inspect)     #=> nil
puts(arr[3].class)       #=> NilClass
p(arr[3])                #=> nil
puts(arr[3].nil?)        #=> true
```

An array may include expressions that yield values. Let's assume you have already created this method:

array2.rb

```
def hello
  return "hello world"
end
```

You can now declare this array:

```
x = [1+2, hello, `dir`]
```

Here, the first element is a mathematical expression that yields the integer 3, and the second is the string "hello world" (returned by the method hello). If you run this on Windows, the third array element will be a string containing a directory listing. This is because `dir` is a back-quoted string, which is executed by the operating system (see Chapter 3). The final "slot" in the array is, therefore, filled with the value returned by the dir command, which happens to be a string of filenames. If you are running on a different operating system, you may need to substitute an appropriate command at this point. (For example, if you're running a Unix-like operating system, you could substitute `ls` to get a similar string of filenames.)

CREATING AN ARRAY OF FILENAMES

A number of Ruby classes have methods that return arrays of values. For example, the Dir class, which is used to perform operations on disk directories, has the entries method. Pass a directory name to the method, and it returns a list of files in an array:

dir_array.rb

```
Dir.entries( 'C:\\' )  # returns an array of files in C:\
```

If you want to create an array of single-quoted strings but can't be bothered to type all the quotation marks, a shortcut is to put unquoted text separated by spaces between parentheses preceded by %w (or use a capital %W for double-quoted strings, as explained in Chapter 3).

array2.rb

```
y = %w( this is an array of strings )
```

The previous code assigns the array shown next to the variable, y:

```
["this", "is", "an", "array", "of", "strings"]
```

You can also create arrays using the usual object construction method, new. Optionally, you can pass an integer to new to create an empty array of a specific size (with each element set to nil), or you can pass two arguments: the first to set the size of the array and the second to specify the element to place at each index of the array, like this:

```
a = Array.new                    # an empty array
a = Array.new(2)                 # [nil,nil]
a = Array.new(2,"hello world")   # ["hello world","hello world"]
```

Multidimensional Arrays

To create a multidimensional array, you can create one array and then add other arrays to each of its "slots." For example, this creates an array containing two elements, each of which is itself an array of two elements:

```
a = Array.new(2)
a[0]= Array.new(2,'hello')
a[1]= Array.new(2,'world')
```

NOTE   *You can also create an Array object by passing an array as an argument to the* new *method. Be careful, though: Ruby considers it a syntax error if you fail to leave a space between the* new *method and the opening square bracket. In other words, this works:* a = Array.new [1,2,3]. *However, this doesn't:* a = Array.new[1,2,3]. *But using parentheses always works, no matter where you put a space:* a = Array.new([1,2,3]).

It is also possible to nest arrays inside one another using square brackets. This creates an array of four arrays, each of which contains four integers:

```
a = [    [1,2,3,4],
     [5,6,7,8],
     [9,10,11,12],
     [13,14,15,16]   ]
```

In the previous code, I have placed the four "subarrays" on separate lines. This is not obligatory, but it does help clarify the structure of the multidimensional array by displaying each subarray as though it were a row, similar to the rows in a spreadsheet. When talking about arrays within arrays, it is convenient to refer to each nested array as a "row" of the "outer" array.

For some more examples of using multidimensional arrays, load the *multi_array.rb* program. This starts by creating an array, multiarr, containing two other arrays. The first of these arrays is at index 0 of multiarr, and the second is at index 1:

multi_array.rb   `multiarr = [['one','two','three','four'],[1,2,3,4]]`

Next you need to find some way to locate the individual elements within arrays, which are themselves contained inside other arrays. You'll consider this problem in the next section.

Iterating over Arrays

You can access the elements of an array by iterating over them using a for loop. In many programming languages, a for loop counts over a fixed number of elements from a starting number (such as 0) to an ending number (such as 10), incrementing a counter variable (such as i) at each pass through the loop. So, in other languages, you might be used to writing a loop something like this: for i = 1 to 10.

In Ruby, the normal for loop counts over all the items *in* a collection and may be referred to as a for..in loop. Its counter variable is assigned each object in a collection, one by one, at each pass through the loop. The syntax may be summarized as for *anObject* in *aCollection*, and at each turn through the loop, the variable anObject is assigned a new item from the collection aCollection until no more items remain. The loop shown next iterates over two elements, namely, the two subarrays at index 0 and 1:

```
for i in multiarr
    puts(i.inspect)
end
```

This displays the following:

```
["one", "two", "three", "four"]
[1, 2, 3, 4]
```

So, how do you iterate over the items (the strings and integers) in each of the two subarrays? If there is a fixed number of items, you could specify a different iterator variable for each, in which case each variable will be assigned the value from the matching array index.

Here you have four subarray slots, so you could use four variables like this:

```
for (a,b,c,d) in multiarr
    print("a=#{a}, b=#{b}, c=#{c}, d=#{d}\n" )
end
```

You could also use a for loop to iterate over all the items in each subarray individually:

multi_array2.rb
```
for s in multiarr[0]
   puts(s)
end
for s in multiarr[1]
   puts(s)
end
```

Both of these techniques (multiple iterator variables and multiple for loops) have two requirements: that you know how many items there are in either the "rows" or the "columns" of the grid of arrays and that each sub-array contains the same number of items as each other.

For a more flexible way of iterating over multidimensional arrays, you could use nested for loops. An outer loop iterates over each row (subarray), and an inner loop iterates over each item in the current row. This technique works even when subarrays have varying numbers of items:

```
for row  in multiarr
    for item in row
        puts(item)
    end
end
```

You'll be looking at for loops and other iterators in more depth in the next chapter.

Indexing into Arrays

As with strings (see Chapter 3), you can index from the end of an array using negative numbers, where −1 is the index of the last element, −2 is the second-to-last, and so on. You can also use ranges, like this:

array_index.rb

```
arr = ['h','e','l','l','o',' ','w','o','r','l','d']

print( arr[0,5] )        #=> hello (or) ["h", "e", "l", "l", "o"]
print( arr[-5,5 ] )      #=> world (or) ["w", "o", "r", "l", "d"]
print( arr[0..4] )       #=> hello (or) ["h", "e", "l", "l", "o"]
print( arr[-5..-1] )     #=> world (or) ["w", "o", "r", "l", "d"]
```

Note that the output displayed by print or puts may vary depending on your version of Ruby. When Ruby 1.8 displays the elements in an array, it shows them one after the other so they look like a single string, as in hello. Ruby 1.9, however, shows the items in array format, as in ["h", "e", "l", "l", "o"].

If you use p instead of print to inspect the array, both Ruby 1.8 and 1.9 display the same result:

```
p( arr[0,5] )    #=> ["h", "e", "l", "l", "o"]
p( arr[0..4] )   #=> ["h", "e", "l", "l", "o"]
```

As with strings, when you provide two integers in order to return a number of contiguous items from an array, the first integer is the start index, while the second is a *count* of the number of items (*not* an index):

```
arr[0,5]    # returns 5 chars - ["h", "e", "l", "l", "o"]
```

You can also make assignments by indexing into an array. Here, for example, I first create an empty array and then put items into indexes 0, 1, and 3. The "empty" slot at index 2 will be filled with a `nil` value:

```
arr = []

arr[0] = [0]
arr[1] = ["one"]
arr[3] = ["a", "b", "c"]

# arr now contains:
# [[0], ["one"], nil, ["a", "b", "c"]]
```

Once again, you can use start-end indexes, ranges, and negative index values:

```
arr2 = ['h','e','l','l','o',' ','w','o','r','l','d']

arr2[0] = 'H'
arr2[2,2] = 'L', 'L'
arr2[4..6] = 'O','-','W'
arr2[-4,4] = 'a','l','d','o'

# arr2 now contains:
# ["H", "e", "L", "L", "O", "-", "W", "a", "l", "d", "o"]
```

Copying Arrays

Note that when you use the assignment operator (`=`) to assign one array variable to another variable, you are actually assigning a *reference* to the array; you are not making a copy. For example, if you assign one array called arr1 to another array called arr2, any changes made to either variable will also alter the value of the other because *both variables refer to the same array*. If you want the variables to reference two different arrays, you can use the `clone` method to make a new copy:

```
arr1=['h','e','l','l','o',' ','w','o','r','l','d']
arr2=arr1  # arr2 is now the same as arr1.
           # Change arr1 and arr2 changes too!
arr3=arr1.clone
           # arr3 is a copy of arr1.
           # Change arr3 and arr2 is unaffected
```

Testing Arrays for Equality

The comparison operator for arrays is `<=>`. This compares two arrays—let's call them arr1 and arr2. It returns -1 if arr1 is less than arr2, it returns 0 if arr1 and arr2 are equal, and it returns 1 if arr2 is greater than arr1. But how does Ruby determine whether one array is "greater than" or "less than" another?

It compares each item in one array with the corresponding item in the other. When two values are not equal, the result of their comparison is returned. In other words, if this comparison were made:

```
[0,10,20] <=> [0,20,20]
```

the value -1 would be returned. This means the first array is "less than" the second, since the integer at index 1 of the first array (10) is less than the integer at index 1 in the second array (20).

If you want to make a comparison based on the array's length rather than the value of its elements, you can use the length method:

```
# Here [2,3,4].length is less than [1,2,3,4].length
p([1,2,3].length<=>[1,2,3,4].length)    #=> -1
p([2,3,4].length<=>[1,2,3,4].length)    #=> -1
```

If you are comparing arrays of strings, then comparisons are made on the ASCII values of the characters that make up those strings. If one array is longer than another and the elements in both arrays are equal, then the longer array is deemed to be "greater." However, if two such arrays are compared and one of the elements in the shorter array is greater than the corresponding element in the longer array, then the *shorter* array is deemed to be greater.

array_compare.rb

```
p([1,2,3]<=>[2,3,4])           #=> -1    (array 1 < array 2)
p([2,3,4]<=>[1,2,3])           #=> 1     (array 1 > array 2)
p([1,2,3,4]<=>[1,2,3])         #=> 1     (array 1 > array 2)all
p([1,2,3,4]<=>[100,200,300])   #=> -1    (array 1 < array 2)
p([1,2,3]<=>["1","2","3"])     #=> nil   (invalid comparison)
```

Sorting Arrays

The sort method compares adjacent array elements using the comparison operator <=>. This operator is defined for many Ruby classes, including Array, String, Float, Date, and Fixnum. The operator is not, however, defined for *all* classes (that is to say, it is not defined for the Object class from which all other classes are derived). One of the unfortunate consequences of this is that it cannot be used to sort arrays containing nil values. However, it is possible to get around this limitation by defining your own sorting routine. This is done by sending a *block* to the sort method. You'll learn about blocks in detail in Chapter 10, but for now it's enough to know a block is a chunk of code delimited either by curly brackets or by the keywords do and end. The following block determines the comparison used by the sort method:

```
arr.sort{
  |a,b|
    a.to_s <=> b.to_s
}
```

Here arr is an array object, and the variables a and b represent two contiguous array elements. I've converted each variable to a string using the to_s method; this converts nil to an empty string that will be sorted "low." Note that although my sorting block defines the sort order of the array items, it does not change the array items themselves. So, nil will remain as nil, and integers will remain as integers. The string conversion is used only to implement the comparison, not to change the array items.

array_sort.rb

```
arr = ['h','e','l','l','o',' ',nil,'w','o','r','l','d',1,2,3,nil,4,5]

# sort ascending from nil upwards
sorted_arr = arr.sort{
    |a,b|
        a.to_s <=> b.to_s
    }

p(sorted_arr )
```

This is the array created and displayed by the previous code:

```
[nil, nil, " ", 1, 2, 3, 4, 5, "d", "e", "h", "l", "l", "l", "o", "o", "r", "w"]
```

The *array_sort.rb* program supplied in the code archive also contains a method to sort in descending order. This is done simply by changing the order of the items on either side of the comparison operator:

```
reverse_sorted_arr = arr.sort{
    |a,b|
        b.to_s <=> a.to_s
    }
```

Comparing Values

The comparison "operator" <=> (which is, in fact, a method) is defined in the Ruby module named Comparable. For now, you can think of a module as a sort of reusable code library. You'll be looking more closely at modules in Chapter 12.

You can include the Comparable module in your own classes. This lets you override the <=> method to enable you to define exactly how comparisons will be made between specific object types. For example, you may want to subclass Array so that comparisons are made based purely on the length of two arrays rather than on the value of each item in the array (which is the default, as explained in "Testing Arrays for Equality" on page 53). This is how you might do this:

comparisons.rb

```
class MyArray < Array
  include Comparable

  def <=> ( anotherArray )
    self.length <=> anotherArray.length
  end
end
```

Now, you can initialize two MyArray objects like this:

```
myarr1 = MyArray.new([0,1,2,3])
myarr2 = MyArray.new([1,2,3,4])
```

And you can use the <=> method defined in MyArray to make comparisons:

```
                          # Two MyArray objects
myarr1 <=> myarr2         #=> 0
```

This comparison returns 0, which indicates that the two arrays are equal (since our <=> method evaluates equality according to length alone). If, on the other hand, you were to initialize two standard arrays with exactly the same integer values, the Array class's own <=> method would perform the comparison:

```
                          # Two Array objects
arr1 <=> arr2             #=> -1
```

Here the comparison returns -1, which indicates that the first array evaluates to "less than" the second array, since the Array class's <=> method compares the numerical values of each item in arr1 and these are less than the values of the items at the same indexes in arr2.

But what if you want to make "less than," "equal to," and "greater than" comparisons using the traditional programming notation?

```
<                  # less than
==                 # equal to
>                  # greater than
```

In the MyArray class, you can make comparisons of this sort without writing any additional code. This is because the Comparable module, which has been included in the MyArray class, automatically supplies these three comparison methods; each method makes its comparison based on the definition of the <=> method. Since our <=> makes its evaluation based on the number of items in an array, the < method evaluates to true when the first array is shorter than the second, == evaluates to true when both arrays are of equal length, and > evaluates to true when the second array is longer than the first:

```
p( myarr1 < myarr2 )      #=> false
p( myarr1 == myarr2 )     #=> true
```

The standard Array class does not include the Comparable module. So if you try to compare two ordinary arrays using <, ==, or >, Ruby will display an error message telling you that the method is undefined.

However, it's easy to add these three methods to a subclass of Array. All you have to do is include Comparable, like this:

```
class Array2 < Array
  include Comparable
end
```

The Array2 class will now perform its comparisons based on the <=> method of Array—that is, by testing the values of the items stored in the array rather than merely testing the length of the array. Assuming that the Array2 objects, arr1 and arr2, are initialized with the same arrays that you previously used for myarr1 and myarr2, you would now see these results:

```
p( arr1 < arr2 )        #=> true
p( arr1 > arr2 )        #=> false
```

Array Methods

Several of the standard array methods modify the array itself rather than returning a modified copy of the array. These include the methods marked with a terminating exclamation point, such as sort!, reverse!, flatten!, and compact!. These also include the << method, which modifies the array to its left by adding to it the array on its right; clear, which removes all the elements from the given array; and delete and delete_at, which remove selected elements. Table 4-1 shows some of the more commonly used Array methods.

Table 4-1: Commonly Used Array Methods

Array	Task
&	Returns common elements of two arrays, no duplicates
+	Returns array concatenating two arrays
-	Returns array with items in second array removed from first
<<	Modifies first array by appending items from second array
clear	Modifies array by removing all elements
compact	Returns array with nil items removed
compact!	Modifies array by removing nil items
delete(object)	Modifies array by deleting object
delete_at(index)	Modifies array by deleting item at index
flatten	Unpacks nested array items and returns array
flatten!	Modifies array by unpacking nested array items
length	Returns number of elements in array
reverse	Returns array with elements in reverse order
reverse!	Modifies array by reversing element order
sort	Returns array sorted using <=>
sort!	Modifies array sorted using <=>

You can try the previous methods in the *array_methods.rb* sample program. Here are a few examples:

array_methods.rb
```
arr1 = [1,1,2,2,3,3]
arr2 = [1,2,3,4,5,6,7,8,9]
arr3 = ['h','e','l','l','o',' ',nil,'w','o','r','l','d']

p(arr1&arr2 )       #=> [1, 2, 3]
p(arr1+arr2)        #=> [1, 1, 2, 2, 3, 3, 1, 2, 3, 4, 5, 6, 7, 8, 9]
p(arr1-arr2)        #=> []
p(arr2-arr1)        #=> [4, 5, 6, 7, 8, 9]
arr1<<arr2
p(arr1)             #=> [1, 1, 2, 2, 3, 3, [1, 2, 3, 4, 5, 6, 7, 8, 9]]
arr1.clear
p(arr1)             #=>[]
```

Although most of the behavior array methods may be deduced from their names, the flatten and compact methods need some explanation. An array is said to be *flattened* when it contains no subarrays. So if you have an array like [1,[2,3]], you can call [1,[2,3]].flatten to return this array: [1,2,3].

An array is said to be *compacted* when it contains no nil items. So if you have an array like [1,2,nil,3], you can call [1,2,nil,3].compact to return this array: [1,2,3]. The methods of Array can be chained together by placing one method call directly after the other:

flatten_compact.rb
```
p( [1,nil,[2,nil,3]].flatten.compact ) #=> [1,2,3]
```

Hashes

Although arrays provide a good way of indexing a collection of items by number, sometimes it would be more convenient to index them in some other way. If, for example, you were creating a collection of recipes, it would be more meaningful to have each recipe indexed by name, such as "Rich Chocolate Cake" and "Coq au Vin," rather than by numbers.

Ruby has a class that lets you do just that, called a *hash*. This is the equivalent of what some other languages call a dictionary or associative array. Just like a real dictionary, each entry is indexed by a unique *key* (in a real-life dictionary, this would be a word) that is associated with a value (in a dictionary, this would be the definition of the word).

Creating Hashes

Just like an array, you can create a hash by creating a new instance of the Hash class:

hash1.rb
```
h1 = Hash.new
h2 = Hash.new("Some kind of ring")
```

Both the previous examples create an empty Hash object. A Hash object always has a default value—that is, a value that is returned when no specific value is found at a given index. In these examples, h2 is initialized with the default value "Some kind of ring"; h1 is not initialized with a value, so its default value will be nil.

Having created a Hash object, you can add items to it using an arraylike syntax—that is, by placing the index in square brackets and using = to assign a value. The obvious difference is that, with an array, the index (or *key*) must be an integer; with a hash, it can be any unique data item:

```
h2['treasure1'] = 'Silver ring'
h2['treasure2'] = 'Gold ring'
h2['treasure3'] = 'Ruby ring'
h2['treasure4'] = 'Sapphire ring'
```

Often, the key may be a number or, as in the previous code, a string. In principle, however, a key can be any type of object. For example, given some class X, the following assignment is perfectly legal:

```
x1 = X.new('my Xobject')
h2[x1] = 'Diamond ring'
```

UNIQUE KEYS?

Take care when assigning keys to hashes. If you use the same key twice in a hash, you will end up overwriting the original value. This is just like assigning a value twice to the same index in an array. Consider this example:

```
h2['treasure1'] = 'Silver ring'
h2['treasure2'] = 'Gold ring'
h2['treasure3'] = 'Ruby ring'
h2['treasure1'] = 'Sapphire ring'
```

Here the key 'treasure1' has been used twice. As a consequence, the original value, 'Silver ring', has been replaced by 'Sapphire ring', resulting in this hash:

```
{"treasure1"=>"Sapphire ring", "treasure2"=>"Gold ring", "treasure3"=>"Ruby ring"}
```

There is a shorthand way of creating Hashes and initializing them with key-value pairs. Just add a key followed by => and its associated value; each key-value pair should be separated by a comma and the whole lot placed inside a pair of curly brackets:

```
h1 = {    'room1'=>'The Treasure Room',
          'room2'=>'The Throne Room',
          'loc1'=>'A Forest Glade',
          'loc2'=>'A Mountain Stream' }
```

Indexing into a Hash

To access a value, place its key between square brackets:

```
puts(h1['room2'])               #=> 'The Throne Room'
```

If you specify a key that does not exist, the default value is returned. Recall that you have not specified a default value for h1, but you have for h2:

```
p(h1['unknown_room'])           #=> nil
p(h2['unknown_treasure'])       #=> 'Some kind of ring'
```

Use the default method to get the default value and the default= method to set it (see Chapter 2 for more information on get and set accessor methods):

```
p(h1.default)
h1.default = 'A mysterious place'
```

Copying a Hash

As with an array, you can assign one Hash variable to another, in which case both variables will refer to the same hash, and a change made using either variable will affect that hash:

hash2.rb
```
h4 = h1
h4['room1']='A new Room'
puts(h1['room1'])          #=> 'A new Room'
```

If you want the two variables to refer to the same items in different Hash objects, use the clone method to make a new copy:

```
h5 = h1.clone
h5['room1'] = 'An even newer Room'
puts(h1['room1'])            #=> 'A new room' (i.e., its value is unchanged)
```

Hash Order

The ordering of elements in a hash varies according to which version of Ruby you are using. In Ruby 1.8, a hash is generally stored in the order defined by its key where, for example, key 1 is less than key 2. When new items are added, these are inserted in key order. In Ruby 1.9, the hash is stored in the order in which it is defined. When new items are added, these are appended to the end of the hash.

As a general principle, it is best to make no assumptions about the order of elements in a hash. Most programming languages treat hashes or dictionaries as unordered collections. If you make the assumption that hash order is unpredictable, not only will you avoid bugs that may occur when running programs with different Ruby implementations, but you will also avoid problems that may arise when keys are of different types. Remember, a single hash may contain a mix of integer, string, and floating-point keys whose relative orders may not be self-evident.

hash_order.rb

```
h = {2=>"two", 1=>"one", 4=>"four" }
p( h )
h[3] = "three"
p( h )
h2 = {"one"=>1, 2=>"two", 4.5=>"four" }
p (h2)
```

When this code is run, Ruby 1.8 produces this output:

```
{1=>"one", 2=>"two", 4=>"four"}
{1=>"one", 2=>"two", 3=>"three", 4=>"four"}
{4.5=>"four", 2=>"two", "one"=>1}
```

But Ruby 1.9 shows this:

```
{2=>"two", 1=>"one", 4=>"four"}
{2=>"two", 1=>"one", 4=>"four", 3=>"three"}
{2=>"two", "one"=>1, 4.5=>"four"}
```

Sorting a Hash

If you want to ensure that the elements of a hash are in a specific order, you may sort them. As with the Array class, you may find a slight problem with the sort method of Hash. It expects to be dealing with keys of the same data type, so if, for example, you merge two arrays, one of which uses integer keys and another of which uses strings, you won't be able to sort the merged hash. The solution to this problem is, as with Array, to write some code to perform a custom type of comparison and pass this to the sort method. You might give it a method, like this:

hash_sort.rb

```
def sorted_hash( aHash )
  return aHash.sort{
    |a,b|
      a.to_s <=> b.to_s
  }
end
```

This performs the sort based on the string representation (to_s) of each key in the hash. In fact, the Hash sort method converts the hash to a nested array of *[key, value]* arrays and sorts them using the Array sort method.

Hash Methods

The Hash class has numerous built-in methods. For example, to delete an item from a hash using its key, use the delete method:

```
aHash.delete( someKey )To test if a key or value exists, use the has_key? and
has_value? methods:aHash.has_key?( someKey )
aHash.has_value?( someValue )
```

To combine two hashes, use the merge method: hash1.merge(hash2).

To return a new hash created using the original hash's values as keys and its keys as values, use aHash.invert. To return an array populated with the hash's keys or values, use aHash.keys and aHash.values.

Here's an example that uses some of these methods:

hash_methods.rb
```
h1 = {
    'room1'=>'The Treasure Room',
    'room2'=>'The Throne Room',
    'loc1'=>'A Forest Glade',
    'loc2'=>'A Mountain Stream'
    }

h2 = {1=>'one', 2=>'two', 3=> 'three'}

h1['room1'] = 'You have wandered into a dark room'
h1.delete('loc2')
p(h1)
                            #=> {"room1"=>"You have wandered into a dark room",
                            #=> "room2"=>"The Throne Room",
                            #=> "loc1"=>"A Forest Glade"}
p(h1.has_key?('loc2'))      #=> false
p(h2.has_value?("two"))     #=>true
p(h2.invert)                #=> {"one"=>1, "two"=>2, "three"=>3}
p(h2.keys)                  #=>[1, 2, 3]
p(h2.values)                #=>["one", "two", "three"]
```

If you want to find the position of an item in a hash, use the index method with Ruby 1.8 and the key method in Ruby 1.9. The index method is still present in Ruby 1.9 but is deprecated, so it may be removed in future versions:

```
h2.index("two")    # use this with Ruby 1.8
h2.key("two")      # use this Ruby 1.9
```

DIGGING DEEPER

In this section you will learn more ways of manipulating arrays and hashes as well as the fundamentals of matrices, vectors and sets.

Treating Hashes as Arrays

The keys and values methods of Hash each return an array, so you can use various Array methods to manipulate them. Here are a few simple examples (remember the order of the keys and value may differ according to the version of Ruby being used):

hash_ops.rb

```
h1 = {'key1'=>'val1', 'key2'=>'val2', 'key3'=>'val3', 'key4'=>'val4'}
h2 = {'key1'=>'val1', 'KEY_TWO'=>'val2', 'key3'=>'VALUE_3', 'key4'=>'val4'}

p( h1.keys & h2.keys )                    # set intersection (keys)
#=> ["key1", "key3", "key4"]

p( h1.values & h2.values )                # set intersection (values)
#=> ["val1", "val2", "val4"]

p( h1.keys+h2.keys )                       # concatenation
#=> [ "key1", "key2", "key3", "key4", "key1", "key3", "key4", "KEY_TWO"]

p( h1.values-h2.values )                   # difference
#=> ["val3"]

p( (h1.keys << h2.keys) )                  # append
#=> ["key1", "key2", "key3", "key4", ["key1", "key3", "key4", "KEY_TWO"]]

p( (h1.keys << h2.keys).flatten.reverse )   # 'un-nest' arrays and reverse
#=> ["KEY_TWO", "key4", "key3", "key1", "key4", "key3", "key2", "key1"]
```

Appending vs. Concatenating

Be careful to note the difference between concatenating using + to add the *values* from the second array to the first and appending using << to add the second *array* itself as the final element of the first:

append_concat.rb

```
a =[1,2,3]
b =[4,5,6]
c = a + b          #=> c=[1, 2, 3, 4, 5, 6]   a=[1, 2, 3]
a << b             #=> a=[1, 2, 3, [4, 5, 6]]
```

In addition, << modifies the first (the *receiver*) array, whereas + returns a new array but leaves the receiver array unchanged.

In object-oriented terminology, the object to which a method belongs is called the receiver. The idea is that instead of calling functions as in procedural languages, "messages" are sent to objects. For example, the message + 1 might be sent to an integer object, while the message reverse might be sent to a string object. The object that "receives" a message tries to find a way (that is, a method) of responding to the message. A string object, for example, has a reverse method and so is able to respond to the reverse message, whereas an integer object has no such method so cannot respond.

You can use the `flatten` method to clean up two arrays you've combined with `<<`, like this:

```
a=[1, 2, 3, [4, 5, 6]]
a.flatten          #=> [1, 2, 3, 4, 5, 6]
```

Vectors and Matrices

For the benefit of mathematicians, Ruby provides a Vector class and a Matrix class. A *vector* is an ordered set of elements upon which certain mathematical operations may be performed. A *matrix* is a collection of rows and columns, and each row is itself a vector. Matrices allow you to perform matrix manipulations, which is a subject beyond the scope of this book and is only likely to be of interest to mathematical programmers. However, you'll look at some simple examples here.

First, given two Matrix objects, m1 and m2, you can add the values of each corresponding cell in the matrices with the plus sign, like this: `m3 = m1+m2`. You must import Matrix using a require directive in order to use it:

matrix.rb

```
require "Matrix"    # This is essential!

m1 = Matrix[ [1,2,3,4],
             [5,6,7,8],
             [9,10,11,12],
             [13,14,15,16]  ]

m2 = Matrix[ [10,20,30,40],
             [50,60,70,80],
             [90,100,110,120],
             [130,140,150,160]  ]

m3 = m1+m2
p(m3)
```

This outputs the following matrix:

```
Matrix[[11, 22, 33, 44], [55, 66, 77, 88], [99, 110, 121, 132], [143, 154, 165, 176]]
```

The following example creates a matrix from two vectors. By passing vectors to the `Matrix.columns()` method, you construct a matrix whose rows are arrays of arrays. Here the matrix has two columns created from the vectors v and v2, with each row containing two items, one from each column:

```
v = Vector[1,2,3,4,5]
v2 = Vector[6,7,8,9,10]
m4 = Matrix.columns([v,v2])
p( m4 )
```

This outputs the following:

```
Matrix[[1, 6], [2, 7], [3, 8], [4, 9], [5, 10]]
```

If, on the other hand, you pass the same two vectors to the `Matrix.rows()` method, you would end up by creating a matrix that contains two rows, each of which is a vector:

```
m5 = Matrix.rows([v,v2])
p( m5 )
```

This outputs the following:

```
Matrix[Vector[1, 2, 3, 4, 5], Vector[6, 7, 8, 9, 10]]
```

Sets

The Set class implements a collection of unordered values with no duplicates. You can initialize a Set with an array of values, in which case duplicates are ignored:

sets.rb

```
s1 = Set.new( [1,2,3,4,5,2] )
s2 = Set.new( [1,1,2,3,4,4,5,1] )
s3 = Set.new( [1,2,100] )
weekdays = Set.new( %w( Monday, Tuesday, Wednesday, Thursday,
        Friday, Saturday, Sunday ) )
```

You can add new values using the add method:

```
s1.add( 1000 )
```

The merge method combines values of one set with another:

```
s1.merge(s2)
```

You can use == to test for equality. Two sets that contain the same values (remembering that duplicates will be removed when a set is created) are considered to be equal:

```
p( s1 == s2 )                    #=> true
```

If you display the contents of a set, the order may differ according to the version of Ruby being used. If order is important, you may convert a set to an array using the to_a method and use a standard or custom sort, as explained in "Sorting Arrays" on page 54:

```
p( weekdays.to_a.sort ) # sort alphabetically
#=> ["Friday,", "Monday,", "Saturday,", "Sunday", "Thursday,", "Tuesday,", "Wednesday,"]
```

5

LOOPS AND ITERATORS

Much of programming is concerned with repetition. Maybe you want your program to beep 10 times, read lines from a file as long as there are more lines to read, or display a warning until the user presses a key. Ruby provides a number of ways of performing this kind of repetition.

for Loops

In many programming languages, when you want to run a bit of code a certain number of times, you can just put it inside a for loop. In most languages, you give a for loop a variable initialized with a starting value that is incremented by 1 on each turn through the loop until it meets some specific ending value. When the ending value is met, the for loop stops running.

Here's a version of this traditional type of for loop written in Pascal:

```
(* This is Pascal code, not Ruby! *)
for i := 1 to 3 do
   writeln( i );
```

You may recall from the previous chapter that Ruby's for loop doesn't work like this at all! Instead of giving it starting and ending values, you give the for loop a list of items, and it iterates over them, one by one, assigning each value in turn to a loop variable until it gets to the end of the list.

For example, here is a for loop that iterates over the items in an array, displaying each in turn:

for_loop.rb

```
# This is Ruby code...
for i in [1,2,3] do
   puts( i )
end
```

The for loop is more like the "for each" iterator provided by some other programming languages. The items over which the loop iterates don't have to be integers. This works just as well:

```
for s in ['one','two','three'] do
   puts( s )
end
```

The author of Ruby describes for as "syntax sugar" for the each method, which is implemented by collection types such as Arrays, Sets, Hashes, and Strings (a String being, in effect, a collection of characters). For the sake of comparison, this is one of the for loops shown earlier rewritten using the each method:

each_loop.rb

```
[1,2,3].each  do |i|
   puts( i )
end
```

As you can see, there isn't really all that much difference. To convert the for loop to an each iterator, all I've had to do is delete for and in and append .each to the array. Then I've put the iterator variable, i, between a pair of upright bars after do. Compare these other examples to see just how similar for loops are to each iterators.

for_each.rb

```
# --- Example 1 ---
# i) for
for s in ['one','two','three'] do
   puts( s )
end
```

```
# ii) each
['one','two','three'].each do |s|
   puts( s )
end


# --- Example 2 ---
# i) for
for x in [1, "two", [3,4,5] ] do puts( x ) end

# ii) each
[1, "two", [3,4,5] ].each do |x| puts( x ) end
```

Note, incidentally, that the do keyword is optional in a for loop that spans multiple lines, but it is obligatory when it is written on a single line:

```
# Here the 'do' keyword can be omitted
for s in ['one','two','three']
   puts( s )
end


# But here it is required
for s in ['one','two','three'] do puts( s ) end
```

This example shows how both for and each can be used to iterate over the values in a range:

for_each2.rb

```
# for
for s in 1..3
   puts( s )
end

# each
(1..3).each do |s|
   puts(s)
end
```

HOW TO WRITE A "NORMAL" FOR LOOP

If you miss the traditional type of for loop, you can always fake it in Ruby by using a for loop to iterate over the values in a range. For example, this is how to use a for loop variable to count up from 1 to 10, displaying its value at each turn through the loop:

for_to.rb

```
for i in (1..10) do
   puts( i )
end
```

Note, incidentally, that a range expression such as 1..3 must be enclosed between parentheses when used with the each method, or Ruby assumes you are attempting to use each as a method of the final integer (a Fixnum) rather than of the entire expression (a Range). The parentheses are optional when a range is used in a for loop.

Blocks and Block Parameters

In Ruby, the body of an iterator is called a *block*, and any variables declared between upright bars at the top of a block are called *block parameters*. In a way, a block works like a function, and the block parameters work like a function's argument list. The each method runs the code inside the block and passes to it the arguments supplied by a collection (such as the array, multiarr). In the example from the previous section, the each method repeatedly passes an array of four elements to the block, and those elements initialize the four block parameters, a, b, c, d. Blocks can be used for other things, in addition to iterating over collections.

Ruby also has an alternative syntax for delimiting blocks. Instead of using do..end, you can use curly brackets {..} like this:

block_syntax.rb
```
# do..end
[[1,2,3],[3,4,5],[6,7,8]].each do
    |a,b,c|
        puts( "#{a}, #{b}, #{c}" )
end

# curly brackets {..}
[[1,2,3],[3,4,5],[6,7,8]].each{
    |a,b,c|
        puts( "#{a}, #{b}, #{c}" )
}
```

No matter which block delimiters you use, you must ensure that the opening delimiter, { or do, is placed on the same line as the each method. Inserting a line break between each and the opening block delimiter is a syntax error. I'll have more to say on blocks in Chapter 10.

Iterating upto and downto

If you need to count from a specific low value up to a high value, you may use the upto() method of an integer. A block argument may optionally be used if you want to display the value at each iteration:

upto_downto.rb
```
0.upto(10) do
    | i |
        puts( i )
end
```

The previous code displays the integers 0 to 10. You may also count down from a high to a low value using the downto() method:

```
10.downto(0) do
    | i |
    puts( i )
end
```

As you can probably guess, this code displays 10 to 0.

Multiple Iterator Arguments

In the previous chapter, you used a for loop with more than one loop variable to iterate over a multidimensional array. On each turn through the for loop, a variable was assigned one row (that is, one "subarray") from the outer array:

multi_array.rb

```
# Here multiarr is an array containing two 'rows'
# (subarrays) at index 0 and 1
multiarr = [    ['one','two','three','four'],
                [1,2,3,4]
            ]
# This for loop runs twice (once for each 'row' of multiarr)
for (a,b,c,d) in multiarr
    print("a=#{a}, b=#{b}, c=#{c}, d=#{d}\n" )
end
```

The previous loop prints this:

```
a=one, b=two, c=three, d=four
a=1, b=2, c=3, d=4
```

However, you could also use the each method to iterate over this four-item array by passing four block parameters—a, b, c, d—into the block delimited by do and end at each iteration:

```
multiarr.each do |a,b,c,d|
    print("a=#{a}, b=#{b}, c=#{c}, d=#{d}\n" )
end
```

And, of course, the alternative block syntax, delimited by curly brackets, works just as well:

```
multiarr.each{  |a,b,c,d|
    print("a=#{a}, b=#{b}, c=#{c}, d=#{d}\n" )
}
```

Both of the previous examples pass the two elements from the `multiarr` array into the iterator block. The first element is itself an array of four strings: `['one','two','three','four']`. Since the block has four parameters declared between a pair of upright bars, `|a,b,c,d|`, the four strings are assigned to the matching parameters, which are then printed with the `print` statement. Then the `each` method passes the second element of `multiarr` into the block. This is another four-element array, this time containing integers: `[1,2,3,4]`. These are again assigned to the block parameters, `|a,b,c,d|`, and the `print` statement displays them. Note that the output is identical as when you used the `for` loop:

```
a=one, b=two, c=three, d=four
a=1, b=2, c=3, d=4
```

while Loops

Ruby has a few other loop constructs too. This is how to do a `while` loop:

```
while tired
    sleep
end
```

Or, here's another way to put it:

```
sleep while tired
```

Even though the syntax of these two examples is different, they perform the same function. In the first example, the code between `while` and `end` (here a call to a method named `sleep`) executes just as long as the Boolean condition (which, in this case, is the value returned by a method called `tired`) evaluates to true. As in `for` loops, the keyword `do` may optionally be placed between the test condition and the code to be executed when these appear on separate lines; the `do` keyword is obligatory when the test condition and the code to be executed appear on the same line.

while Modifiers

In the second version of the loop (`sleep while tired`), the code to be executed (`sleep`) precedes the test condition (`while tired`). This syntax is called a *while modifier*. When you want to execute several expressions using this syntax, you can put them between the `begin` and `end` keywords:

```
begin
    sleep
    snore
end while tired
```

Here is an example showing the various alternative syntaxes:

```ruby
$hours_asleep = 0

def tired
    if $hours_asleep >= 8 then
        $hours_asleep = 0
      return false
    else
        $hours_asleep += 1
        return true
    end
end

def snore
    puts('snore....')
end

def sleep
    puts("z" * $hours_asleep )
end

while tired do sleep end    # a single-line while loop

while tired                 # a multiline while loop
    sleep
end

sleep while tired           # single-line while modifier

begin                       # multiline while modifier
    sleep
    snore
end while tired
```

The last example in the previous code (the multiline while modifier)
needs close consideration because it introduces some important new behavior. When a block of code delimited by begin and end precedes the while test,
that code always executes at least once. In the other types of while loop, the
code may never execute at all if the Boolean condition initially evaluates
to false.

Ensuring a while Loop Executes at Least Once

Usually a while loops executes zero or more times since the Boolean test is
evaluated before the loop executes; if the test returns false at the outset, the
code inside the loop never runs. However, when the while test follows a block
of code enclosed between begin and end, the loop executes one or more times
as the Boolean expression is evaluated after the code inside the loop executes.

These examples should help clarify:

```
x = 100

    # The code in this loop never runs
while (x < 100) do puts('x < 100') end

    # The code in this loop never runs
puts('x < 100') while (x < 100)

    # But the code in loop runs once
begin puts('x < 100') end while (x < 100)
```

until Loops

Ruby also has an until loop, which can be thought of as a *while not* loop. Its syntax and options are the same as those applying to while—that is, the test condition and the code to be executed can be placed on a single line (in which case the do keyword is obligatory) or can be placed on separate lines (in which case do is optional). There is also an until modifier that lets you put the code before the test condition and an option to enclose the code between begin and end in order to ensure that the code block is run at least once.

Here are some simple examples of until loops:

```
i = 10

until i == 10 do puts(i) end      # never executes

until i == 10                     # never executes
    puts(i)
    i += 1
end

puts(i) until i == 10             # never executes

begin                             # executes once
    puts(i)
end until i == 10
```

Both while and until loops can, just like a for loop, be used to iterate over arrays and other collections. For example, the following code shows two ways of iterating over all the elements in an array:

```
arr= [1,2,3,4,5]
i = 0

while i < arr.length
    puts(arr[i])
    i += 1
end
```

```
i=0
until i == arr.length
    puts(arr[i])
    i +=1
end
```

loop

Unlike for and while, the loop command does not evaluate a test condition to determine whether to continue looping. To break out of the loop, you have to explicitly use the break keyword, as you can see in the following examples:

3loops.rb

```
i=0
loop do
    puts(arr[i])
    i+=1
    if (i == arr.length) then
        break
    end
end

loop {
    puts(arr[i])
    i+=1
    if (i == arr.length) then
        break
    end
}
```

These use the loop method repeatedly to execute the block of code that follows. These blocks are just like the iterator blocks you used earlier with the each method. Once again, you have a choice of block delimiters, either curly brackets or do and end.

In each case, the code iterates through the array, arr, by incrementing a counter variable, i, and breaking out of the loop when the (i == arr.length) condition evaluates to true. Note that without a break, these would loop forever.

DIGGING DEEPER

Ruby provides a number of ways of iterating over items in structures such as arrays and ranges. Here we discover the inner details of the enumerations and comparisons.

The Enumerable Module

Hashes, Arrays, Ranges, and Sets all include a Ruby module called Enumerable. It provides these data structures with a number of useful methods such as include?, which returns true if a specific value is found; min, which returns the smallest value; max, which returns the largest; and collect, which creates a new structure made up of values returned from a block. In the following code, you can see some of these functions being used on an array:

enum.rb

```
x = (1..5).collect{ |i| i }
p( x )                        #=> [1, 2, 3, 4, 5]

arr = [1,2,3,4,5]
y = arr.collect{ |i| i }
p( y )                        #=> [1, 2, 3, 4, 5]
z = arr.collect{ |i| i * i }
p( z )                        #=> [1, 4, 9, 16, 25]

p( arr.include?( 3 ) )        #=> true
p( arr.include?( 6 ) )        #=> false
p( arr.min )                  #=> 1
p( arr.max )                  #=> 5
```

These same methods are available to other collection classes too, as long as those classes include Enumerable. Here's an example using the Hash class:

enum2.rb

```
h = {'one'=>'for sorrow',
    'two'=>'for joy',
    'three'=>'for a girl',
    'four'=>'for a boy'}

y = h.collect{ |i| i }
p( y )
```

This code outputs the following:

```
[["one", "for sorrow"], ["two", "for joy"], ["three", "for a girl"], ["four", "for a boy"]]
```

Note that because of changes in the way hashes are stored, the order of the items displayed when this code runs differs in Ruby 1.8 and Ruby 1.9. Remember too that the items in a Hash are not indexed in sequential order, so when you use the min and max methods, these return the items that are lowest and highest according to their numerical value—here the items are strings, and the numerical value is determined by the ASCII codes of the characters in the key.

```
p( h.min )    #=> ["one", "for sorrow"]
p( h.max )    #=> ["two", "for joy"]
```

Custom Comparisons

What if you want min and max to return items based on some other criterion (say the length of a string)? The easiest way to do this would be to define the nature of the comparison inside a block. This is done in a similar manner to the sorting blocks I defined in Chapter 4. You may recall that you sorted a hash (here the variable h) by passing a block to the sort method like this:

```
h.sort{ |a,b| a.to_s <=> b.to_s }
```

The two parameters, a and b, represent two items from the hash that are compared using the <=> comparison method. You can similarly pass blocks to the max and min methods:

```
h.min{ |a,b| a[0].length <=> b[0].length }
h.max{|a,b| a[0].length <=> b[0].length }
```

When a hash passes items into a block, it does so in the form of arrays, each of which contains a key-value pair. So, if a hash contains items like this:

```
{'one'=>'for sorrow', 'two'=>'for joy'}
```

then the two block arguments, a and b, would be initialized to two arrays:

```
a = ['one', 'for sorrow']
b = ['two', 'for joy']
```

This explains why the two blocks in which I have defined custom comparisons for the max and min methods specifically compare the first elements, at index 0, of the two block parameters:

```
a[0].length <=> b[0].length
```

This ensures that the comparisons are based on the *keys* in the hash. There is a potential pitfall here, however. As explained in the previous chapter, the default ordering of hashes is different in Ruby 1.8 and Ruby 1.9. This means that if you sort by the length of the key, as I did with my custom comparator earlier, and more than one key has the same length, the first match returned will be different in different versions of Ruby. For example, in my hash, the first two keys ("one" and "two") have the same length. So when I use `min` with a comparison based on the key length, the result will be different in Ruby versions 1.8 and 1.9:

```
p( h.min{|a,b| a[0].length <=> b[0].length } )
```

Ruby 1.8 displays the following:

```
["two", "for joy"]
```

Ruby 1.9 displays the following:

```
["one", "for sorrow"]
```

This is another illustration of why it is always safer to make no assumptions of the ordering of the elements in a hash. Now let's assume you want to compare the *values* rather than the keys. In the previous example, you could do this quite simply by changing the array indexes from 0 to 1:

enum3.rb
```
p( h.min{|a,b| a[1].length <=> b[1].length } )
p( h.max{|a,b| a[1].length <=> b[1].length } )
```

The value with the lowest length is "for joy" and the value with the highest length is "for a secret never to be told," so the previous code displays the following:

```
["two", "for joy"]
["seven", "for a secret never to be told"]
```

You could, of course, define other types of custom comparisons in your blocks. Let's suppose, for example, that you want the strings "one," "two," "three," and so on, to be evaluated in the order in which you would speak them. One way of doing this would be to create an ordered array of strings:

```
str_arr=['one','two','three','four','five','six','seven']
```

Now, if a hash, h, contains these strings as keys, a block can use `str_array` as a reference in order to determine the minimum and maximum values. This also assures that we obtain the same results no matter which version of Ruby is used:

```
h.min{|a,b| str_arr.index(a[0]) <=> str_arr.index(b[0])}
h.max{|a,b| str_arr.index(a[0]) <=> str_arr.index(b[0])}
```

This displays the following:

```
["one", "for sorrow"]
["seven", "for a secret never to be told"]
```

All the previous examples use the min and max methods of the Array and Hash classes. Remember that these methods are provided to those classes by the Enumerable module, which is "included" in the Array and Hash classes.

There may be occasions when it would be useful to be able to apply Enumerable methods such as max, min, and collect to classes that do not descend from existing classes (such as Array) that implement those methods. You can do that by including the Enumerable module in your class and then writing an iterator method called each like this:

include_enum1.rb
```
class MyCollection
    include Enumerable

    def initialize( someItems )
      @items = someItems
    end

    def each
      @items.each{ |i|
        yield( i )
      }
    end
end
```

Here you initialize a MyCollection object with an array, which will be stored in the instance variable, @items. When you call one of the methods provided by the Enumerable module (such as min, max, or collect), this will call the each method to obtain each piece of data one at a time. So, here the each method passes each value from the @items array into the block where that item is assigned to the block parameter i. The keyword yield is a special bit of Ruby magic that runs a block of code that was passed to the each method. You'll look at this in much more depth when I discuss Ruby blocks in Chapter 10.

Now you can use the Enumerable methods with your MyCollection objects:

include_enum2.rb
```
things = MyCollection.new(['x','yz','defgh','ij','klmno'])

p( things.min )        #=> "defgh"
p( things.max )        #=> "yz"
p( things.collect{ |i| i.upcase } )
                       #=> ["X", "YZ", "DEFGH", "IJ", "KLMNO"]
```

You could similarly use your MyCollection class to process arrays such as the keys or values of hashes. Currently the min and max methods adopt the default behavior: They perform comparisons based on numerical values. This means that "xy" is considered to have a "higher" value than "abcd" on the basis of the characters' ASCII values. If you want to perform some other type of comparison—say, by string length, so that "abcd" would be deemed to be higher than "xz"—you can override the min and max methods:

```
def min
  @items.to_a.min{|a,b| a.length <=> b.length }
end

def max
  @items.to_a.max{|a,b| a.length <=> b.length }
end
```

Here is the complete class definition with its versions of each, min, and max:

include_enum3.rb

```
class MyCollection
  include Enumerable

    def initialize( someItems )
        @items = someItems
    end

    def each
        @items.each{ |i| yield i }
    end

    def min
        @items.to_a.min{|a,b| a.length <=> b.length }
    end

    def max
        @items.to_a.max{|a,b| a.length <=> b.length }
    end
end
```

A MyCollection object can now be created, and its overridden methods can be used in this way:

```
things = MyCollection.new(['z','xy','defgh','ij','abc','klmnopqr'])
x = things.collect{ |i| i }
p( x ) #=> ["z", "xy", "defgh", "ij", "abc", "klmnopqr"]
y = things.max
p( y ) #=> "klmnopqr"
z = things.min
p( z ) #=> "z"
```

each and yield

So what is really going on when a method from the Enumerable module uses the each method that you've written? It turns out that the Enumerable methods (min, max, collect and so forth) pass to the each method a block of code. This block of code expects to receive one piece of data at a time (namely, each item from a collection of some sort). Your each method supplies it with that item in the form of a block parameter, such as the parameter i here:

```
def each
   @items.each{ |i|
      yield( i )
   }
end
```

As mentioned earlier, the keyword yield tells the code to run the block that was passed to the each method—that is, to run the code supplied by the Enumerable module's min, max, or collect methods. This means that the code of those methods can be used with all kinds of different types of collections. All you have to do is include the Enumerable module into your class and write an each method that determines which values will be used by the Enumerable methods.

6

CONDITIONAL STATEMENTS

Computer programs, like life itself, are full of difficult decisions waiting to be made. Things like "If I stay in bed, I will get more sleep, else I will have to go to work; if I go to work, I will earn some money, else I will lose my job," and so on. You've already performed a number of if tests in previous programs. To take a simple example, this is from the Tax calculator in Chapter 1:

```
if (subtotal < 0.0) then
    subtotal = 0.0
end
```

In this program, the user was prompted to enter a value, subtotal, that was then used in order to calculate the tax due on it. If the user, in a fit of madness, enters a value less than 0, the if test spots this since the test (subtotal < 0.0) evaluates to true, which causes the body of the code between the if test and the end keyword to be executed; here, this sets the value of subtotal to 0.

if..then..else

A simple test like this has only one of two possible results. Either a bit of code is run or it isn't, depending on whether the test evaluates to true or not. Often, you will need to have more than two possible outcomes. Let's suppose, for example, that your program needs to follow one course of action if the day is a weekday and a different course of action if it is a weekend. You can test these conditions by adding an else section after the if section, like this:

if_else.rb
```
if aDay == 'Saturday' or aDay == 'Sunday'
    daytype = 'weekend'
else
    daytype = 'weekday'
end
```

NOTE   *Like many other programming languages, Ruby uses one equal sign (=) to assign a value and two (==) to test a value.*

The if condition here is straightforward. It tests two possible conditions: if the value of the variable aDay is equal to the string "Saturday" and if the value of aDay is equal to the string "Sunday." If either of those conditions is true, then the next line of code executes daytype = 'weekend'; in all other cases, the code after else executes daytype = 'weekday'.

When an if test and the code to be executed are placed on separate lines, the then keyword is optional. When the test and the code are placed on a single line, the then keyword is obligatory:

if_then.rb
```
if x == 1 then puts( 'ok' ) end    # with 'then'
if x == 1 puts( 'ok' ) end         # syntax error!
```

In Ruby 1.8, a colon character (:) was permitted as an alternative to then. This syntax is not supported in Ruby 1.9:

```
if x == 1 : puts( 'ok' ) end    # This works with Ruby 1.8 only
```

An if test isn't restricted to evaluating just two conditions. Let's suppose, for example, that your code needs to work out whether a certain day is a working day or a holiday. All weekdays are working days; all Saturdays are holidays, but Sundays are only holidays when you are not working overtime. This is my first attempt to write a test to evaluate all these conditions:

and_or_wrong.rb
```
working_overtime = true
if aDay == 'Saturday' or aDay == 'Sunday' and not working_overtime
    daytype = 'holiday'
    puts( "Hurrah!" )
else
    daytype = 'working day'
end
```

Unfortunately, this doesn't have quite the effect intended. Remember that Saturday is always a holiday. But this code insists that Saturday is a working day. This is because Ruby takes the test to mean "If the day is Saturday and I am not working overtime or if the day is Sunday and I am not working overtime," whereas what I really meant was "If the day is Saturday or if the day is Sunday and I am not working overtime." The easiest way to resolve this ambiguity is to put parentheses around any code to be evaluated as a single unit, like this:

and_or.rb

```
if aDay == 'Saturday' or (aDay == 'Sunday' and not working_overtime)
```

and, or, and not

Incidentally, Ruby has two different syntaxes for testing Boolean (true/false) conditions. In the previous example, I've used the English-language style operators: and, or, and not. If you prefer, you could use alternative operators similar to those used in many other programming languages, namely, && (and), || (or), and ! (not).

Be careful, though: The two sets of operators aren't completely interchangeable. For one thing, they have different precedence, which means that when multiple operators are used in a single test, the parts of the test may be evaluated in different orders depending on which operators you use. For example, look at this test:

days.rb

```
if aDay == 'Saturday' or aDay == 'Sunday' and not working_overtime
    daytype = 'holiday'
end
```

Assuming that the Boolean variable working_overtime is true, would this test succeed if the variable aDay were initialized with the string "Saturday"? In other words, would daytype be assigned the value "holiday" if aDay is "Saturday"? The answer is no, it wouldn't. The test will succeed only if aDay is either "Saturday" or "Sunday" and working_overtime is not true. So, when or is used in the previous code, Saturday would be deemed to be a working day.

Now consider this test:

```
if aDay == 'Saturday' || aDay == 'Sunday' &&  !working_overtime
    daytype = 'holiday'
end
```

On the face of it, this is the same test as the last one; the only difference is that this time I've used the alternative syntax for the operators. However, the change is more than cosmetic since if aDay is "Saturday," this test evaluates to true and daytype is initialized with the value "holiday." This is because the || operator has a higher precedence than the or operator. So, this test succeeds either if aDay is "Saturday" *or* if aDay is "Sunday" and working_overtime is not true. So, when || is used in the previous code, Saturday would be deemed to be a holiday.

Refer to "Digging Deeper" on page 93 for more on this. As a general principle, you would do well to decide which set of operators you prefer—stick to them and use parentheses to avoid ambiguity.

Negation

In the previous example, I used the negation operator (!) in the expression !working_overtime, which can be read as "not working_overtime." The negation operator can be used at the start of an expression; as an alternative, you can use the "not equals" (!=) operator between the left and right sides of an expression:

negation.rb

```
!(1==1)          #=> false
1!=1             #=> false
```

Alternatively, you can use not instead of !:

```
not( 1==1 )      #=> false
```

if..elsif

There will no doubt be occasions when you will need to take multiple different actions based on several alternative conditions. One way of doing this is by evaluating one if condition followed by a series of other test conditions placed after the keyword elsif. The whole lot must then be terminated using the end keyword.

For example, here I am repeatedly taking input from a user inside a while loop. An if condition tests whether the user enters "q" (I've used chomp() to remove the carriage return from the input). If "q" is not entered, the first elsif condition tests whether the integer value of the input (input.to_i) is greater than 800; if this test fails, the next elsif condition tests whether it is less than or equal to 800:

if_elsif.rb

```
while input != 'q' do
   puts("Enter a number between 1 and 1000 (or 'q' to quit)")
   print("?- ")
   input = gets().chomp()
   if input == 'q'
      puts( "Bye" )
   elsif input.to_i > 800
      puts( "That's a high rate of pay!" )
   elsif input.to_i <= 800
      puts( "We can afford that" )
   end
end
```

The problem with this program is that, even though it asks the user to enter a value between 1 and 1,000, it accepts values less than 1 (incidentally, if you really want a salary in negative figures, I'll be glad to offer you a job!) and greater than 1,000 (in which case, don't look to me for employment!).

You can fix this by rewriting the two `elsif` conditions and adding an `else` section that executes if all the preceding tests fail:

if_elsif2.rb

```ruby
if input == 'q'
    puts( "Bye" )
elsif input.to_i > 800 && input.to_i <= 1000
    puts( "That's a high rate of pay!" )
elsif input.to_i <= 800 && input.to_i > 0
    puts( "We can afford that" )
else
    puts( "I said: Enter a number between 1 and 1000!" )
end
```

SHORTHAND NOTATION FOR IF..THEN..ELSE

Ruby also has a short-form notation for if..then..else in which a question mark (?) replaces the if..then part and a colon (:) acts as else. Formally, this may be known either as a *ternary operator* or as a *conditional operator*.

```
< Test Condition > ? <if true do this> : <else do this>
```

For example:

if_else_alt.rb

```ruby
x == 10 ? puts("it's 10") : puts( "it's some other number" )
```

When the test condition is complex (if it uses ands and ors), you should enclose it in parentheses. If the tests and code span several lines, the ? must be placed on the same line as the preceding condition and the : must be placed on the same line as the code immediately following the ?. In other words, if you put a newline before the ? or the :, you will generate a syntax error. This is an example of a valid multiline code block:

```ruby
(aDay == 'Saturday' or aDay == 'Sunday') ?
    daytype = 'weekend' :
    daytype = 'weekday'
```

Here's another example of a longer sequence of if..elsif sections followed by a catchall else section. This time the trigger value, i, is an integer:

days2.rb

```ruby
def showDay( i )
    if i == 1 then puts("It's Monday" )
    elsif i == 2 then puts("It's Tuesday" )
    elsif i == 3 then puts("It's Wednesday" )
    elsif i == 4 then puts("It's Thursday" )
    elsif i == 5 then puts("It's Friday" )
```

```
    elsif (6..7) === i then puts( "Yippee! It's the weekend! " )
    else puts( "That's not a real day!" )
    end
end
```

Notice that I've used the range (6..7) to match the two integer values for Saturday and Sunday. The === method (that is, three = characters) tests whether a value (here i) is a member of the range. In the previous example, the following:

```
(6..7) === i
```

could be rewritten as this:

```
(6..7).include?(i)
```

The === method is defined by the Object class and overridden in descendant classes. Its behavior varies according to the class. As you will see shortly, one of its fundamental uses is to provide meaningful tests for case statements.

unless

Ruby also can also perform unless tests, which are the exact opposite of if tests:

unless.rb
```
unless aDay == 'Saturday' or aDay == 'Sunday'
    daytype = 'weekday'
else
    daytype = 'weekend'
end
```

Think of unless as being an alternative way of expressing "if not." The following is equivalent to the previous code; both consider Saturday and Sunday to be the weekend and other days to be weekdays:

```
if !(aDay == 'Saturday' or aDay == 'Sunday')
    daytype = 'weekday'
else
    daytype = 'weekend'
end
```

if and unless Modifiers

You may recall the alternative syntax for while loops mentioned in Chapter 5. Instead of writing this:

```
while tired do sleep end
```

you can write this:

```
sleep while tired
```

This alternative syntax, in which the while keyword is placed between the code to execute and the test condition, is called a *while modifier*. It turns out that Ruby has if and unless modifiers too. Here are a few examples:

if_unless_mod.rb
```
sleep if tired

begin
   sleep
   snore
end if tired

sleep unless not tired

begin
   sleep
   snore
end unless not tired
```

The terseness of this syntax is useful when you repeatedly need to take some well-defined action if some condition is true. You might, for example, pepper your code with debugging output if a constant called DEBUG is true:

```
puts( "somevar = #{somevar}" ) if DEBUG
```

Case Statements

When you need to take a variety of different actions based on the value of a single variable, multiple if..elsif tests are verbose and repetitive.

A neater alternative is provided by a case statement. This begins with the word case followed by the variable name to test. Then comes a series of when sections, each of which specifies a "trigger" value followed by some code.

This code executes only when the test variable equals the trigger value:

case.rb
```
case( i )
   when 1 then puts("It's Monday" )
   when 2 then puts("It's Tuesday" )
   when 3 then puts("It's Wednesday" )
   when 4 then puts("It's Thursday" )
   when 5 then puts("It's Friday" )
   when (6..7) then puts( "Yippee! It's the weekend! " )
   else puts( "That's not a real day!" )
end
```

In principle, constants are objects whose values never change. For example, PI in Ruby's Math module is a constant. Constants in Ruby begin with a capital letter. Class names are also constants. You can obtain a list of all defined constants using the constants method:

constants.rb

```
Object.constants
```

Ruby provides the const_get and const_set methods to get and set the value of named constants specified as symbols (identifiers preceded by a colon such as :RUBY_VERSION). Note that, unlike the constants in many other programming languages, Ruby's constants may be assigned new values:

```
RUBY_VERSION = "1.8.7"
RUBY_VERSION = "2.5.6"
```

The previous reassignment of the RUBY_VERSION constant produces an "already initialized constant" warning but not an error! You can even reassign constants declared in Ruby's standard class library. For example, here I reassign the value of PI. Although this displays a warning, the assignment succeeds nonetheless:

math_pi.rb

```
puts Math::PI      #=> 3.141592653589793
Math::PI = 100     #=> warning: already initialized constant PI
puts Math::PI      #=> 100
```

You need to be aware that the constancy of Ruby's constants is a programming *convention*, rather than a rigorously enforced *rule*. Naturally, it is not good programming practice to reassign constants.

In the previous example, I've used the then keyword to separate each when test from the code to execute. In Ruby 1.8, just as with if tests mentioned earlier, you could use a colon as an alternative, but this syntax is not supported in Ruby 1.9:

```
when 1 : puts("It's Monday" )  # This works in Ruby 1.8 only!
```

The then can be omitted if the test and the code to be executed are on separate lines. Unlike case statements in C-like languages, there is no need to enter a break keyword when a match is made in order to prevent execution trickling down through the remainder of the sections. In Ruby, once a match is made, the case statement exits:

case_break.rb

```
def showDay( i )
    case( i )
    when 5 then puts("It's Friday" )
        puts("...nearly the weekend!")
    when 6 then puts("It's Saturday!" )
```

```
        # the following never executes
    when 5 then puts( "It's Friday all over again!" )
    end
end

showDay( 5 )
showDay( 6 )
```

This displays the following:

```
It's Friday
...nearly the weekend!
It's Saturday!
```

You can include several lines of code between each when condition, and you can include multiple values separated by commas to trigger a single when block, like this:

```
when 6, 7 then puts( "Yippee! It's the weekend! " )
```

The condition in a case statement is not obliged to be a simple variable; it can be an expression like this:

case2.rb

```
case( i + 1 )
```

You can also use noninteger types such as a string. If multiple trigger values are specified in a when section, they may be of varying types—for example, both string and integers:

```
when 1, 'Monday', 'Mon' then puts( "Yup, '#{i}' is Monday" )
```

Here is a longer example, illustrating some of the syntactical elements mentioned earlier:

case3.rb

```
case( i )
    when 1 then puts("It's Monday" )
    when 2 then puts("It's Tuesday" )
    when 3 then puts("It's Wednesday" )
    when 4 then puts("It's Thursday" )
    when 5 then puts("It's Friday" )
        puts("...nearly the weekend!")
    when 6, 7
        puts("It's Saturday!" ) if i == 6
        puts("It's Sunday!" ) if i == 7
        puts( "Yippee! It's the weekend! " )
        # the following never executes
    when 5 then puts( "It's Friday all over again!" )
    else puts( "That's not a real day!" )
end
```

The === Method

As mentioned earlier, the when tests on an object used in a case statement are performed using the === method. So, for example, just as the === method returns true when an integer forms part of a range, a when test returns true when an integer variable in a case statement forms part of a range expression:

```
when (6..7) then puts( "Yippee! It's the weekend! " )
```

If in doubt on the effect of the === method for a specific object, refer to the Ruby documentation on that object's class. Ruby's standard classes are documented in the core API here: *http://www.ruby-doc.org/*.

Alternative Case Syntax

There is an alternative form of the case statement that is like a shorthand form of a series of if..then..else statements. Each when section can perform some arbitrary test and execute one or more lines of code. No case variable is required. Each when section returns a value that, just like a method, is the result of the last piece of code that's evaluated. This value can be assigned to a variable preceding the case statement:

case4.rb

```
salary = 2000000
season = 'summer'

happy = case
    when salary > 10000 && season == 'summer' then
        puts( "Yes, I really am happy!" )
        'Very happy'
    when salary > 500000 && season == 'spring' then 'Pretty happy'
    else puts( 'miserable' )
end

puts( happy ) #=> 'Very happy'
```

DIGGING DEEPER

There is more to Ruby comparison operators than meets the eye. Here you will learn about their effects and side effects and discover how to break out of blocks when a condition is met.

Boolean Operators

The following operators are available in Ruby for testing expressions that may yield true or false values.

and and &&	These operators evaluate the left-hand side; only if the result is true do they then evaluate the right side. and has lower precedence than &&.
or and ||	These operators evaluate the left-hand side; if the result is false, then they evaluate the right side. or has lower precedence than ||.
not and !	These operators negate a Boolean value; in other words, they return true when false and return false when true.

Be careful when using the alternative Boolean operators. Because of the difference in precedence, conditions will be evaluated in different orders and may yield different results.

Consider the following:

boolean_ops.rb

```
# Example 1
if ( 1==3 ) and (2==1) || (3==3) then
    puts('true')
else
    puts('false')
end

# Example 2
if ( 1==3 ) and (2==1) or (3==3) then
    puts('true')
else
    puts('false')
end
```

These may look the same at first sight. In fact, Example 1 prints "false," while Example 2 prints "true." This is entirely because or has lower precedence than ||. As a consequence, Example 1 tests "if 1 equals 3 [*false*] and (either 2 equals 1 or 3 equals 3) [*true*]." Because one of these two necessary conditions is false, the entire test returns false.

Now look at Example 2. This tests "(if 1 equals 3 and 2 equals 1) [*false*] or 3 equals 3 [*true*]." This time, you need only one of the two tests to succeed; the second test evaluates to true so the entire tests returns true.

The side effects of operator precedence in this kind of test can lead to very obscure bugs. You can avoid these by clarifying the meaning of the test using parentheses. Here, I have rewritten Examples 1 and 2; in each case, the addition of one pair of parentheses has inverted the initial Boolean value returned by the test:

```
# Example 1 (b) - now returns true
if (( 1==3 ) and (2==1)) || (3==3) then
   puts('true')
else
   puts('false')
end

# Example 2 (b) - now returns false
if ( 1==3 ) and ((2==1) or (3==3)) then
   puts('true')
else
   puts('false')
end
```

Eccentricities of Boolean Operators

Be warned that Ruby's Boolean operators can sometimes behave in a curious and unpredictable manner. For example:

eccentricities.rb

```
puts( (not( 1==1 )) )        # This is okay
puts( not( 1==1 ) )          # Syntax error in Ruby 1.8
                             # but okay in Ruby 1.9

puts( true && true && !(true) )   # This is okay
puts( true && true and !(true) )  # This is a syntax error

puts( ((true) and (true)) )  # This is okay
puts( true && true )         # This is okay
puts( true and true )        # This is a syntax error
```

In many cases, you can avoid problems by sticking to one style of operator (either and, or, and not *or* &&, ||, and !) rather than mixing the two. In addition, the generous use of parentheses is recommended!

catch and throw

Ruby provides a pair of methods, catch and throw, which can be used to break out of a block of code when some condition is met. This is Ruby's nearest equivalent to a goto in some other programming languages. The block must begin with catch followed by a symbol (that is, a unique identifier preceded by a colon), such as :done or :finished. The block itself may be delimited either by curly brackets or by the keywords do and end, like this:

```
# think of this as a block called :done
catch( :done ){
   # some code here
}
```

```
# and this is a block called :finished
catch( :finished ) do
    # some code here
end
```

Inside the block, you can call throw with a symbol as an argument. Normally you would call throw when some specific condition is met that makes it desirable to skip all the remaining code in the block. For instance, let's assume the block contains some code that prompts the user to enter a number, divides some value by that number, and then goes on to do a multitude of other complex calculations with the result. Obviously, if the user enters 0, then none of the calculations that follow can be completed, so you would want to skip them all by jumping right out of the block and continuing with any code that follows it. This is one way of doing that:

catch_throw.rb

```
catch( :finished) do
    print( 'Enter a number: ' )
    num = gets().chomp.to_i
    if num == 0 then
        throw :finished # if num is 0, jump out of the block
    end
        # Here there may be hundreds of lines of
        # calculations based on the value of num
        # if num is 0 this code will be skipped
end
        # the throw method causes execution to
        # jump to here - outside of the block
puts( "Finished" )
```

You can, in fact, have a call to throw outside the block, like this:

```
def dothings( aNum )
    i = 0
    while true
        puts( "I'm doing things..." )
        i += 1
        throw( :go_for_tea ) if (i == aNum )
                        # throws to end of go_to_tea block
    end
end

catch( :go_for_tea ){   # this is the :go_to_tea block
        dothings(5)
}
```

And you can have catch blocks nested inside other catch blocks, like this:

```
catch( :finished) do
    print( 'Enter a number: ' )
    num = gets().chomp.to_i
```

```
    if num == 0 then throw :finished end
      puts( 100 / num )


    catch( :go_for_tea ){
      dothings(5)
    }

    puts( "Things have all been done. Time for tea!" )
end
```

As with gotos and jumps in other programming languages, catch and throw in Ruby should be used with great care because they break the logic of your code and can, potentially, introduce hard-to-find bugs.

7

METHODS

You've used numerous methods throughout this book. On the whole, they aren't particularly complicated things, so you may wonder why this chapter, which is all about methods, is so long. As you will discover, there is much more to methods than meets the eye.

Class Methods

The methods you've been using so far have been *instance methods*. An instance method belongs to a specific instance of a class—in other words, to an individual object. It is also possible to write *class methods*. (Some other languages refer to this kind of method as a static method.) A class method belongs to the class itself. To define a class method, you must precede the method name with the class name and a full stop.

```
class MyClass
    def MyClass.classMethod
        puts( "This is a class method" )
    end

    def instanceMethod
        puts( "This is an instance method" )
    en
end
```

You should use the class name when calling a class method:

```
MyClass.classMethod
```

A specific object cannot call a class method. Nor can a class call an instance method:

```
MyClass.instanceMethod        #=> Error! This is an 'undefined method'
ob.classMethod                #=> Error! This is an 'undefined method'
```

What Are Class Methods For?

But why, you may reasonably ask, would you ever want to create a class method rather than the more usual instance method? There are two main reasons: First, a class method can be used as a "ready-to-run function" without having to go to the bother of creating an object just to use it, and second, it can be used on those occasions when you need to run a method before an object has been created.

For a few examples of using methods as "ready-to-run functions," consider Ruby's File class. Many of its methods are class methods. This is because most of the time you will be using them to do something to, or return information about, an existing file. You don't need to create a new File object to do that; instead, you pass the filename as an argument to the File class methods. You'll look more closely at the File class in Chapter 13. Here are examples of a few of its class methods in use:

```
fn = 'file_methods.rb'
if File.exist?(fn) then
    puts(File.expand_path(fn))
    puts(File.basename(fn))
    puts(File.dirname(fn))
    puts(File.extname(fn))
    puts(File.mtime(fn))
    puts("#{File.size(fn)} bytes")
else
    puts( "Can't find file!")
end
```

This outputs something like this:

```
C:/bookofruby2/ch7/file_methods.rb
file_methods.rb
.
.rb
2010-10-05 16:14:53 +0100
300 bytes
```

The other occasion when a class method is vital is when you need to use a method before an object has been created. The most important example of this is the `new` method.

You call the `new` method every time you create an object. Until the object has been created, you clearly cannot call one of its instance methods—because you can call instance methods only from an object that already exists. When you use `new`, you are calling a method of the class itself and telling the class to create a new instance of itself.

Class Variables

Class methods may remind you of the class variables you used previously (that is, variables whose names begin with `@@`). You may recall that you used class variables in a simple adventure game (see *2adventure.rb* on page 22) to keep a tally of the total number of objects in the game; each time a new Thing object was created, 1 was added to the `@@num_things` class variable:

```
class Thing
   @@num_things = 0

   def initialize( aName, aDescription )
      @@num_things +=1
   end

end
```

Unlike an instance variable (that is, a variable that belongs to a specific object created from a class), a class variable must be given a value when it is first declared:

```
@@classvar = 1000     # class variables must be initialized
```

Initialization of either instance or class variables within the body of the class affects only the values stored by the class itself. Class variables are available both to the class itself and to the objects created from that class. However, each instance variable is unique; each object has its own copy of any instance variables—*and the class itself may also have its own instance variables.*

To understand how a class may have instance variables, refer to the *class_methods2.rb* program. This defines a class containing one class method and one instance method:

class_methods2.rb

```ruby
class MyClass
    @@classvar = 1000
    @instvar = 1000

    def MyClass.classMethod
        if @instvar == nil then
            @instvar = 10
        else
            @instvar += 10
        end

        if @@classvar == nil then
            @@classvar = 10
        else
            @@classvar += 10
        end
    end

    def instanceMethod
        if @instvar == nil then
            @instvar = 1
        else
            @instvar += 1
        end

        if @@classvar == nil then
            @@classvar = 1
```

```
        else
            @@classvar += 1
        end

    end

    def showVars
        return "(instance method) @instvar = #{@instvar}, @@classvar = #{@@classvar}"
    end

    def MyClass.showVars
        return "(class method) @instvar = #{@instvar}, @@classvar = #{@@classvar}"
    end

end
```

Notice that it declares and initializes a class variable and an instance variable, @@classvar and @instvar, respectively. Its class method, classMethod, increments both these variables by 10, while its instance method, instanceMethod, increments both variables by 1. Notice that I have assigned values to both the class variable and the instance variable:

```
@@classvar = 1000
@instvar = 1000
```

I said earlier that initial values are not normally assigned to instance variables in this way. The exception to the rule is when you assign a value to an instance variable *of the class itself* rather than to an object derived from that class. The distinction should become clearer shortly.

I've written a few lines of code that create three instances of MyClass (the ob variable is initialized with a new instance on each turn through the loop) and then call both the class and instance methods:

```
for i in 0..2 do
    ob = MyClass.new
    MyClass.classMethod
    ob.instanceMethod
    puts( MyClass.showVars )
    puts( ob.showVars )
end
```

The class method, MyClass.showVars, and the instance method, showVars, display the values of @instvar and @@classvar at each turn through the loop. When you run the code, these are the values displayed:

```
(class method) @instvar = 1010, @@classvar = 1011
(instance method) @instvar = 1, @@classvar = 1011
(class method) @instvar = 1020, @@classvar = 1022
(instance method) @instvar = 1, @@classvar = 1022
(class method) @instvar = 1030, @@classvar = 1033
(instance method) @instvar = 1, @@classvar = 1033
```

You may need to look at these results carefully in order to see what is going on here. In summary, this is what is happening: The code in both the class method, MyClass.classMethod, and the instance method, instanceMethod, increments both the class and instance variables, @@classvar and @instvar.

You can see clearly that the class variable is incremented by both these methods (the class method adds 10 to @@classvar whenever a new object is created, while the instance method adds 1 to it). However, whenever a new object is created, its instance variable is initialized to 1 by the instanceMethod. This is the expected behavior since each object has its own copy of an instance variable, but all objects share a unique class variable. Perhaps less obvious is that the class itself also has its own instance variable, @instvar. This is because, in Ruby, a class is an object and therefore can contain instance variables, just like any other object. The MyClass variable, @instvar, is incremented by the class method MyClass.classMethod:

```
@instvar += 10
```

When the instance method, showVars, prints the value of @instvar, it prints the value stored in a specific object, ob; the value of ob's @instvar is initially nil (*not* the value 1,000 with which the MyClass variable @instvar was initialized), and this value is incremented by 1 in instanceMethod.

When the class method, MyClass.showVars, prints the value of @instvar, it prints the value stored in the class itself (in other words, MyClass's @instvar *is a different variable* from ob's @instvar). But when either method prints the value of the class variable, @@classvar, the value is the same.

Just remember that there is only ever one copy of a class variable, but there may be many copies of instance variables. If this is still confusing, take a look at the *inst_vars.rb* program:

inst_vars.rb

```ruby
class MyClass
   @@classvar = 1000
   @instvar = 1000

   def MyClass.classMethod
      if @instvar == nil then
         @instvar = 10
      else
         @instvar += 10
      end
   end

   def instanceMethod
      if @instvar == nil then
         @instvar = 1
      else
         @instvar += 1
      end
   end
end
```

```
ob = MyClass.new
puts MyClass.instance_variable_get(:@instvar)
puts( '--------------' )
for i in 0..2 do
   # MyClass.classMethod
   ob.instanceMethod
   puts( "MyClass @instvar=#{MyClass.instance_variable_get(:@instvar)}")
   puts( "ob @instvar= #{ob.instance_variable_get(:@instvar)}" )
end
```

This time, instead of creating a new object instance at each turn through the loop, you create a single instance (ob) at the outset. When the ob.instanceMethod is called, @instvar is incremented by 1.

Here I've used a little trick to look inside the class and method and retrieve the value of @instvar using Ruby's instance_variable_get method (I'll return to this when I cover dynamic programming in Chapter 20):

```
puts( "MyClass @instvar= #{MyClass.instance_variable_get(:@instvar)}" )
puts( "ob @instvar= #{ob.instance_variable_get(:@instvar)}" )
```

Because you only ever increment the @instvar that belongs to the object ob, the value of its @instvar goes up from 1 to 3 as the for loop executes. But the @instvar that belongs to the MyClass class is never incremented; it remains at its initial value of 1,000:

```
1000
--------------
MyClass @instvar= 1000
ob @instvar= 1
MyClass @instvar= 1000
ob @instvar= 2
MyClass @instvar= 1000
ob @instvar= 3
```

But now let's uncomment this line:

```
MyClass.classMethod
```

This calls a class method that increments @instvar by 10. This time when you run the program, you see that, as before, the @instvar variable of ob is incremented by 1 on each turn through the loop, while the @instvar variable of MyClass is incremented by 10:

```
1000
--------------
MyClass @instvar= 1010
ob @instvar= 1
MyClass @instvar= 1020
ob @instvar= 2
MyClass @instvar= 1030
ob @instvar= 3
```

Ruby Constructors: new or initialize?

I gave a brief explanation of new and initialize in Chapter 1. At that stage, you had not examined the differences between Ruby's class and instance methods and variables, so it was not possible to give a full discussion of how new and initialize work together. Because these are such important methods, you'll look at them in more detail now.

The method responsible for bringing an object into being is called the *constructor*. In Ruby, the constructor method is called new. The new method is a class method that, once it has created an object, will run an instance method named initialize if such a method exists.

In brief then, the new method is the constructor, and the initialize method is used to initialize the values of any variables immediately after an object is created. But why can't you just write your own new method and initialize variables in it? Well, let's try that:

new.rb

```ruby
class MyClass
    def initialize( aStr )
        @avar = aStr
    end

    def MyClass.new( aStr )
        super
        @anewvar = aStr.swapcase
    end
end

ob = MyClass.new( "hello world" )
puts( ob )
puts( ob.class )
```

Here, I've written a MyClass.new method that begins with the super keyword to invoke the new method of its superclass. Then I've created a string instance variable, @anewvar. So what do I end up with? Not, as you might suppose, a new MyClass object containing a string variable. Remember that the last expression evaluated by a method in Ruby is the value returned by that method. The last expression evaluated by the new method here is a string. I evaluate this:

```
ob = MyClass.new( "hello world" )
```

And I display the newly created ob object and its class:

```
puts( ob )
puts( ob.class )
```

This is the output:

```
HELLO WORLD
String
```

This proves that MyClass.new returns a string, and it is this string (*not* a MyClass object) that is assigned to the variable ob. If you find this confusing, don't panic. The moral of the story is that overriding new *is* confusing and is generally a bad idea. Unless you have a very good reason for doing so, you should avoid trying to override the new method.

Singleton Methods

A singleton method is a method that belongs to a single object rather than to an entire class. Many of the methods in the Ruby class library are singleton methods. This is because, as mentioned earlier, each class is an object of the type Class. Or, to put it simply, the class of every class is Class. This is true of all classes—both those you define yourself and those provided by the Ruby class library:

class_classes.rb

```
class MyClass
end

puts( MyClass.class )    #=> Class
puts( String.class )     #=> Class
puts( Object.class )     #=> Class
puts( Class.class )      #=> Class
puts( IO.class )         #=> Class
```

Now, some classes also have class methods—that is, methods that belong to the Class object itself. In that sense, these are singleton methods of the Class object. Indeed, if you evaluate the following, you will be shown an array of method names that match the names of IO class methods:

```
p( IO.singleton_methods )
```

This displays the following:

```
[:new, :open, :sysopen, :for_fd, :popen, :foreach, :readlines, :read,
:binread, :select, :pipe, :try_convert, :copy_stream]
```

As explained earlier, when you write your own class methods, you do so by prefacing the method name with the name of the class:

```
def MyClass.classMethod
```

It turns out that you can use a similar syntax when creating singleton classes for specific objects. This time you preface the method name with the name of the object:

```
def myObject.objectMethod
```

class_hierarchy
.rb

FINDING AN OBJECT'S ANCESTOR CLASSES

Ultimately all classes descend from the Object class. In Ruby 1.9, the Object class itself descends from the BasicObject class (see Chapter 2). This is true even for the Class class! To prove this, try the *class_hierarchy.rb* program:

```
def showFamily( aClass )
    if (aClass != nil) then
        puts( "#{aClass} :: about to recurse with aClass.superclass =
#{aClass.superclass.inspect}" )
        showFamily( aClass.superclass )
    end
end
```

Pass a class name to this method to track back up its family tree of ancestor classes. For example, try this:

```
showFamily(File)
```

In Ruby 1.9, this displays the following:

```
File :: about to recurse with aClass.superclass = IO
IO :: about to recurse with aClass.superclass = Object
Object :: about to recurse with aClass.superclass = BasicObject
BasicObject :: about to recurse with aClass.superclass = nil
```

Let's look at a concrete example. Suppose you have a program containing Creature objects of many different species (maybe you are a veterinarian, the head keeper at a zoo, or, like the author of this book, an enthusiastic player of adventure games); each creature has a method called talk that displays the vocal noise each creature usually makes.

Here's my Creature class and a few creature objects:

singleton_meth1
.rb

```
class Creature
    def initialize( aSpeech )
        @speech = aSpeech
    end
```

```
    def talk
        puts( @speech )
    end
end

cat = Creature.new( "miaow" )
dog = Creature.new( "woof" )
budgie = Creature.new( "Who's a pretty boy, then!" )
werewolf = Creature.new( "growl" )
```

Then you suddenly realize that one of those creatures, and one alone, has additional special behavior. On the night of a full moon, the werewolf not only talks ("growl") but also howls ("How-oo-oo-oo-oo!"). It really needs a howl method.

You could go back and add such a method to the Creature class, but then you'd end up with howling dogs, cats, and budgies too—which is not what you want. You could create a new Werewolf class that descends from Creature, but you will only ever have one werewolf (they are, alas, an endangered species), so why do you want a whole class for just that? Wouldn't it make more sense to have a werewolf *object* that is the same as every other creature object except that it also has a howl method? Okay, let's do that by giving the werewolf its very own singleton method. Here goes:

```
def werewolf.howl
    puts( "How-oo-oo-oo-oo!" )
end
```

Heck, you can do better than that! It howls only on a full moon, so let's make sure that, if asked to howl when the moon is new, it just growls. Here's my finished method:

```
def werewolf.howl
    if FULLMOON then
      puts( "How-oo-oo-oo-oo!" )
    else
      talk
    end
end
```

Notice that, even though this method has been declared outside the Creature class, it is able to call the instance method talk. That's because the howl method now lives "inside" the werewolf object so has the same scope within that object as the talk method. It does not, however, live inside any of the werewolf's fellow creatures; the howl method belongs to him and him alone. Try to make the budgie.howl, and Ruby will inform you that howl is an undefined method.

Now, if you are debugging your code for your own use, having your program blow up thanks to an undefined method may be acceptable; however, if your program does so out in the big, bad world of the "end user," it is definitely *not* acceptable.

If you think undefined methods are likely to be a problem, you can take avoidance measures by testing whether a singleton method exists before trying to use it. The Object class has a `singleton_methods` method that returns an array of singleton method names. You can test a method name for inclusion using the Array class's `include?` method. In *singleton_meth2.rb*, for example, I've programmed an "open the box" game, which has a number of Box objects, only one of which, when opened, contains the star prize. I've named this special Box object starprize and given it a singleton method called congratulate:

singleton_meth2 .rb

```
starprize = Box.new( "Star Prize" )
def starprize.congratulate
    puts( "You've won a fabulous holiday in Grimsby!" )
end
```

The `congratulate` method should be called when the starprize box is opened. This bit of code (in which item is a Box object) ensures that this method (which does not exist in any other object) is not called when some other box is opened:

```
if item.singleton_methods.include?("congratulate") then
    item.congratulate
end
```

An alternative way of checking the validity of a method would be to pass that method name as a symbol (an identifier preceded by a colon) to the Object class's `respond_to?` method:

```
if item.respond_to?( :congratulate ) then
    item.congratulate
end
```

NOTE   *You'll see another way of handling nonexistent methods in Chapter 20.*

Singleton Classes

A singleton method is a method that belongs to a single object. A singleton class, on the other hand, is a class that defines a single object. Confused? Me too. Let's take a closer look.

Let's suppose you create a few dozen objects, each of which is an instance of the Object class. Naturally they all have access to inherited methods such as inspect and class. But now you decide that you want just one special object (for the sake of variety, let's call him ob), which has one special method (let's call it blather).

You don't want to define a whole new class for this one object since you will never again create any more objects with the blather method. So, you create a class especially for little ob.

You don't need to name this class. You just tell it to attach itself to ob by putting a << between the keyword class and the name of the object. Then you add code to the class in the usual way:

singleton_class.rb

```
ob = Object.new
    # singleton class
class << ob
    def blather( aStr )
        puts("blather, blather #{aStr}")
    end
end
```

Now ob, and only ob, has not only all the usual methods of the Object class; it also has the methods (here just the blather method, but there could, in principle, be many more) of its own special anonymous class:

```
ob.blather( "weeble" )    #=> "blather, blather weeble"
```

If you've been paying close attention, you might have noticed that the singleton class seems to be doing something rather similar to a singleton method. With a singleton class, I can create an object and then add extra methods packaged up inside an anonymous class. With singleton methods, I can create an object and then add methods one by one:

singleton_class2 .rb

```
ob2 = Object.new

def ob2.blather( aStr )        # <= this is a singleton method
    puts( "grippity, grippity #{aStr}" )
end

ob2.blather( "ping!" )        #=> grippity, grippity ping!
```

Similarly, I could rewrite the "star prize" program. In the previous version I added a singleton method, congratulate, to an object named starprize. I could just as easily have created a singleton class containing the congratulate method:

```
starprize = MyClass.new( "Star Prize" )

class << starprize
    def congratulate
        puts( "You've won a fabulous holiday in Grimsby!" )
    end
end
```

In fact, the similarity is more than skin deep. The end result of the previous code is that congratulate becomes a singleton method of starprize. I can verify this by checking whether the array of singleton methods available for the item object contains the name congratulate:

```
if item.singleton_methods.include?(:congratulate)     # Ruby 1.9
```

In Ruby 1.9, the singleton_methods method returns an array of symbols representing the method names. This is why I have used the symbol :congratulate in the previous code. However, in Ruby 1.8, singleton_methods returns an array of strings. So, if you are using Ruby 1.8, you should be sure to use the following test using the string argument "congratulate":

```
if item.singleton_methods.include?("congratulate")     # Ruby 1.8
```

NOTE   *What's the difference between a singleton method and a singleton class? The short answer is, not a lot. These two syntaxes provide different ways of adding methods to a specific object rather than building those methods into its defining class.*

Overriding Methods

Sometimes you may want to redefine a method that already exists in some class. You've done this before when, for example, you created classes with their own to_s methods to return a string representation. Every Ruby class, from Object downward, has a to_s method. The to_s method of the Object class returns the class name and a hexadecimal representation of the object's unique identifier. However, many Ruby classes have their own special versions of to_s. For example, Array.to_s concatenates and returns the values in the array.

When a method in one class replaces a method of the same name in an ancestor class, it is said to *override* that method. You can override methods that are defined in the standard class library such as to_s as well as methods defined in your own classes. If you need to add new behavior to an existing method, remember to call the superclass's method using the super keyword at the start of the overridden method.

Here is an example:

override.rb

```
class MyClass
    def sayHello
        return "Hello from MyClass"
    end

    def sayGoodbye
        return "Goodbye from MyClass"
    end
end
```

```
class MyOtherClass < MyClass
    def sayHello            #overrides (and replaces) MyClass.sayHello
        return "Hello from MyOtherClass"
    end

    # overrides MyClass.sayGoodbye   but first calls that method
    # with super. So this version "adds to" MyClass.sayGoodbye
    def sayGoodbye
        return super << " and also from MyOtherClass"
    end

    # overrides default to_s method
    def to_s
        return "I am an instance of the #{self.class} class"
    end
end
```

Public, Protected, and Private Methods

In some cases, you may want to restrict the "visibility" of your methods to ensure that they cannot be called by code outside the class in which the methods occur.

This may be useful when your class defines various "utility" methods that it requires in order to perform certain functions that it does not intend for public consumption. By imposing access restrictions on those methods, you can prevent programmers from using them for their own nefarious purposes. This means you will be able to change the implementation of those methods at a later stage without having to worry you are going to break somebody else's code.

Ruby provides three levels of method accessibility:

- public
- protected
- private

As the name suggests, public methods are the most accessible, and private methods are the least accessible. All your methods are public unless you specify otherwise. When a method is public, it is available to be used by the world outside the object in whose class it is defined.

When a method is private, it can be used only by other methods inside the object in whose class it is defined.

A protected method generally works in the same way as a private method with one tiny but important difference: In addition to being visible to the methods of the current object, a protected method is also visible to objects of the same type when the second object is within the scope of the first object.

The distinction between private and protected methods will probably be easier to understand when you see a working example. Consider this class:

```
class MyClass

    private
        def priv
            puts( "private" )
        end

    protected
        def prot
            puts( "protected" )
        end

    public
        def pub
            puts( "public" )
        end

        def useOb( anOb )
            anOb.pub
            anOb.prot
            anOb.priv
        end
end
```

I've declared three methods, one for each level of accessibility. These levels are set by putting private, protected, or public prior to one or more methods. The specified accessibility level remains in force for all subsequent methods until some other access level is specified.

NOTE   *public, private, and protected may look like keywords. But they are, in fact, methods of the Module class.*

Finally, my class has a public method, useOb, which takes a MyOb object as an argument and calls the three methods pub, prot, and priv of that object. Now, let's see how a MyClass object can be used. First, I'll create two instances of the class:

```
myob = MyClass.new
myob2 = MyClass.new
```

Now, I try to call each of the three methods in turn:

```
myob.pub     # This works! Prints out "public"
myob.prot    # This doesn't work! I get an error
myob.priv    # This doesn't work either - another error
```

From the previous, it would seem that the public method is (as expected) visible from the world outside the object to which it applies. But both the private and the protected methods are invisible. This being so, what is the protected method for? Another example should help clarify this:

```
myob.useOb( myob2 )
```

This time, I am calling the public method useOb of the myob object, and I am passing to it a second object, myob2, as an argument. The important thing to note is that myob and myob2 are instances of the same class. Now, recall what I said earlier: *In addition to being visible to the methods of the current object, a protected method is also visible to objects of the same type when the second object is within the scope of the first object.*

This may sound like gobbledygook. Let's see if I can make some sense out of it. In the program, the first MyClass object (here myob) has a second MyClass object within its scope when myob2 is passed as an argument to a method of myob. When this happens, you can think of myob2 as being present "inside" myob. Now myob2 shares the scope of the "containing" object, myob. In this special circumstance—when two objects of the same class are within the scope defined by that class—the protected methods of any objects of this class become visible.

In the present case, the protected method prot of the object myob2 (or, at any rate, of the argument that "receives" myob2, here called anob) becomes visible and can be executed. Its private arguments, however, are not visible:

```
def useOb( anOb )
   anOb.pub
   anOb.prot    # protected method can be called
   anOb.priv    # calling a private method results in an error
end
```

DIGGING DEEPER

Here you will learn more about the visibility of code inside methods and another way of defining singleton methods.

Protected and Private Methods in Descendant Classes

The same access rules described in this chapter also apply when calling the methods of ancestor and descendant objects. That is, when you pass an object to a method (as an argument) that has the same class as the receiver object (in other words, the object to which the method belongs), the argument object can call the public and protected methods of the class but not its private methods.

For an example of this, take a look at the *protected.rb* program. Here I have created a MyClass object called myob and a MyOtherClass object, myotherob, where MyOtherClass descends from MyClass:

protected.rb

```ruby
class MyClass

    private
        def priv( aStr )
            return aStr.upcase
        end

    protected
        def prot( aStr )
            return aStr << '!!!!!!'
        end

    public

        def exclaim( anOb )   # calls a protected method
            puts( anOb.prot( "This is a #{anOb.class} - hurrah" ) )
        end

        def shout( anOb )     # calls a private method
            puts( anOb.priv( "This is a #{anOb.class} - hurrah" ) )
        end

end

class MyOtherClass < MyClass

end

class MyUnrelatedClass

end
```

I now create objects from each of these three classes, and I try to pass myotherob as an argument to the myob public method, shout:

```
myob = MyClass.new
myotherob = MyOtherClass.new
myunrelatedob = MyUnrelatedClass.new
```

If you load this program from the code archive, you will see that it contains a number of lines of code in which these three objects attempt to execute the shout and exclaim methods. Many of these attempts are doomed to failure and so have been commented out. However, when testing the code, you may want to uncomment each method call one by one to see the results. This is my first attempt:

```
myob.shout( myotherob )      # fails
```

Here the shout method calls the private method priv on the argument object:

```
def shout( anOb )    # calls a private method
   puts( anOb.priv( "This is a #{anOb.class} - hurrah" ) )
end
```

This won't work! Ruby complains that the priv method is private.
Similarly, were I to do it the other way around—that is, by passing the ancestor object myob as the argument and invoking the method shout on the descendant object—I would encounter the same error:

```
myotherob.shout( myob )      # fails
```

The MyClass class also has another public method, exclaim. This one calls a protected method, prot:

```
def exclaim( anOb )  # calls a protected method
   puts( anOb.prot( "This is a #{anOb.class} - hurrah" ) )
end
```

Now, I can pass either the MyClass object, myob, or the MyOtherClass object, myotherob, as an argument to the exclaim method, and no error will occur when the protected method is called:

```
myob.exclaim( myotherob )        # This is OK
myotherob.exclaim( myob )        # And so is this...
myob.exclaim( myunrelatedob )    # But this won't work
```

Needless to say, this works only when the two objects (the receiver object to the left of the dot and the argument passed to the method) share the same line of descent. If you send an unrelated object as an argument, you would not be able to call methods of the receiver class, no matter what their protection levels.

Invading the Privacy of Private Methods

The whole point of a private method is that it cannot be called from outside the scope of the object to which it belongs. So, this won't work:

send.rb

```
class X
    private
        def priv( aStr )
            puts("I'm private, " << aStr)
        end
end

ob = X.new
ob.priv( "hello" )      # This fails
```

However, it turns out that Ruby provides a "get out clause" (or maybe I should say a "get in" clause?) in the form of a method called send.

The send method invokes the method whose name matches that of a symbol (an identifier beginning with a colon such as :priv), which is passed as the first argument to send like this:

```
ob.send( :priv, "hello" )    # This succeeds
```

Any arguments supplied after the symbol (like the string "hello") are passed in the normal way to the specified method.

Using send to gain public access to a private method is not generally a good idea. After all, if you need access to a certain method, why make it private in the first place? Use this technique with caution or not at all.

Singleton Class Methods

Earlier, I created class methods by appending a method name to the name of the class like this:

```
def MyClass.classMethod
```

There is a "shortcut" syntax for doing this. Here is an example:

class_methods3.rb

```
class MyClass

    def MyClass.methodA
        puts("a")
    end
```

```
class << self
    def methodB
        puts("b")
    end

    def methodC
        puts("c")
    end
end

end
```

Here, `methodA`, `methodB`, and `methodC` are all class methods of MyClass; `methodA` is declared using the syntax used previously:

```
def ClassName.methodname
```

But `methodB` and `methodC` are declared using the syntax of instance methods:

```
def methodname
```

So, why do they end up as class methods? It's all because the method declarations have been placed inside this code:

```
class << self
    # some method declarations
end
```

This may remind you of the syntax used for declaring singleton classes. For example, in the *singleton_class.rb* program, you may recall that I first created an object named `ob` and then gave it its very own method, `blather`:

```
class << ob
    def blather( aStr )
        puts("blather, blather #{aStr}")
    end
end
```

The `blather` method here is a singleton method of the `ob` object. Similarly, in the *class_methods3.rb* program, the `methodB` and `methodC` methods are singleton methods of `self`—and `self` happens to be the MyClass class. You can similarly add singleton methods from outside the class definition by using `<<` followed by the class name, like this:

```
class << MyClass
    def methodD
        puts( "d" )
    end
end
```

Finally, the code checks that all four methods really are singleton methods by first printing the names of all available singleton methods and then calling them:

```
puts( MyClass.singleton_methods.sort )
MyClass.methodA
MyClass.methodB
MyClass.methodC
MyClass.methodD
```

This displays the following:

```
methodA
methodB
methodC
methodD
a
b
c
d
```

Nested Methods

You can nest methods; that is, you can write methods that contain other methods. This gives you a way of dividing a long method into reusable chunks. So, for example, if method x needs to do calculation y at several different points, you can put the y method inside the x method (the methods in the following example are called outer_x, nested_y, and nested_z for clarity):

nested_methods
.rb

```
class X

    def outer_x
        print( "x:" )

        def nested_y
            print("ha! ")
        end

        def nested_z
            print( "z:" )
            nested_y
        end

        nested_y
        nested_z
    end

end
```

Nested methods are not initially visible outside the scope in which they are defined. So, in the previous example, although nested_y and nested_z may be called from inside outer_x, they may not be called by any other code:

```
ob = X.new
ob.outer_x          #=> x:ha! z:ha!
```

If, instead of ob.outer_x in the previous code, you were to call ob.nested_y or ob.nested_z, you would see an error message since the nested_y and nested_z methods would not, at this stage, be visible. However, when you run a method that encloses nested methods, those nested methods *will* be brought into scope outside that method!

*nested_methods2
.rb*

```
class X
    def x
        print( "x:" )
        def y
            print("y:")
        end

        def z
            print( "z:" )
            y
        end
    end
end


ob = X.new
ob.x          #=> x:
puts
ob.y          #=> y:
puts
ob.z          #=> z:y:
```

To see another example of this, try running the *nested_methods.rb* code again, but this time uncomment all three method calls. This time, when the outer_x method executes, it brings nested_y and nested_z into scope so the calls to the two nested methods now succeed:

```
ob.outer_x      #=> x:ha! z:ha!
ob.nested_y     #=> ha!
ob.nested_z     #=> z:ha!
```

Method Names

As a final point, it's worth mentioning that method names in Ruby almost always begin with a lowercase character like this:

```
def fred
```

However, that is a *convention*, not an *obligation*. It is also permissible to begin method names with capital letters, like this:

```
def Fred
```

Since the `Fred` method looks like a constant (it starts with a capital letter), you would need to tell Ruby that it is a method when calling it by adding parentheses:

method_names.rb
```
Fred          # <= Ruby complains 'uninitialized constant'
Fred()        # <= Ruby calls the Fred method
```

On the whole, it is better to stick to the convention of using method names that begin with a lowercase character.

8

PASSING ARGUMENTS AND RETURNING VALUES

In this chapter, you'll be looking at many of the effects (and side effects) of passing arguments and returning values to and from methods. First, though, I'll take a moment to summarize the types of methods you've used up to now.

Summarizing Instance, Class, and Singleton Methods

An instance method is declared inside a class definition and is intended for use by a specific object or "instance" of the class, like this:

methods.rb

```
class MyClass
    # declare instance method
    def instanceMethod
        puts( "This is an instance method" )
    end
end
```

```
    # create object
ob = MyClass.new
    # use instance method
ob.instanceMethod
```

A class method may be declared inside a class definition, in which case the method name may be preceded by the class name, or a class << self block may contain a "normal" method definition. Either way, a class method is intended for use by the class itself, not by a specific object, like this:

```
class MyClass
    # a class method
    def MyClass.classmethod1
        puts( "This is a class method" )
    end

    # another class method
    class << self
        def classmethod2
            puts( "This is another class method" )
        end
    end
end

    # call class methods from the class itself
MyClass.classmethod1
MyClass.classmethod2
```

Singleton methods are methods that are added to a single object and cannot be used by other objects. A singleton method may be defined by appending the method name to the object name followed by a dot or by placing a "normal" method definition inside an *ObjectName* << self block like this:

```
    # create object
ob = MyClass.new

    # define a singleton method
def ob.singleton_method1
    puts( "This is a singleton method" )
end

    # define another singleton method
class << ob
    def singleton_method2
        puts( "This is another singleton method" )
    end
end

    # use the singleton methods
ob.singleton_method1
ob.singleton_method2
```

Returning Values

In many programming languages, a distinction is made between functions or methods that return a value to the calling code and those that do not. In Pascal, for example, a *function* returns a value, but a *procedure* does not. No such distinction is made in Ruby. All methods always return a value, though of course you are not obliged to use it.

When no return value is specified, Ruby methods return the result of the last expression evaluated. Consider this method:

return_vals.rb

```
def method1
    a = 1
    b = 2
    c = a + b    # returns 3
end
```

The last expression evaluated is a + b, which happens to return 3, so that is the value returned by this method. There may often be times when you don't want to return the last expression evaluated. In such cases, you can specify the return value using the return keyword:

```
def method2
    a = 1
    b = 2
    c = a + b
    return b    # returns 2
end
```

A method is not obliged to make any assignments in order to return a value. If a simple piece of data happens to be the last thing evaluated in a method, that will be the value the method returns. When nothing is evaluated, nil is returned:

```
def method3
    "hello"      # returns "hello"
end

def method4
    a = 1 + 2
    "goodbye"    # returns "goodbye"
end

def method5
end              # returns nil
```

My own programming prejudice is to write code that is clear and unambiguous whenever possible. For that reason, whenever I plan to use the value returned by a method, I prefer to specify it using the return keyword; only when I do not plan to use the returned value do I omit this. However, this is not obligatory—Ruby leaves the choice to you.

Returning Multiple Values

But what about those occasions when you need a method to return more than one value? In other program languages, you may be able to "fake" this by passing arguments by reference (pointers to the original data items) rather than by value (a copy of the data); when you alter the values of "by reference" arguments, you alter the original values without explicitly having to return any values to the calling code.

Ruby doesn't make a distinction between "by reference" and "by value," so this technique is not available to you (though you will see some exceptions to the rule shortly). However, Ruby is capable of returning multiple values all in one go, as shown here:

return_many.rb

```
def ret_things
    greeting = "Hello world"
    a = 1
    b = 2.0
    return a, b, 3, "four", greeting, 6 * 10
end
```

Multiple return values are placed into an array. If you were to evaluate ret_things.class, Ruby would inform you that the returned object is an Array. You could, however, explicitly return a different collection type such as a Hash:

```
def ret_hash
    return {'a'=>'hello', 'b'=>'goodbye', 'c'=>'fare thee well'}
end
```

Default and Multiple Arguments

Ruby lets you specify default values for arguments. Default values can be assigned in the parameter list of a method using the usual assignment operator:

```
def aMethod( a=10, b=20 )
```

If an unassigned variable is passed to that method, the default value will be assigned to it. If an assigned variable is passed, however, the assigned value takes precedence over the default. Here I use the p() method to inspect and print the return values:

```
def aMethod( a=10, b=20 )
    return a, b
end
```

```
p( aMethod )          #=> displays: [10,  20]
p( aMethod( 1 ))      #=> displays: [1, 20]
p( aMethod( 1, 2 ))   #=> displays: [1, 2]
```

In some cases, a method may need to be capable of receiving an uncertain number of arguments—say, for example, a method that processes a variable-length list of items. In this case, you can "mop up" any number of trailing items by preceding the final argument with an asterisk:

default_args.rb

```
def aMethod( a=10, b=20, c=100, *d )
    return a, b, c, d
end

p( aMethod( 1,2,3,4,6 ) )    #=> displays: [1, 2, 3, [4, 6]]
```

Assignment and Parameter Passing

Most of the time, Ruby methods come with two access points—like the doors into and out of a room. The argument list provides the way in; the return value provides the way out. Modifications made to the input arguments do not affect the original data for the simple reason that when Ruby evaluates an expression, the result of that evaluation creates a new object, so any changes made to an argument affect only the new object, not the original piece of data. But there are exceptions to this rule, which I'll show you now.

Let's start by looking at the simplest case—a method that takes one value as a named parameter and returns another value:

in_out.rb

```
def change( x )
    x += 1
    return x
end
```

On the face of it, you might think you are dealing with a single object, x, here: The object x goes into the change method, and the same object x is returned. In fact, that is not the case. One object goes in (the argument), and a different object comes out (the return value). You can easily verify this using the object_id method to show a number that uniquely identifies each object in your program:

```
num = 10
puts( "num.object_id=#{num.object_id}" )
num = change( num )
puts( "num.object_id=#{num.object_id}" )
```

The identifier of the variable, num, is different before and after you call the change method. This shows that even though the variable name remains the same, the num object that is returned by the change method is different from the num object that was sent to it.

The method call itself has nothing to do with the change of the object. You can verify this by running *method_call.rb*. This simply passes the num object to the change method and returns it:

```
def nochange( x )
    return x
end
```

In this case, the object_id is the same after num is returned as it was before num was sent to the method. In other words, the object that went into the method is the same object as the one that came out again. That leads to the inevitable conclusion that there is something about the *assignment* in the change method (x += 1) that caused the creation of a new object.

But assignment itself isn't the whole explanation. If you simply assign a variable to itself, no new object is created:

```
num = 10
num = num      # a new num object is not created
```

If you now display the object_id of the num variable, the number is the same before an after assignment, proving that this really is the same object. So, what if you assign to the object the same value that it already has?

```
num = 10
num = 10       # a new num object is not created
```

Once again, the object_id is unchanged after the assignment. This demonstrates that assignment alone does not necessarily create a new object. Now let's try assigning a new value:

```
num = 10
num += 1       # this time a new num object is created
```

This time, if you display num.object_id before and after the assignment, you will see a different number—say 21 before and 23 after. The actual numbers are automatically determined by Ruby and may vary. The important thing to understand is that a different object ID indicates a different object. If the same variable returns a different object_id when a value is assigned to it, that means a new object has been created.

Most data items are treated as unique, so one string "hello" is considered to be different from another string "hello," and one float 10.5 is considered to be different from another float 10.5. Thus, any string or float assignment will create a new object.

But when working with integers, only when the assignment value is *different* from the previous value is a new object created. You can do all kinds of complicated operations on the right side of the assignment, but if the yielded value is the same as the original value, no new object is created.

```
num = 11
puts( "num.object_id=#{num.object_id}" )
num = (((num + 1 - 1) * 100) / 100)
puts( "num.object_id=#{num.object_id}" )
```

In the previous code, the first assignment creates a new num object with the integer value 11. Even though the result of a fairly complex expression is used in the next assignment, this still has the value 11. Since the value of num is not changed, no new objects are created, and its object_id remains the same:

```
num.object_id=23
num.object_id=23
```

Integers Are Special

In Ruby, an integer (or Fixnum) has a fixed identity. Every instance of the number 10 or every variable to which the value 10 is assigned will have the same object_id. The same cannot be said of other data types. Each instance of a floating-point number such as 10.5 or of a string such as "hello world" will be a different object with a unique object_id. Be aware that when you assign an integer to a variable, that variable will have the object_id *of the integer itself*. But when you assign some other type of data to a variable, a new object will be created even if the data itself is the same at each assignment:

object_ids.rb
```
# 10 and x after each assignment are the same object
puts( 10.object_id )
x = 10
puts( x.object_id )
x = 10
puts( x.object_id )

# 10.5 and x after each assignment are 3 different objects!
puts( 10.5.object_id )
x = 10.5
puts( x.object_id )
x = 10.5
puts( x.object_id )
```

But why does all this matter?

It matters because of a few rare exceptions to the rule. As I said earlier, most of the time, a method has a well-defined way in and a well-defined way out. Once an argument goes inside a method, it enters a closed room. Any code outside that method has no way of learning about any changes that have been made to the argument until it comes out again in the form of a returned value. This is, in fact, one of the deep secrets of "pure" object orientation. The implementation details of methods should, in principle, be hidden away, or *encapsulated*. This ensures that code outside an object cannot be dependent on things that happen inside that object.

The One-Way-In, One-Way-Out Principle

In most modern object-oriented languages such as Java and C#, encapsulation and information hiding are not rigorously enforced. In Smalltalk, on the other hand—the most famous and influential object-oriented language—encapsulation and information hiding are fundamental principles: If you send a variable x to a method y and the value of x is changed inside y, you cannot obtain the changed value of x from outside the method—*unless the method explicitly returns that value.*

ENCAPSULATION OR INFORMATION HIDING?

Often these two terms are used interchangeably. To be nitpicky, however, there is a difference. *Encapsulation* refers to the grouping together of an object's "state" (its data) and the operations that may alter or interrogate its state (its methods). *Information hiding* refers to the fact that data is sealed off and can be accessed only using well-defined routes in and out—in object-oriented terms, this implies "accessor methods" to get or return values. In procedural languages, information hiding may take other forms; for example, you might have to define interfaces to retrieve data from code "units" or "modules" rather than from objects.

In object-oriented terms, encapsulation and information hiding are almost synonymous—true encapsulation necessarily implies that the internal data of an object is hidden. However, many modern object-oriented languages such as Java, C#, C++, and Object Pascal are quite permissive in the degree to which information hiding is enforced (if at all).

Usually, Ruby adheres to this principle: Arguments go into a method, but any changes made inside the method cannot be accessed from the outside unless Ruby returns the changed value:

hidden.rb

```
def hidden( aStr, anotherStr )
    anotherStr = aStr + " " + anotherStr
    return anotherStr.reverse
end

str1 = "dlrow"
str2 = "olleh"
str3 = hidden(str1, str2)
puts( str1 )    #=> dlrow
puts( str2 )    #=> olleh
puts( str3 )    #=> hello world
```

In the previous code, the string value of the second object, str2, is received by the anotherStr argument of the hidden method. The argument is assigned a new string value and reversed. Even so, neither of the original variables, str1 or str2, is changed. Only the variable assigned the return value, str3, contains the changed "hello world" string.

It turns out that there are occasions when arguments passed to a Ruby method can be used like the "by reference" arguments of other languages (that is, changes made *inside* the method may affect variables *outside* the method). This is because some Ruby methods modify the original object rather than yielding a value and assigning this to a new object.

For example, there are some methods ending with an exclamation mark that alter the original object. Similarly, the String append method << concatenates the string on its right to the string on its left but does not create a new string object in the process: So, the value of the string on the left is modified, but the string object itself retains its original object_id.

The consequence of this is that if you use the << operator instead of the + operator in a method, your results will change:

not_hidden.rb

```
def nothidden( aStr, anotherStr )
    anotherStr = aStr << " " << anotherStr
    return anotherStr.reverse
end

str1 = "dlrow"
str2 = "olleh"
str3 = nothidden(str1, str2)
puts( str1 )        #=> dlrow olleh
puts( str2 )        #=> olleh
puts( str3 )        #=> hello world
```

In the previous code, the anotherStr argument is concatenated with a space and the aStr argument using <<, and the resulting string is reversed when returned. If information hiding were rigorously enforced, this might be expected to produce the same results as in the previous program—that is, str1 and str2 would remain unchanged. However, the use of << has had profound effects because it has caused the modifications made to the aStr argument *inside* the nothidden method to change the value of the str1 object *outside* the method.

This behavior, incidentally, would be the same if the nothidden method were placed into a separate class:

nothidden2.rb

```
class X
    def nothidden( aStr, anotherStr )
        anotherStr = aStr << " " << anotherStr
        return anotherStr.reverse
    end
end
ob = X.new
str1 = "dlrow"
str2 = "olleh"
str3 = ob.nothidden(str1, str2)
puts( str1 )     #=> dlrow olleh
```

This shows that, in certain cases, the internal implementation details of an object's methods may accidentally alter the code that calls it. It is generally safer to make implementation details hidden; otherwise, when code is rewritten inside a class, the changes may have side effects on code that uses that class.

Modifying Receivers and Yielding New Objects

You may recall from Chapter 4 that I made the distinction between methods that modify their receiver and those that do not. (Remember that a *receiver* is the object that "owns" the method.) In most cases, Ruby methods do not modify the receiver object. However, some methods, such as those ending with !, do modify their receiver.

The *str_reverse.rb* sample program should help clarify this. This shows that when you use the reverse method, for example, no change is made to the receiver object (that is, an object such as str1). But when you use the reverse! method, a change *is* made to the object (its letters are reversed). Even so, no new object is created: str1 is the same object before and after the reverse! method is called.

Here reverse operates like most Ruby methods: It yields a value, and in order to use that value, you must assign it to a new object. Consider the following:

str_reverse.rb
```
str1 = "hello"
str1.reverse
```

Here, str1 is unaffected by calling reverse. It still has the value "hello" and still has its original object_id. Now look at this:

```
str1 = "hello"
str1.reverse!
```

This time, str1 *is* changed (it becomes "olleh"). Even so, no new object is created: str1 has the same object_id with which it started. So, how about this:

```
str1 = "hello"
str1 = str1.reverse
```

This time, the value yielded by str1.reverse is assigned to str1. The yielded value is a new object, so str1 is now assigned the reversed string ("olleh"), and it now has a new object_id.

Refer to the sample program *concat.rb* for an example of the string concatenation method, <<, which, just like those methods that end with !, modifies the receiver object without creating a new object (once again, the actual object_id numbers may be different when you run the code):

concat.rb
```
str1 = "hello"      #object_id = 23033940
str2 = "world"      #object_id = 23033928
str3 = "goodbye"    #object_id = 23033916
```

```
str3 = str2 << str1
puts( str1.object_id )  #=> 23033940 # unchanged
puts( str2.object_id )  #=> 23033928 # unchanged
puts( str3.object_id )  #=> 23033928 # now the same as str2!
```

In this example, str1 is never modified, so it has the same object_id
throughout; str2 *is* modified through concatenation. However, the << operator does not create a new object, so str2 also retains its original object_id.

But str3 is a different object at the end than at the beginning, because
it is assigned the value yielded by this expression: str2 << str1. This value
happens to be the str2 object itself, so the object_id of str3 is now identical
to that of str2 (that is, str2 and str3 *now reference the same object*).

In summary, then, methods ending with a ! such as reverse!, plus some
other methods such as the << concatenation method, change the value of the
receiver object. Most other methods do not change the value of the receiver
object. To use any new value yielded as a result of calling one of these methods, you have to assign that value to a variable (or pass the yielded value as an
argument to a method).

NOTE   *The fact that a few methods modify the receiver object whereas most do not may seem
harmless enough, but beware: This behavior provides you with the ability to retrieve
the values of arguments "by reference" rather than retrieving values that are explicitly
returned. Doing so breaks encapsulation by allowing your code to rely upon the internal implementation details of a method. This can potentially lead to unpredictable
side effects and, in my view, should be avoided.*

Potential Side Effects of Reliance on Argument Values

For a simple (but, in real-world programming, potentially serious) example
of how relying on the modified values of arguments rather than on explicit
return values can introduce undesirable dependencies on implementation
details, see *side_effects.rb*. Here is a method called stringProcess that takes two
string arguments, messes about with them, and returns the results:

side_effects.rb
```
def stringProcess( aStr, anotherStr )
    aStr.capitalize!
    anotherStr.reverse!.capitalize!
    aStr = aStr +  " " + anotherStr.reverse!
    return aStr
end
```

Let's assume the object of the exercise is to take two lowercase strings
and return a single string that combines these two strings, separated by a
space and with the first and last letters capitalized. So, the two original strings
might be "hello" and "world," and the returned string is "Hello worlD." This
works fine:

```
str1 = "hello"
str2 = "world"
```

```
str3 = stringProcess( str1, str2 )
puts( "#{str3}" )      #=> Hello worlD
```

But now there is an impatient programmer who can't be bothered with return values. He notices that the modifications made inside the method change the values of the ingoing arguments. So, heck! (he decides), he might as well use the arguments themselves! This is his version:

```
puts( "#{str1} #{str2}" ) #=> Hello worlD
```

By using the values of the input arguments, str1 and str2, he has obtained the same result as if he had used the returned value, str3. He then goes away and writes a fabulously complicated text-processing system with thousands of bits of code reliant on the changed values of those two arguments.

But now the programmer who originally wrote the stringProcess method decides that the original implementation was inefficient or inelegant and so rewrites the code confident in the knowledge that the return value is unchanged (if "hello" and "world" are sent as arguments, "Hello worlD" is returned just as it was by the previous version):

```
def stringProcess( aStr, anotherStr )
    myStr = aStr.capitalize!
    anotherStr.reverse!.capitalize!
    myStr = myStr + " " + anotherStr.reverse
    return myStr
end

str1 = "hello"
str2 = "world"
str3 = stringProcess( str1, str2 )

puts( "#{str3}" )            #=> Hello worlD
puts( "#{str1} #{str2}" )    #=> Hello Dlrow
```

Aha! But the new implementation causes the values of the input arguments to be changed inside the body of the method. So, the impatient programmer's text-processing system, which relies on those *arguments* rather than on the return value, is now filled with bits of text saying "hello Dlrow" instead of the "Hello worlD" he was expecting (actually, it turns out that his program was processing the works of Shakespeare, so a generation of actors will end up declaiming, "To eb or ton to eb, that si the noitseuq..."). This is the kind of unexpected side effect that can easily be avoided by following the one-way-in, one-way-out principle.

Parallel Assignment

I mentioned earlier that it is possible for a method to return multiple values, separated by commas. Often you will want to assign these returned values to a set of matching variables.

In Ruby, you can do this in a single operation by parallel assignment. This means you can have several variables to the left or an assignment operator and several values to the right. The values to the right will be assigned, in order, to the variables on the left, like this:

parallel_assign.rb

```
s1, s2, s3 = "Hickory", "Dickory", "Dock"
```

This ability not only gives you a shortcut way to make multiple assignments; it also lets you swap the values of variables (you just change their orders on either side of the assignment operator):

```
i1 = 1
i2 = 2

i1, i2 = i2, i1          #=> i1 is now 2, i2 is 1
```

And you can make multiple assignments from the values returned by a method:

```
def returnArray( a, b, c )
    a = "Hello, " + a
    b = "Hi, " + b
    c = "Good day, " + c
    return a, b, c
end
x, y, z = returnArray( "Fred", "Bert", "Mary" )
```

If you specify more variables to the left than there are values on the right of an assignment, any "trailing" variables will be assigned nil:

```
x, y, z, extravar = returnArray( "Fred", "Bert", "Mary" ) # extravar = nil
```

Multiple values returned by a method are put into an array. When you put an array to the right of a multiple-variable assignment, its individual elements will be assigned to each variable, and once again if too many variables are supplied, the extra ones will be assigned nil:

```
s1, s2, s3 = ["Ding", "Dong", "Bell"]
```

DIGGING DEEPER

In this section we look at some of the inner workings of parameter-passing and object equality. I also discuss the value of parentheses for code clarity.

By Reference or By Value?

Earlier, I said that Ruby does not make a distinction between arguments that are passed "by value" and "by reference." Even so, if you search the Internet, you'll soon discover that Ruby programmers often get into arguments about how exactly arguments are passed. In many procedural programming languages such as Pascal or C, there is a clear distinction between arguments passed by value or by reference.

A *by value* argument is a *copy* of the original variable; you can pass it to a function and mess around with it, and the value of the original variable remains unchanged.

A *by reference* argument, on the other hand, is a *pointer* to the original variable. When this gets passed to a procedure, you are not passing a new copy but a reference to the bit of memory in which the original data is stored. So, any changes made inside the procedure are made to the original data and necessarily affect the value of the original variable.

So, which way does Ruby pass arguments? It's actually pretty easy to resolve this issue. If Ruby passes by value, then it makes a copy of the original variable, and that copy will therefore have a different object_id. In fact, this is not the case. Try the *arg_passing.rb* program to prove this point.

arg_passing.rb

```ruby
def aMethod( anArg )
    puts( "#{anArg.object_id}\n\n" )
end

class MyClass
end


i = 10
f = 10.5
s = "hello world"
ob = MyClass.new


puts( "#{i}.object_id = #{i.object_id}" )
aMethod( i )
puts( "#{f}.object_id = #{f.object_id}" )
aMethod( f )
puts( "#{s}.object_id = #{s.object_id}" )
aMethod( s )
puts( "#{ob}.object_id = #{ob.object_id}" )
aMethod( ob )
```

This prints out the object IDs of an integer, a floating-point number, a string, and a custom object both when they are originally declared and when they are passed as arguments to the aMethod() method. In each case, the ID of the argument is the same as the ID of the original variable, so the arguments must be passed by reference.

Now, it may well be that in certain circumstances the passing of arguments could, "behind the scenes" so to speak, be *implemented* as "by value." However, such implementation details should be of interest to writers of Ruby interpreters and compilers rather than to Ruby programmers. The plain fact of the matter is that if you program in a "pure" object-oriented way—by passing arguments into methods but only subsequently using the values that those methods return—the implementation details (by value or by reference) will be of no consequence to you.

Nevertheless, because Ruby can occasionally modify arguments (for example, using ! methods or <<, as explained in "Modifying Receivers and Yielding New Objects" on page 130), some programmers have formed the habit of using the modified values of the arguments themselves (equivalent to using by reference arguments in C) rather than using the values returned. In my view, this is a bad practice. It makes your programs reliant upon the implementation details of methods and should, therefore, be avoided.

Are Assignments Copies or References?

I said earlier that a new object is created when a value is *yielded* by some expression. So, for example, if you assign a new value to a variable called x, the object after the assignment will be a different object from the one before the assignment (that is, it will have a different object_id):

```
x = 10      # this x has one object_id
x +=1       # and this x has a different one
```

But it isn't the assignment that creates a new object. It is the value that is yielded that causes a new object to be created. In the previous example, +=1 is an expression that yields a value (x+=1 is equivalent to the expression x=x+1).

Simple assignment of one variable to another does not create a new object. So, let's assume you have one variable called num and another called num2. If you assign num2 to num, both variables will refer to the same object. You can test this using the equal? method of the Object class:

assign_ref.rb
```
num = 11.5
num2 = 11.5

    # num and num 2 are not equal
puts( "#{num.equal?(num2)}" )    #=> false

num = num2
    # but now they are equal
puts( "#{num.equal?(num2)}" )    #=> true
```

Tests for Equality: == or equal?

By default (as defined in Ruby's Kernel module), a test using == returns true when both objects being tested are the same object. So, it will return false if the values are the same but the objects are different:

equal_tests.rb

```
ob1 = Object.new
ob2 = Object.new
puts( ob1==ob2 ) #=> false
```

In fact, == is frequently overridden by classes such as String and will then return true when the values are the same but the objects are different:

```
s1 = "hello"
s2 = "hello"
puts( s1==s2 ) #=> true
```

For that reason, the equal? method is preferable when you want to establish whether two variables refer to the same object:

```
puts( ob1.equal?(ob2) )    #=> false
puts( s1.equal?(s2) )      #=> false
```

When Are Two Objects Identical?

As a general rule, if you initialize 10 variables with 10 values, each variable will refer to a different object. For example, if you create two strings like this:

identical.rb

```
s1 = "hello"
s2 = "hello"
```

then s1 and s2 will refer to independent objects. The same goes for two floats:

```
f1 = 10.00
f2 = 10.00
```

But, as mentioned earlier, integers are different. Create two integers with the same value, and they will end up referencing the same object:

```
i1 = 10
i2 = 10
```

This is even true with literal integer values. If in doubt, use the equals? method to test whether two variables or values reference exactly the same object:

```
10.0.equal?(10.0) # compare floats - returns false
10.equal?(10)     # compare integers (Fixnums) - returns true
```

Parentheses Avoid Ambiguity

Methods may share the same name as local variables. For example, you might have a variable called name and a method called name. If it is your habit to call methods without parentheses, it may not be obvious whether you are referring to a method or a variable. Once again, parentheses avoid ambiguity:

parentheses.rb

```
greet = "Hello"
name = "Fred"

def greet
    return "Good morning"
end

def name
    return "Mary"
end

def sayHi( aName )
    return "Hi, #{aName}"
end

puts( greet )                  #=> Hello
puts greet                     #=> Hello
puts greet()                   #=> good morning
puts( sayHi( name ) )          #=> Hi, Fred
puts( sayHi( name() ) )        #=> Hi, Mary
```

9

EXCEPTION HANDLING

Even the most carefully written program will sometimes encounter unforeseen errors. For example, if you write a program that needs to read some data from disk, it works on the assumption that the specified disk is actually available and the data is valid. If your program does calculations based on user input, it works on the assumption that the input is suitable to be used in a calculation.

Although you may try to anticipate some potential problems before they arise—for example, by writing code to check that a file exists before reading data from it or checking that user input is numerical before doing a calculation—you will never be able to predict every possible problem in advance.

The user may remove a data disk after you've already started reading data from it, for example; or some obscure calculation may yield 0 just before your code attempts to divide by this value. When you know that there is the possibility that your code may be "broken" by some unforeseen circumstances at runtime, you can attempt to avoid disaster by using *exception handling*.

An *exception* is an error that is packaged into an object. The object is an instance of the Exception class (or one of its descendants). You can handle exceptions by trapping the Exception object, optionally using information that it contains (to print an appropriate error message, for instance) and taking any actions needed to recover from the error—perhaps by closing any files that are still open or assigning a sensible value to a variable that may have been assigned some nonsensical value as the result of an erroneous calculation.

rescue: Execute Code When Error Occurs

The basic syntax of exception handling can be summarized as follows:

```
begin
    # Some code which may cause an exception
rescue <Exception Class>
    # Code to recover from the exception
end
```

When an exception is unhandled, your program may crash, and Ruby is likely to display a relatively unfriendly error message:

div_by_zero.rb
```
x = 1/0
puts( x )
```

The program terminates with this error:

```
C:/bookofruby/ch9/div_by_zero.rb:3:in `/': divided by 0 (ZeroDivisionError)
from C:/bookofruby/ch9/div_by_zero.rb:3:in `<main>'
```

To prevent this from happening, you should handle exceptions yourself. Here is an example of an exception handler that deals with an attempt to divide by zero:

exception1.rb
```
begin
    x = 1/0
rescue Exception
    x = 0
    puts( $!.class )
    puts( $! )
end
puts( x )
```

When this runs, the code following rescue Exception executes and displays this:

```
ZeroDivisionError
divided by 0
0
```

The code between begin and end is my exception-handling block. I've placed the troublesome code after begin. When an exception occurs, it is handled in the section beginning with rescue. The first thing I've done is to set the variable x to a meaningful value. Next come these two inscrutable statements:

```
puts( $!.class )
puts( $! )
```

In Ruby, $! is a global variable to which is assigned the last exception. Printing $!.class displays the class name, which here is ZeroDivisionError; printing the variable $! alone has the effect of displaying the error message contained by the Exception object, which here is "divided by 0."

I am not generally keen on relying upon global variables, particularly when they have names as undescriptive as $!. Fortunately, there is an alternative. You can associate a variable name with the exception by placing the "assoc operator" (=>) after the class name of the exception and before the variable name:

exception2.rb

```
rescue Exception => exc
```

You can now use the variable name (here exc) to refer to the Exception object:

```
puts( exc.class )
puts( exc )
```

Although it may seem pretty obvious that when you divide by zero, you are going to get a ZeroDivisionError exception, in real-world code there may be times when the type of exception is not so predictable. Let's suppose, for instance, that you have a method that does a division based on two values supplied by a user:

```
def calc( val1, val2 )
    return val1 / val2
end
```

This could potentially produce a variety of different exceptions. Obviously, if the second value entered by the user is 0, you will get a ZeroDivisionError.

exception_tree.rb

```
ZeroDivisionError
StandardError
Exception
Object
BasicObject
```

However, if the *second* value is a string, the exception will be a TypeError, whereas if the *first* value is a string, it will be a NoMethodError (because the String class does not define the "division operator," which is /). Here the rescue block handles all possible exceptions:

multi_except.rb

```
def calc( val1, val2 )
    begin
        result = val1 / val2
    rescue Exception => e
        puts( e.class )
        puts( e )
        result = nil
    end
    return result
end
```

You can test this by deliberately generating different error conditions:

```
calc( 20, 0 )
    #=> ZeroDivisionError
    #=> divided by 0
calc( 20, "100" )
    #=> TypeError
    #=> String can't be coerced into Fixnum
calc( "100", 100 )
    #=> NoMethodError
    #=> undefined method `/' for "100":String
```

Often it will be useful to take different actions for different exceptions. You can do that by adding multiple rescue clauses. Each rescue clause can handle multiple exception types, with the exception class names separated by commas. Here my calc method handles TypeError and NoMethodError exceptions in one clause with a catchall Exception handler to deal with other exception types:

multi_except2.rb

```
def calc( val1, val2 )
    begin
        result = val1 / val2
    rescue TypeError, NoMethodError => e
        puts( e.class )
        puts( e )
        puts( "One of the values is not a number!" )
        result = nil
    rescue Exception => e
        puts( e.class )
        puts( e )
        result = nil
    end
    return result
end
```

This time, when a TypeError or NoMethodError is handled (but no other sort of error), my additional error message is displayed like this:

```
NoMethodError
undefined method `/' for "100":String
One of the values is not a number!
```

When handling multiple exception types, you should always put the rescue clauses dealing with specific exceptions first and then follow these with rescue clauses dealing with more generalized exceptions.

When a specific exception such as TypeError is handled, the begin..end exception block exits so the flow of execution won't "trickle down" to more generalized rescue clauses. However, if you put a generalized exception-handling rescue clause first, that will handle all exceptions, so any more specific clauses lower down will never execute.

If, for example, I had reversed the order of the rescue clauses in my calc method, placing the generalized Exception handler first, this would match all exception types so the clause for the specific TypeError and NoMethodError exceptions would never be run:

multi_except_err .rb

```
# This is incorrect...
rescue Exception => e
    puts( e.class )
    result = nil
rescue TypeError, NoMethodError => e
    puts( e.class )
    puts( e )
    puts( "Oops! This message will never be displayed!" )
    result = nil
end
```

```
calc( 20, 0 )       #=> ZeroDivisionError
calc( 20, "100" )   #=> TypeError
calc( "100", 100 )  #=> NoMethodError
```

ensure: Execute Code Whether or Not an Error Occurs

There may be some circumstances in which you want to take some particular action whether or not an exception occurs. For example, whenever you are dealing with some kind of unpredictable input/output—say, when working with files and directories on disk—there is always the possibility that the location (the disk or directory) or the data source (the file) either may not be there at all or may provide some other kinds of problems—such as the disk being full when you attempt to write to it or the file containing the wrong kind of data when you attempt to read from it.

You may need to perform some final "cleanup" procedures whether or not you have encountered any problems, such as logging onto a specific working directory or closing a file that was previously opened. You can do this by following a begin..rescue block of code with another block starting with the ensure keyword. The code in the ensure block will always execute, whether or not an exception has arisen beforehand.

Let's look at two simple examples. In the first one, I try to log onto a disk and display the directory listing. At the end of this, I want to be sure that my working directory (given by Dir.getwd) is always restored to its original location. I do this by saving the original directory in the startdir variable and once again making this the working directory in the ensure block:

ensure.rb

```
startdir = Dir.getwd

begin
   Dir.chdir( "X:\\" )
   puts( `dir` )
rescue Exception => e
   puts e.class
   puts e
ensure
   Dir.chdir( startdir )
end
```

When I run this, the following is displayed:

```
We start out here: C:/Huw/programming/bookofruby/ch9
Errno::ENOENT
No such file or directory - X:\
We end up here: C:/Huw/programming/bookofruby/ch9
```

Let's now see how to deal with the problem of reading the incorrect data from a file. This might happen if the data is corrupt, if you accidentally open the wrong file, or—quite simply—if your program code contains a bug.

Here I have a file, *test.txt*, containing six lines. The first five lines are numbers; the sixth line is a string, "six." My code opens this file and reads in all six lines:

ensure2.rb

```
f = File.new( "test.txt" )
begin
    for i in (1..6) do
        puts("line number: #{f.lineno}")
        line = f.gets.chomp
        num = line.to_i
        puts( "Line '#{line}' is converted to #{num}" )
        puts( 100 / num )
    end
rescue Exception => e
    puts( e.class )
    puts( e )
ensure
    f.close
    puts( "File closed" )
end
```

The lines are read in as strings (using gets), and the code attempts to convert them to integers (using to_i). No error is produced when the conversion fails; instead, Ruby returns the value 0. The problem arises in the next line of code, which attempts a division by the converted number.

Having opened the data file at the outset, I want to ensure that the file is closed whether or not an error occurs. If, for example, I read in only the first five lines by editing the range in the for loop to (1..5), then there would be no exception. I would still want to close the file. But it would be no good putting the file-closing code (f.close) in the rescue clause because it would not, in this case, be executed. By putting it in the ensure clause, however, I can be certain that the file will be closed whether or not an exception occurs.

else: Execute Code When No Error Occurs

If the rescue section executes when an error occurs and ensure executes whether or not an error occurs, how can you specifically execute some code only when an error does *not* occur?

The way to do this is to add an optional else clause after the rescue section and before the ensure section (if there is one), like this:

```
begin
        # code which may cause an exception
rescue [Exception Type]
else    # optional section executes if no exception occurs
ensure  # optional exception always executes
end
```

This is an example:

```
def doCalc( aNum )
    begin
        result = 100 / aNum.to_i
    rescue Exception => e         # executes when there is an error
        result = 0
        msg = "Error: " + e.to_s
    else                          # executes when there is no error
        msg = "Result = #{result}"
    ensure                        # always executes
        msg = "You entered '#{aNum}'. " + msg
    end
    return msg
end
```

Try running the previous program and enter a number such as 10, which won't cause an error, so msg will be assigned in the else clause; then try entering 0, which will cause an error, so msg will be assigned in the rescue clause. Whether or not there is an error, the ensure section will execute to create a msg string that begins with "You entered " followed by any other messages. For example:

```
You entered '5'. Result = 20
You entered '0'. Error: divided by 0
```

Error Numbers

If you ran the *ensure.rb* program earlier and you were watching closely, you may have noticed something unusual when you tried to log onto a non-existent drive (for example, on my system that might be the *X:* drive). Often, when an exception occurs, the exception class is an instance of a specific named type such as ZeroDivisionError or NoMethodError. In this case, however, the class of the exception is shown to be Errno::ENOENT.

It turns out that there is quite a variety of Errno errors in Ruby. Try *disk_err.rb*. This defines a method, chDisk, which attempts to log onto a disk identified by the character, aChar. So if you pass "A" as an argument to chDisk, it will try to log onto the *A:* drive. I've called the chDisk method three times, passing to it a different string each time:

```
def chDisk( aChar )
    startdir = Dir.getwd
    begin
        Dir.chdir( "#{aChar}:\\" )
        puts( `dir` )
    rescue Exception => e
        #showFamily( e.class ) # to see ancestors, uncomment
        puts e.class           # ...and comment out this
        puts e
```

```
    ensure
        Dir.chdir( startdir )
    end
end

chDisk( "F" )
chDisk( "X" )
chDisk( "ABC" )
```

You might, of course, need to edit the paths to something different on your computer. On my PC, *F:* is my DVD drive. At the moment, it is empty, and when my program tries to log onto it, Ruby returns an exception of this type: `Errno::EACCES`.

I have no *X:* drive on my PC, and when I try to log onto that, Ruby returns an exception of this type: `Errno::ENOENT`.

In the previous example, I pass the string parameter "ABC," which is invalid as a disk identifier, and Ruby returns an exception of this type: `Errno::EINVAL`.

Errors of this type are descendants of the SystemCallError class. You can easily verify this by uncommenting the line of code to show the class's family where indicated in the source code of *disk_err.rb*. This calls the same `showFamily` method, which you used earlier in the *exception_tree.rb* program.

These Error classes, in effect, wrap up integer error values that are returned by the underlying operating system. Both the names and the values of constants may vary according to the operating system and the version of Ruby. Here `Errno` is the name of the module containing the constants, such as `EACCES` and `ENOENT`, which match the integer error values.

To see a complete list of `Errno` constants, run this:

errno.rb

```
puts( Errno.constants )
```

To view the corresponding numerical value of any given constant, append `::Errno` to the constant name, like this:

```
Errno::EINVAL::Errno
```

You can use the following code to display a list of all `Errno` constants along with their numerical values (here the `eval` method evaluates the expression passed to it—you'll look at how this works in Chapter 20):

```
for err in Errno.constants do
    errnum = eval( "Errno::#{err}::Errno" )
    puts( "#{err}, #{errnum}" )
end
```

retry: Attempt to Execute Code Again After an Error

If you think an error condition may be transient or may be corrected (by the user, perhaps?), you can rerun all the code in a begin..end block using the keyword retry, as in this example that prompts the user to re-enter a value if an error such as ZeroDivisionError occurs:

retry.rb

```
def doCalc
    begin
        print( "Enter a number: " )
        aNum = gets().chomp()
        result = 100 / aNum.to_i
    rescue Exception => e
        result = 0
        puts( "Error: " + e.to_s + "\nPlease try again." )
        retry              # retry on exception
    else
        msg = "Result = #{result}"
    ensure
        msg = "You entered '#{aNum}'. " + msg
    end
    return msg
end
```

NOTE *When you want to append the message from an exception object such as* e *to a string such as* "Error: "*, Ruby 1.9 insists that you explicitly convert* e *to a string* ("Error: " + e.to_s)*, whereas Ruby 1.8 does the conversion for you* ("Error: " + e)*.*

There is, of course, the danger that the error may not be as transient as you think, so if you use retry, you may want to provide a clearly defined exit condition to ensure that the code stops executing after a fixed number of attempts.

You could, for example, increment a local variable in the begin clause. (If you do this, make sure it is incremented *before* any code that is liable to generate an exception since once an exception occurs, the remainder of the code prior to the rescue clause will be skipped!) Then test the value of that variable in the rescue section, like this:

```
rescue Exception => e
    if aValue < someValue then
        retry
    end
```

Here is a complete example, in which I test the value of a variable named tries to ensure no more than three tries to run the code without error before the exception-handling block exits:

retry2.rb

```
def doCalc
    tries = 0
    begin
        print( "Enter a number: " )
        tries += 1
```

```
        aNum = gets().chomp()
        result = 100 / aNum.to_i
    rescue Exception => e
        msg = "Error: " + e.to_s
        puts( msg )
        puts( "tries = #{tries}" )
        result = 0
        if tries < 3 then # set a fixed number of retries
            retry
        end
    else
        msg = "Result = #{result}"
    ensure
        msg = "You entered '#{aNum}'. " + msg
    end
    return msg
end
```

If the user were to enter 0 three times in a row, this would be the output:

```
Enter a number: 0
Error: divided by 0
tries = 1
Enter a number: 0
Error: divided by 0
tries = 2
Enter a number: 0
Error: divided by 0
tries = 3
You entered '0'. Error: divided by 0
```

raise: Reactivate a Handled Error

Sometimes you may want to keep an exception "alive" even after it has been trapped in an exception-handling block. You can do this, for example, to defer the handling of the exception, say by passing it on to some other method. You can do this using the raise method. You need to be aware, however, that, once raised, an exception needs to be rehandled; otherwise, it may cause your program to crash. Here is a simple example of raising a ZeroDivisionError exception and passing on the exception to a method called, in this case, handleError:

raise.rb

```
begin
    divbyzero
rescue Exception => e
    puts( "A problem just occurred. Please wait..." )
    x = 0
    begin
        raise
    rescue
        handleError( e )
    end
end
```

Here divbyzero is the name of a method in which the divide-by-zero operation takes place, and handleError is a method that prints more detailed information on the exception:

```
def handleError( e )
    puts( "Error of type: #{e.class}" )
    puts( e )
    puts( "Here is a backtrace: " )
    puts( e.backtrace )
end
```

Notice that this uses the backtrace method, which displays an array of strings showing the filenames and line numbers where the error occurred and, in this case, the line that called the error-producing divbyzero method. This is an example of this program's output:

```
A problem just occurred. Please wait...
Error of type: ZeroDivisionError
divided by 0
Here is a backtrace:
C:/Huw/programming/bookofruby/ch9/raise.rb:11:in `/'
C:/Huw/programming/bookofruby/ch9/raise.rb:11:in `divbyzero'
C:/Huw/programming/bookofruby/ch9/raise.rb:15:in `<main>'
```

You can also specifically raise your exceptions to force an error condition even when the program code has not caused an exception. Calling raise on its own raises an exception of the type RuntimeError (or whatever exception is in the global variable $!):

```
raise        # raises RuntimeError
```

By default, this will have no descriptive message associated with it. You can add a message as a parameter, like this:

```
raise "An unknown exception just occurred!"
```

You can raise a specific type of error:

```
raise ZeroDivisionError
```

You can also create an object of a specific exception type and initialize it with a custom message:

```
raise ZeroDivisionError.new( "I'm afraid you divided by Zero" )
```

This is a simple example:

raise2.rb

```ruby
begin
    raise ZeroDivisionError.new( "I'm afraid you divided by Zero" )
rescue Exception => e
    puts( e.class )
    puts( "message: " + e.to_s )
end
```

This outputs the following:

```
ZeroDivisionError
message: I'm afraid you divided by Zero
```

If the standard exception types don't meet your requirements, you can, of course, create new ones just by subclassing existing exceptions. Provide your classes with a to_str method in order to give them a default message.

raise3.rb

```ruby
class NoNameError < Exception
    def to_str
        "No Name given!"
    end
end
```

Here is an example of how you might raise a custom exception:

```ruby
def sayHello( aName )
    begin
        if (aName == "") or (aName == nil) then
            raise NoNameError
        end
    rescue Exception => e
        puts( e.class )
        puts( "error message: " + e.to_s )
        puts( e.backtrace )
    else
        puts( "Hello #{aName}" )
    end
end
```

If you now enter sayHello(nil), this would be the output:

```
NoNameError
error message: NoNameError
C:/Huw/programming/bookofruby/ch9/raise3.rb:12:in `sayHello'
C:/Huw/programming/bookofruby/ch9/raise3.rb:23:in `<main>'
```

DIGGING DEEPER

When trapping exceptions, the begin keyword may, in some circumstances, be omitted. Here you will learn about this syntax. I will also clarify some potential confusion about catch and throw.

Omitting begin and end

You can optionally omit begin and end when trapping exceptions inside a method, a class, or a module. For example, all the following are legal:

omit_begin_end
.rb

```
def calc
        result = 1/0
    rescue Exception => e
        puts( e.class )
        puts( e )
        result = nil
    return result
end

class X
        @@x = 1/0
    rescue Exception => e
        puts( e.class )
        puts( e )
end

module Y
        @@x = 1/0
    rescue Exception => e
        puts( e.class )
        puts( e )
end
```

In all the previous cases, the exception-handling will also work if you place the begin and end keywords at the start and end of the exception-handling code in the usual way.

catch..throw

In some languages, exceptions are trapped using the keyword catch and may be raised using the keyword throw. Although Ruby provides catch and throw methods, these are not directly related to its exception handling. Instead, catch and throw are used to break out of a defined block of code when some condition is met. You could, of course, use catch and throw to break out of a block of code when an exception occurs (though this may not be the most elegant way of handling errors). For example, this code will exit the block delimited by curly brackets if a ZeroDivisionError occurs:

```ruby
catch( :finished) {
    print( 'Enter a number: ' )
    num = gets().chomp.to_i
    begin
        result = 100 / num
    rescue Exception => e
        throw :finished        # jump to end of block
    end
    puts( "The result of that calculation is #{result}" )
}    # end of :finished catch block
```

See Chapter 6 for more on catch and throw.

10

BLOCKS, PROCS, AND LAMBDAS

When programmers talk about blocks, they often mean some arbitrary "chunks" of code. In Ruby, however, a block is special. It is a unit of code that works somewhat like a method but, unlike a method, it has no name.

Blocks are very important in Ruby, but they can be difficult to understand. In addition, there are some important differences in the behavior of blocks in Ruby 1.8 and Ruby 1.9. If you fail to appreciate those differences, your programs may behave in unexpected ways when run in different versions of Ruby. This chapter looks at blocks in great detail. Not only does it explain how they work and why they are special, but it also provides guidance on ensuring that they continue to work consistently no matter which version of Ruby you happen to be using.

What Is a Block?

Consider this code:

1blocks.rb

```
3.times do |i|
    puts( i )
end
```

It's probably pretty obvious that this code is intended to execute three times. What may be less obvious is the value that i will have on each successive turn through the loop. In fact, the values of i in this case will be 0, 1, and 2. The following is an alternative form of the previous code. This time, the block is delimited by curly brackets rather than by do and end.

```
3.times { |i|
    puts( i )
}
```

According to the Ruby documentation, times is a method of Integer (let's call the Integer int), which iterates a block "int times, passing in values from 0 to int -1." So here, the code within the block is run three times. The first time it is run, the variable i is given the value 0; each subsequent time, i is incremented by 1 until the final value, 2 (that is, int-1), is reached.

The two code examples shown earlier are functionally identical. A block can be enclosed either by curly brackets or by the do and end keywords, and the programmer can use either syntax according to personal preference.

NOTE *Some Ruby programmers like to delimit blocks with curly brackets when the entire code of the block fits onto a single line and with do..end when the block spans multiple lines. My personal prejudice is to be consistent, irrespective of code layout, so I generally use curly brackets when delimiting blocks. Usually your choice of delimiters makes no difference to the behavior of the code—but see "Precedence Rules" on page 170.*

If you are familiar with a C-like language such as C# or Java, you may, perhaps, assume that Ruby's curly brackets can be used, as in those languages, simply to group together arbitrary "blocks" of code—for example, a block of code to be executed when a condition evaluates to true. This is not the case. In Ruby, a block is a special construct that can be used only in very specific circumstances.

Line Breaks Are Significant

You must place the opening block delimiter on the same line as the method with which it is associated.

For example, these are okay:

```
3.times do |i|
    puts( i )
end
```

```
3.times { |i|
    puts( i )
}
```

But these contain syntax errors:

```
3.times
do |i|
    puts( i )
end

3.times
{ |i|
    puts( i )
}
```

Nameless Functions

A Ruby block may be regarded as a sort of nameless function or method, and its most frequent use is to provide a means of iterating over items from a list or range of values. If you have never come across nameless functions, this may sound like gobbledygook. With luck, by the end of this chapter, things will have become a little clearer. Let's look back at the simple example given earlier. I said a block is like a nameless function. Take this block as an example:

```
{ |i|
    puts( i )
}
```

If that were written as a normal Ruby method, it would look something like this:

```
def aMethod( i )
    puts( i )
end
```

To call that method three times and pass values from 0 to 2, you might write this:

```
for i in 0..2
    aMethod( i )
end
```

When you create a nameless method (that is, a block), variables declared between upright bars such as |i| can be treated like the arguments to a named method. I will refer to these variables as *block parameters*.

Look again at my earlier example:

```
3.times { |i|
    puts( i )
}
```

The `times` method of an integer passes values to a block from 0 to the specified integer value minus 1.

So, this:

```
3.times{ |i| }
```

is very much like this:

```
for i in 0..2
    aMethod( i )
end
```

The chief difference is that the second example has to call a named method to process the value of i, whereas the first example uses the nameless method (the code between curly brackets) to process i.

Look Familiar?

Now that you know what a block is, you may notice that you've seen them before. Many times. For example, you previously used do..end blocks to iterate over ranges like this:

```
(1..3).each do |i|
    puts(i)
end
```

You have also used do..end blocks to iterate over arrays (see *for_each2.rb* on page 69):

```
arr = ['one','two','three','four']
arr.each do |s|
    puts(s)
end
```

And you have executed a block repeatedly by passing it to the loop method (see *3loops.rb* on page 75):

```
i=0
loop {
    puts(arr[i])
    i+=1
    if (i == arr.length) then
        break
    end
}
```

The previous `loop` example is notable for two things: It has no list of items (such as an array or a range of values) to iterate over, and it is pretty darn ugly. These two features are not entirely unrelated! The `loop` method is part of the Kernel class, which is "automatically" available to your programs. Because it has no "end value," it will execute the block forever unless you explicitly break out of it using the `break` keyword. Usually there are more elegant ways to perform this kind of iteration—by iterating over a sequence of values with a finite range.

Blocks and Arrays

Blocks are commonly used to iterate over arrays. The Array class, consequently, provides a number of methods to which blocks are passed.

One useful method is called `collect`; this passes each element of the array to a block and creates a new array to contain each of the values returned by the block. Here, for example, a block is passed to each of the integers in an array (each integer is assigned to the variable x); the block doubles its value and returns it. The `collect` method creates a new array containing each of the returned integers in sequence:

2blocks.rb

```
b3 = [1,2,3].collect{|x| x*2}
```

The previous example assigns this array to b3:

```
[2,4,6]
```

In the next example, the block returns a version of the original strings in which each initial letter is capitalized:

```
b4 = ["hello","good day","how do you do"].collect{|x| x.capitalize }
```

So, b4 is now as follows:

```
["Hello", "Good day", "How do you do"]
```

The each method of the Array class may look rather similar to `collect`; it too passes each array element in turn to be processed by the block. However, unlike `collect`, the each method does not create a new array to contain the returned values:

```
b5 = ["hello","good day","how do you do"].each{|x| x.capitalize }
```

This time, b5 is unchanged:

```
["hello", "good day", "how do you do"]
```

Recall, however, that some methods—notably those ending with an exclamation mark (!)—actually alter the original objects rather than yielding new values. If you wanted to use the each method to capitalize the strings in the original array, you could use the capitalize! method:

```
b6 = ["hello","good day", "how do you do"].each{|x| x.capitalize! }
```

So, b6 is now as follows:

```
["Hello", "Good day", "How do you do"]
```

With a bit of thought, you could also use a block to iterate over the characters in a string. First, you need to split off each character from a string. This can be done using the split method of the String class like this:

```
"hello world".split(//)
```

The split method divides a string into substrings based on a delimiter and returns an array of these substrings. Here // is a regular expression that defines a zero-length string; this has the effect of returning a single character, so you end up creating an array of all the characters in the string. You can now iterate over this array of characters, returning a capitalized version of each:

```
a = "hello world".split(//).each{ |x| newstr << x.capitalize }
```

At each iteration, a capitalized character is appended to newstr, and the following is displayed:

```
H
HE
HEL
HELL
HELLO
HELLO
HELLO W
HELLO WO
HELLO WOR
HELLO WORL
HELLO WORLD
```

Because you are using the capitalize method here (with no terminating ! character), the characters in the array a remain as they began, all lowercase, since the capitalize method does not alter the receiver object (here the receiver objects are the characters passed into the block).

Be aware, however, that this code would not work if you were to use the `capitalize!` method to modify the original characters. This is because `capitalize!` returns `nil` when no changes are made, so when the space character is encountered, `nil` would be returned, and your attempt to append (`<<`) a `nil` value to the string `newstr` would fail.

You could also capitalize a string using the `each_byte` method. This iterates through the string characters, passing each byte to the block. These bytes take the form of ASCII codes. So, "hello world" would be passed in the form of these numeric values: 104 101 108 108 111 32 119 111 114 108 100.

Obviously, you can't capitalize an integer, so you need to convert each ASCII value to a character. The `chr` method of String does this:

```
a = "hello world".each_byte{|x| newstr << (x.chr).capitalize }
```

Procs and Lambdas

In the examples up to now, blocks have been used in cahoots with methods. This has been a requirement since nameless blocks cannot have an independent existence in Ruby. You cannot, for example, create a stand-alone block like this:

```
{|x| x = x*10; puts(x)}          # This is not allowed!
```

This is one of the exceptions to the rule that "everything in Ruby is an object." A block clearly is not an object. Every object is created from a class, and you can find an object's class by calling its `class` method.

Do this with a hash, for example, and the class name "Hash" will be displayed:

```
puts({1=>2}.class)
```

Try this with a block, however, and you will only get an error message:

```
puts({|i| puts(i)}.class) #<= error!
```

Block or Hash?

Ruby uses curly brackets to delimit both blocks and hashes. So, how can you (and Ruby) tell which is which? The answer, basically, is that it's a hash when it *looks* like a hash, and otherwise it's a block. A hash looks like a hash when curly brackets contain key-value pairs:

```
puts( {1=>2}.class )      #<= Hash
```

or when they are empty:

block_or_hash.rb
```
puts( {}.class )          #<= Hash
```

However, if you omit the parentheses, there is an ambiguity. Is this an empty hash, or is it a block associated with the puts method?

```
puts{}.class
```

Frankly, I have to admit I don't know the answer to that question, and I can't get Ruby to tell me. Ruby accepts this as valid syntax but does not, in fact, display anything when the code executes. So, how about this?

```
print{}.class
```

Once again, this prints nothing at all in Ruby 1.9, but in Ruby 1.8 it displays nil (not, you will notice, the actual *class* of nil, which is NilClass, but nil itself). If you find all this confusing (as I do!), just remember that this can all be clarified by the judicious use of parentheses:

```
print( {}.class )     #<= Hash
```

Creating Objects from Blocks

Although blocks may not be objects by default, they can be "turned into" objects. There are three ways of creating objects from blocks and assigning them to variables—here's how:

proc_create.rb
```
a = Proc.new{|x| x = x*10; puts(x) }    #=> Proc
b = lambda{|x| x = x*10; puts(x) }       #=> Proc
c = proc{|x| x.capitalize! }             #=> Proc
```

In each of the three cases, you will end up creating an instance of the Proc class—which is the Ruby "object wrapper" for a block.

Let's take a look at a simple example of creating and using a Proc object. First, you can create an object calling Proc.new and passing to it a block as an argument:

3blocks.rb
```
a = Proc.new{|x| x = x*10; puts(x)}
```

Second, you can execute the code in the block to which a refers using the Proc class's call method with one or more arguments (matching the block parameters) to be passed into the block; in the previous code, you could pass an integer such as 100, and this would be assigned to the block variable x:

```
a.call(100)       #=> 1000
```

Finally, you can also create a Proc object by calling the `lambda` or `proc` methods, which are supplied by the Kernel class. The name `lambda` is taken from the Scheme (Lisp) language and is a term used to describe an anonymous method, or *closure*.

```
b = lambda{|x| x = x*10; puts(x) }
b.call(100)              #=> 1000

c = proc{|x| x.capitalize! }
c1 = c.call( "hello" )
puts( c1 )               #=> Hello
```

Here is a slightly more complicated example that iterates over an array of strings, capitalizing each string in turn. The array of capitalized strings is then assigned to the `d1` variable:

```
d = lambda{|x| x.capitalize! }
d1 = ["hello","good day","how do you do"].each{ |s| d.call(s)}
puts(d1.inspect)         #=> ["Hello", "Good day", "How do you do"]
```

There is one important difference between creating a Proc object using `Proc.new` and creating a Proc object using a `lambda` method—`Proc.new` does not check that the number of arguments passed to the block matches the number of block parameters. `lambda` does. The behavior of the proc method is different in Ruby 1.8 and 1.9. In Ruby 1.8, `proc` is equivalent to `lambda`—it checks the number of arguments. In Ruby 1.9, `proc` is equivalent to `Proc.new`—it does *not* check the number of arguments:

proc_lamba.rb
```
a = Proc.new{|x,y,z| x = y*z; puts(x) }
a.call(2,5,10,100)       # This is not an error

b = lambda{|x,y,z| x = y*z; puts(x) }
b.call(2,5,10,100)       # This is an error

puts('---Block #2---' )
c = proc{|x,y,z| x = y*z; puts(x) }
c.call(2,5,10,100)       # This is an error in Ruby 1.8
                         # Not an error in Ruby 1.9
```

What Is a Closure?

A *closure* is a function that has the ability to store (that is, to "enclose") values of local variables within the scope in which the block was created (think of this as the block's "native scope"). Ruby's blocks are closures. To understand this, look at this example:

block_closure.rb
```
x = "hello world"

ablock = Proc.new { puts( x ) }
```

```
def aMethod( aBlockArg )
    x = "goodbye"
    aBlockArg.call
end

puts( x )
ablock.call
aMethod( ablock )
ablock.call
puts( x )
```

Here, the value of the local variable x is "hello world" within the scope of ablock. Inside aMethod, however, a local variable named x has the value "goodbye." In spite of that, when ablock is passed to aMethod and called within the scope of aMethod, it prints "hello world" (that is, the value of x within the block's native scope) rather than "goodbye," which is the value of x within the scope of aMethod. The previous code, therefore, only ever prints "hello world."

NOTE *See "Digging Deeper" on page 175 for more on closures.*

yield

Let's see a few more blocks in use. The *4blocks.rb* program introduces something new, namely, a way of executing a nameless block when it is passed to a method. This is done using the keyword yield. In the first example, I define this simple method:

4blocks.rb
```
def aMethod
    yield
end
```

It doesn't really have any code of its own. Instead, it expects to receive a block, and the yield keyword causes the block to execute. This is how I pass a block to it:

```
aMethod{ puts( "Good morning" ) }
```

Notice that this time the block is not passed as a named argument. It would be an error to try to pass the block between parentheses, like this:

```
aMethod( { puts( "Good morning" ) } )    # This won't work!
```

Instead, you simply put the block right next to the method to which you are passing it, just as you did in the first example in this chapter. That method receives the block without having to declare a named parameter for it, and it calls the block with yield.

Here is a slightly more useful example:

```
def caps( anarg )
    yield( anarg )
end

caps( "a lowercase string" ){ |x| x.capitalize! ; puts( x ) }
```

Here the caps method receives one argument, anarg, and passes this argument to a nameless block, which is then executed by yield. When I call the caps method, I pass it a string argument ("a lowercase string") using the normal parameter-passing syntax. The nameless block is passed *after the end* of the parameter list.

When the caps method calls yield(anarg), then the string argument is passed into the block; it is assigned to the block variable x. This capitalizes it and displays it with puts(s), which shows that the initial letter has been capitalized: "A lowercase string."

Blocks Within Blocks

You've already seen how to use a block to iterate over an array. In the next example (also in *4blocks.rb*), I use one block to iterate over an array of strings, assigning each string in turn to the block variable s. A second block is then passed to the caps method in order to capitalize the string:

```
["hello","good day","how do you do"].each{
    |s|
    caps( s ){ |x| x.capitalize!
        puts( x )
    }
}
```

This results in the following output:

```
Hello
Good day
How do you do
```

Passing Named Proc Arguments

Up to now, you have passed blocks to procedures either anonymously (in which case the block is executed with the yield keyword) or in the form of a named argument, in which case it is executed using the call method. There is another way to pass a block. When the last argument in a method's list of parameters is preceded by an ampersand (&), it is considered to be a Proc object. This gives you the option of passing an anonymous block to a procedure using the same syntax as when passing a block to an iterator, and yet the procedure itself can receive the block as a named argument. Load *5blocks.rb* to see some examples of this.

First, here is a reminder of the two ways you've already seen of passing blocks. This method has three parameters, a, b, and c:

5blocks.rb

```
def abc( a, b, c )
    a.call
    b.call
    c.call
    yield
end
```

You call this method with three named arguments (which here happen to be blocks but could, in principle, be anything) plus an unnamed block:

```
a = lambda{ puts "one" }
b = lambda{ puts "two" }
c = proc{ puts "three" }
abc(a, b, c ){ puts "four" }
```

The abc method executes the named block arguments using the call method and the unnamed block using the yield keyword. The results are shown in the #=> comments here:

```
a.call     #=> one
b.call     #=> two
c.call     #=> three
yield      #=> four
```

The next method, abc2, takes a single argument, &d. The ampersand here is significant because it indicates that the &d parameter is a block. Instead of using the yield keyword, the abc2 method is able to execute the block using the name of the argument (without the ampersand):

```
def abc2( &d )
    d.call
end
```

So, a block argument with an ampersand is called in the same way as one without an ampersand. However, there is a difference in the way the object matching that argument is passed to the method. To match an ampersand-argument, an unnamed block is passed by appending it to the method name:

```
abc2{ puts "four" }
```

You can think of ampersand-arguments as type-checked block parameters. Unlike normal arguments (without an ampersand), the argument cannot match any type; it can match only a block. You cannot pass some other sort of object to abc2:

```
abc2( 10 )    # This won't work!
```

The abc3 method is essentially the same as the abc method except it specifies a fourth formal block-typed argument (&d):

```
def abc3( a, b, c, &d)
```

The arguments a, b, and c are called, while the argument &d may be either called or yielded, as you prefer:

```
def abc3( a, b, c, &d)
    a.call
    b.call
    c.call
    d.call        # first call block &d
    yield         # then yield block &d
end
```

This means the calling code must pass to this method three formal arguments plus a block, which may be nameless:

```
abc3(a, b, c){ puts "five" }
```

The previous method call would result in this output (bearing in mind that the final block argument is executed twice since it is both called and yielded):

```
one
two
three
five
five
```

You can also use a preceding ampersand in order to pass a named block to a method when the receiving method has no matching named argument, like this:

```
myproc = proc{ puts("my proc") }
abc3(a, b, c, &myproc )
```

An ampersand block variable such as &myproc in the previous code may be passed to a method even if that method does not declare a matching variable in its argument list. This gives you the choice of passing either an unnamed block or a Proc object:

```
xyz{ |a,b,c| puts(a+b+c) }
xyz( &myproc )
```

Be careful, however! Notice in one of the previous examples, I have used block parameters (|a,b,c|) with the same names as the three local variables to which I previously assigned Proc objects: a, b, c:

```
a = lambda{ puts "one" }
b = lambda{ puts "two" }
c = proc{ puts "three" }
xyz{ |a,b,c| puts(a+b+c) }
```

In principle, block parameters should be visible only within the block itself. However, it turns out that assignment to block parameters has profoundly different effects in Ruby 1.8 and Ruby 1.9. Let's look first at Ruby 1.8. Here, assignment to block parameters can initialize the values of any local variables with the same name within the block's native scope (see "What Is a Closure?" on page 163).

Even though the variables in the xyz method are named x, y, and z, it turns out that the integer assignments in that method are actually made to the variables a, b, and c when this block:

```
{ |a,b,c| puts(a+b+c) }
```

is passed the values of x, y, and z:

```
def xyz
    x = 1
    y = 2
    z = 3
    yield( x, y, z )    # 1,2,3 assigned to block parameters a,b,c
end
```

As a consequence, the Proc variables a, b, and c within the block's native scope (the main scope of my program) are initialized with the integer values of the block variables x, y, and z once the code in the block has been run. So, a, b, and c, which began as Proc objects, end up as integers.

In Ruby 1.9, on the contrary, the variables inside the block are sealed off from the variables declared outside the block. So, the values of the xyz method's x, y, and z variables are not assigned to the block's a, b, and c parameters. That means once the block has executed, the values of the a, b, and c variables declared outside that method are unaffected: They began as Proc objects, and they end up as Proc objects.

Now let's suppose you execute the following code, remembering that a, b, and c are Proc objects at the outset:

```
xyz{ |a,b,c| puts(a+b+c) }
puts( a, b, c )
```

In Ruby 1.8, the puts statement shown earlier displays the end values of a, b, and c, showing that they have been initialized with the integer values that were passed into the block when it was yielded (yield(x, y, z)) in the xyz method. As a consequence, they are now integers:

```
1
2
3
```

But in Ruby 1.9, a, b, and c are not initialized by the block parameters and remain, as they began, as Proc objects:

```
#<Proc:0x2b65828@C:/bookofruby/ch10/5blocks.rb:36 (lambda)>
#<Proc:0x2b65810@C:/bookofruby/ch10/5blocks.rb:37 (lambda)>
#<Proc:0x2b657f8@C:/bookofruby/ch10/5blocks.rb:38>
```

This behavior can be difficult to understand, but it is worth taking the time to do so. The use of blocks is commonplace in Ruby, and it is important to know how the execution of a block may (or may not) affect the values of variables declared outside the block. To clarify this, try the simple program in *6blocks.rb*:

6blocks.rb

```
a = "hello world"

def foo
    yield 100
end

puts( a )
foo{ |a| puts( a ) }

puts( a )
```

Here a is a string within the scope of the main program. A different variable with the same name, a, is declared in the block, which is passed to foo and yielded. When it is yielded, an integer value, 100, is passed into the block, causing the block's parameter, a, to be initialized to 100. The question is, does the initialization of the block argument, a, also initialize the string variable, a, in the main scope? And the answer is, *yes* in Ruby 1.8 but *no* in Ruby 1.9.

Ruby 1.8 displays this:

```
hello world
100
100
```

Ruby 1.9 displays this:

```
hello world
100
hello world
```

If you want to make sure that block parameters do not alter the values of variables declared outside the block, no matter which version of Ruby you use, just ensure that the block parameter names do not duplicate names used elsewhere. In the current program, you can do this simply by changing the name of the block argument to ensure that it is unique to the block:

```
foo{ |b| puts( b ) }    # the name 'b' is not used elsewhere
```

This time, when the program is run, Ruby 1.8 and Ruby 1.9 both produce the same results:

```
hello world
100
hello world
```

This is an example of one of the pitfalls into which it is all too easy to fall in Ruby. As a general rule, when variables share the same scope (for example, a block declared within the scope of the main program here), it is best to make their names unique in order to avoid any unforeseen side effects. For more on scoping, see "Blocks and Local Variables" on page 177.

Precedence Rules

Blocks within curly brackets have stronger precedence than blocks within do and end. Let's see what that means in practice. Consider these two examples:

```
foo bar do |s| puts( s ) end
foo bar{ |s| puts(s) }
```

Here, foo and bar are both methods, and the code between curly brackets and do and end are blocks. So, to which of the two methods is each of these blocks passed? It turns out that the do..end block would be passed to the leftmost method, foo, whereas the block in curly brackets would be sent to the rightmost method, bar. This is because curly brackets are said to have higher precedence than do and end.

Consider this program:

precedence.rb

```
def foo( b )
    puts("---in foo---")
    a = 'foo'
    if block_given?
        puts( "(Block passed to foo)" )
        yield( a )
    else
        puts( "(no block passed to foo)" )
    end
    puts( "in foo, arg b = #{b}" )
    return "returned by " << a
end

def bar
    puts("---in bar---")
    a = 'bar'
    if block_given?
        puts( "(Block passed to bar)" )
        yield( a )
    else
        puts( "(no block passed to bar)" )
    end
    return "returned by " << a
end

foo bar do |s| puts( s ) end        # 1) do..end block
foo bar{ |s| puts(s) }              # 2) {..} block
```

Here the do..end block has lower precedence, and the method foo is given priority. This means both bar and the do..end block are passed to foo. Thus, these two expressions are equivalent:

```
foo bar do |s| puts( s ) end
foo( bar ) do |s| puts( s ) end
```

A curly bracket block, on the other hand, has stronger precedence, so it tries to execute immediately and is passed to the first possible receiver method (bar). The result (that is, the value returned by bar) is then passed as an argument to foo, but this time, foo does not receive the block itself. Thus, the two following expressions are equivalent:

```
foo bar{ |s| puts(s) }
foo( bar{ |s| puts(s) } )
```

If you are confused by all this, take comfort in that you are not alone! The potential ambiguities result from the fact that, in Ruby, the parentheses around argument lists are optional. As you can see from the alternative versions I gave earlier, the ambiguities disappear when you use parentheses.

NOTE   *A method can test whether it has received a block using the* block_given? *method. You can find examples of this in the* precedence.rb *program.*

Blocks as Iterators

As mentioned earlier, one of the primary uses of blocks in Ruby is to provide iterators to which a range or list of items can be passed. Many standard classes such as Integer and Array have methods that can supply items over which a block can iterate. For example:

```
3.times{ |i| puts( i ) }
[1,2,3].each{|i| puts(i) }
```

You can, of course, create your own iterator methods to provide a series of values to a block. In the *iterate1.rb* program, I have defined a simple timesRepeat method that executes a block a specified number of times. This is similar to the times method of the Integer class except it begins at index 1 rather than at index 0 (here the variable i is displayed in order to demonstrate this):

iterate1.rb
```
def timesRepeat( aNum )
    for i in 1..aNum do
        yield i
    end
end
```

Here is an example of how this method might be called:

```
timesRepeat( 3 ){  |i| puts("[#{i}] hello world") }
```

This displays the following:

```
[1] hello world
[2] hello world
[3] hello world
```

I've also created a timesRepeat2 method to iterate over an array:

```
def timesRepeat2( aNum, anArray )
    anArray.each{ |anitem|
        yield( anitem )
    }
end
```

This could be called in this manner:

```
timesRepeat2( 3, ["hello","good day","how do you do"] ){ |x| puts(x) }
```

This displays the following:

```
hello
good day
how do you do
```

Of course, it would be better (truer to the spirit of object orientation) if an object itself contained its own iterator method. I've implemented this in the next example. Here I have created MyArray, a subclass of Array:

```
class MyArray < Array
```

It is initialized with an array when a new MyArray object is created:

```
def initialize( anArray )
    super( anArray )
end
```

It relies upon its own each method (an object refers to itself as self), which is provided by its ancestor, Array, to iterate over the items in the array, and it uses the times method of Integer to do this a certain number of times. This is the complete class definition:

iterate2.rb

```
class MyArray < Array
    def initialize( anArray )
        super( anArray )
    end

    def timesRepeat( aNum )
        aNum.times{            # start block 1...
            | num |
            self.each{         # start block 2...
                | anitem |
                yield( "[#{num}] :: '#{anitem}'" )
            }                  # ...end block 2
        }                      # ...end block 1
    end
end
```

Notice that, because I have used two iterators (aNum.times and self.each), the timesRepeat method comprises two nested blocks. This is an example of how you might use this:

```
numarr = MyArray.new( [1,2,3] )
numarr.timesRepeat( 2  ){ |x| puts(x) }
```

This would output the following:

```
[0] :: '1'
[0] :: '2'
[0] :: '3'
[1] :: '1'
[1] :: '2'
[1] :: '3'
```

In *iterate3.rb*, I have set myself the problem of defining an iterator for an array containing an arbitrary number of subarrays, in which each subarray has the same number of items. In other words, it will be like a table or matrix with a fixed number of rows and a fixed number of columns. Here, for example, is a multidimensional array with three "rows" (subarrays) and four "columns" (items):

iterate3.rb

```
multiarr =
[ ['one','two','three','four'],
  [1,    2,    3,      4     ],
  [:a,   :b,   :c,     :d    ]
]
```

I've tried three alternative versions of this. The first version suffers from the limitation of only working with a predefined number (here 2 at indexes [0] and [1]) of "rows" so it won't display the symbols in the third row:

```
multiarr[0].length.times{|i|
    puts(multiarr[0][i], multiarr[1][i])
}
```

The second version gets around this limitation by iterating over each element (or "row") of multiarr and then iterating along each item in that row by obtaining the row length and using the Integer's times method with that value. As a result, it displays the data from all three rows:

```
multiarr.each{ |arr|
    multiarr[0].length.times{|i|
        puts(arr[i])
    }
}
```

The third version reverses these operations: The outer block iterates along the length of row 0, and the inner block obtains the item at index i in each row. Once again, this displays the data from all three rows:

```
multiarr[0].length.times{|i|
    multiarr.each{ |arr|
        puts(arr[i])
    }
}
```

However, although versions 2 and 3 work in a similar way, you will find that they iterate through the items in a different order. Version 2 iterates through each complete row one at a time. Version 3 iterates down the items in each column. Run the program to verify that. You could try creating your own subclass of Array and adding iterator methods like this—one method to iterate through the rows in sequence and one to iterate through the columns.

DIGGING DEEPER

Here we look at important differences between block scoping in Ruby 1.8 and 1.9 and also learn about returning blocks from methods.

Returning Blocks from Methods

Earlier, I explained that blocks in Ruby may act as closures. A closure may be said to enclose the "environment" in which it is declared. Or, to put it another way, it carries the values of local variables from its original scope into a different scope. The example I gave previously showed how the block named ablock captures the value of the local variable x:

block_closure.rb

```
x = "hello world"
ablock = Proc.new { puts( x ) }
```

It is then able to "carry" that variable into a different scope. Here, for example, ablock is passed to aMethod. When ablock is called inside that method, it runs the code puts(x). This displays "hello world" and not "goodbye":

```
def aMethod( aBlockArg )
    x = "goodbye"
    aBlockArg.call              #=> "hello world"
end
```

In this particular example, this behavior may seem like a curiosity of no great interest. In fact, block/closures can be used more creatively.

For example, instead of creating a block and sending it to a method, you could create a block *inside a method* and return that block to the calling code. If the method in which the block is created happens to take an argument, the block could be initialized with that argument.

This gives you a simple way of creating multiple blocks from the same "block template," each instance of which is initialized with different data. Here, for example, I have created two blocks and assigned them to the variables salesTax and vat, each of which calculates results based on different values (0.10) and (0.175):

block_closure2.rb

```
def calcTax( taxRate )
    return lambda{
        |subtotal|
            subtotal * taxRate
    }
end

salesTax = calcTax( 0.10 )
vat = calcTax( 0.175 )
```

```
print( "Tax due on book = ")
print( salesTax.call( 10 ) )          #=> 1.0

print( "\nVat due on DVD = ")
print( vat.call( 10 ) )               #=> 1.75
```

Blocks and Instance Variables

One of the less obvious features of blocks is the way in which they use variables. If a block may truly be regarded as a nameless function or method, then, logically, it should be able to contain its own local variables and have access to the instance variables of the object to which the block belongs.

Let's look first at instance variables. Load the *closures1.rb* program. This provides another illustration of a block acting as a closure—by capturing the values of the local variables in the scope in which it was created. Here I have created a block using the lambda method:

closures1.rb
```
aClos = lambda{
    @hello << " yikes!"
}
```

This block appends the string " yikes!" to the instance variable @hello. Notice that at this stage in the proceedings, no value has previously been assigned to @hello. I have, however, created a separate method, aFunc, which does assign a value to a variable called @hello:

```
def aFunc( aClosure )
    @hello = "hello world"
    aClosure.call
end
```

When I pass my block (the aClosure argument) to the aFunc method, the method brings @hello into being. I can now execute the code inside the block using the call method. And sure enough, the @hello variable contains the "hello world" string. The same variable can also be used by calling the block outside of the method. Indeed, now, by repeatedly calling the block, I will end up repeatedly appending the string " yikes!" to @hello:

```
aFunc(aClos)     #<= @hello = "hello world yikes!"
aClos.call       #<= @hello = "hello world yikes! yikes!"
aClos.call       #<= @hello = "hello world yikes! yikes! yikes!"
aClos.call       # ...and so on
```

If you think about it, this is not too surprising. After all, @hello is an instance variable, so it exists within the scope of an object. When you run a Ruby program, an object called main is automatically created. So, you should expect any instance variable created within that object (the program) to be available to everything inside it.

The question now arises: What would happen if you were to send the block to a method of some *other* object? If that object has its own instance variable, @hello, which variable will the block use—the @hello from the scope in which the block was created or the @hello from the scope of the object in which the block is called? Let's try that. You'll use the same block as before, except this time it will display a bit of information about the object to which the block belongs and the value of @hello:

```
aClos = lambda{
    @hello << " yikes!"
    puts("in #{self} object of class #{self.class}, @hello = #{@hello}")
}
```

Now, create a new object from a new class (X), and give it a method that will receive the block b and call the block:

```
class X
    def y( b )
        @hello = "I say, I say, I say!!!"
        puts( "    [In X.y]" )
        puts("in #{self} object of class #{self.class}, @hello = #{@hello}")
        puts( "    [In X.y] when block is called..." )
        b.call
    end
end

x = X.new
```

To test it, just pass the block aClos to the y method of x:

```
x.y( aClos )
```

And this is what is displayed:

```
    [In X.y]
in #<X:0x32a6e64> object of class X, @hello = I say, I say, I say!!!
    [In X.y] when block is called...
in main object of class Object, @hello = hello world yikes! yikes! yikes!
yikes! yikes! yikes!
```

So, it is clear that the block executes in the scope of the object in which it was *created* (main) and retains the instance variable from that object even though the object in whose scope the block is *called* has an instance variable with the same name and a different value.

Blocks and Local Variables

Now let's see how a block/closure deals with local variables. In the *closures2.rb* program, I declare a variable, x, which is local to the context of the program:

closures2.rb

```
x = 3000
```

The first block/closure is called c1. Each time I call this block, it picks up the value of x defined outside the block (3,000) and returns x + 100:

```
c1 = proc{
    x + 100
}
```

Incidentally, even though this returns a value (in ordinary Ruby methods, the default value is the result of the last expression to be evaluated), in Ruby 1.9 you cannot explicitly use the return statement here like this:

```
return x + 1
```

If you do this, Ruby 1.9 throws a LocalJumpError exception. Ruby 1.8, on the other hand, does not throw an exception.

This block has no block parameters (that is, there are no "block-local" variables between upright bars), so when it is called with a variable, someval, that variable is discarded, unused. In other words, c1.call(someval) has the same effect as c1.call().

So, when you call the block c1, it returns x+100 (that is, 3,100); this value is then assigned to someval. When you call c1 a second time, the same thing happens all over again, so once again someval is assigned 3,100:

```
someval=1000
someval=c1.call(someval); puts(someval)    #<= someval is now 3100
someval=c1.call(someval); puts(someval)    #<= someval is now 3100
```

NOTE   *Instead of repeating the call to c1, as shown earlier, you could place the call inside a block and pass this to the times method of Integer like this:*

```
2.times{ someval=c1.call(someval); puts(someval) }
```

However, because it can be hard enough to work out what just one block is up to (such as the c1 block here), I've deliberately avoided using any more blocks than are absolutely necessary in this program!

The second block is named c2. This declares the "block parameter" z. This too returns a value:

```
c2 = proc{
    |z|
    z + 100
}
```

However, this time the returned value can be reused since the block parameter acts like an incoming argument to a method—so when the value of someval is changed after it is assigned the return value of c2, this changed value is subsequently passed as an argument:

```
someval=1000
someval=c2.call(someval); puts(someval)        #<= someval is now 1100
someval=c2.call(someval); puts(someval)        #<= someval is now 1200
```

The third block, c3, looks, at first sight, pretty much the same as the second block, c2. In fact, the only difference is that its block parameter is called x instead of z:

```
c3 = proc{
    |x|
    x + 100
}
```

The name of the block parameter has no effect on the return value. As before, someval is first assigned the value 1,100 (that is, its original value, 1,000, plus the 100 added inside the block). Then, when the block is called a second time, someval is assigned the value 1,200 (its previous value, 1,100, plus 100 assigned inside the block).

But now look at what happens to the value of the local variable x. This was assigned 3,000 at the top of the unit. Remember that, in Ruby 1.8, an assignment to a block parameter can change the value of a variable with the same name in its surrounding context. In Ruby 1.8, then the local variable x changes when the block parameter x is changed. It now has the value, 1,100—that is, the value that the block parameter, x, last had when the c3 block was called:

```
x = 3000
someval=1000
someval=c3.call(someval); puts(someval)     #=> 1100
someval=c3.call(someval); puts(someval)     #=> 1200
puts( x ) # Ruby 1.8, x = 1100. Ruby 1.9, x = 3000
```

Incidentally, even though block-local variables and block parameters can affect similarly named local variables outside the block in Ruby 1.8, the block variables themselves have no "existence" outside the block. You can verify this using the defined? keyword to attempt to display the type of variable if it is, indeed, defined:

```
print("x=[#{defined?(x)}],z=[#{defined?(z)}]")
```

This demonstrates that only x, and not the block variable z, is defined in the main scope:

```
x=[local-variable], z=[]
```

Matz, the creator of Ruby, has described the scoping of local variables within a block as "regrettable." Although Ruby 1.9 has addressed some issues, it is worth noting that one other curious feature of block scoping remains: Namely, local variables within a block are invisible to the method containing that block. This may be changed in future versions. For an example of this, look at this code:

*local_var_scope
.rb*

```
def foo
    a = 100
    [1,2,3].each do |b|
        c = b
        a = b
        print("a=#{a}, b=#{b}, c=#{c}\n")
    end
    print("Outside block: a=#{a}\n")    # Can't print #{b} and #{c} here!!!
end
```

Here, the block parameter, b, and the block-local variable, c, are both visible only when inside the block. The block has access to both these variables and to the variable a (local to the foo method). However, outside of the block, b and c are inaccessible, and only a is visible.

Just to add to the confusion, whereas the block-local variable, c, and the block parameter, b, are both inaccessible outside the block in the previous example, they are accessible when you iterate a block with for, as in the following example:

```
def foo2
    a = 100
    for b in [1,2,3] do
        c = b
        a = b
        print("a=#{a}, b=#{b}, c=#{c}\n")
    end
    print("Outside block: a=#{a}, b=#{b}, c=#{b}\n")
end
```

11

SYMBOLS

Many newcomers to Ruby are confused by symbols. A symbol is an identifier whose first character is a colon (:), so :this is a symbol and so is :that. Symbols are, in fact, not at all complicated—and, in certain circumstances, they may be extremely useful, as you will see shortly.

Let's first be clear about what a symbol is *not*: It is not a string, it is not a constant, and it is not a variable. A symbol is, quite simply, an identifier with no intrinsic meaning other than its own name. Whereas you might assign a value to a variable like this . . .

```
name = "Fred"
```

you would *not* assign a value to a symbol:

```
:name = "Fred"    # Error!
```

The value of a symbol is itself. So, the value of a symbol called :name is :name.

NOTE *For a more technical account of what a symbol is, refer to "Digging Deeper" on page 190.*

You have, of course, used symbols before. In Chapter 2, for instance, you created attribute readers and writers by passing symbols to the attr_reader and attr_writer methods, like this:

```
attr_reader( :description )
attr_writer( :description )
```

You may recall that the previous code causes Ruby to create a @description instance variable plus a pair of getter (reader) and setter (writer) methods called description. Ruby takes the value of a symbol literally. The attr_reader and attr_writer methods create, from that name, variables and methods with matching names.

Symbols and Strings

It is a common misconception that a symbol is a type of string. After all, isn't the symbol :hello pretty similar to the string "hello"? In fact, symbols are quite unlike strings. For one thing, each string is different—so, as far as Ruby is concerned, "hello", "hello", and "hello" are three separate objects with three separate object_ids.

symbol_ids.rb
```
# These 3 strings have 3 different object_ids
puts( "hello".object_id ) #=> 16589436
puts( "hello".object_id ) #=> 16589388
puts( "hello".object_id ) #=> 16589340
```

But a symbol is unique, so :hello, :hello, and :hello all refer to the same object with the same object_id.

```
# These 3 symbols have the same object_id
puts( :hello.object_id ) #=> 208712
puts( :hello.object_id ) #=> 208712
puts( :hello.object_id ) #=> 208712
```

In this respect, a symbol has more in common with an integer than with a string. Each occurrence of a given integer value, you may recall, refers to the same object, so 10, 10, and 10 may be considered to be the same object, and they have the same object_id. Remember that the actual IDs assigned to objects will change each time you run a program. The number itself is not significant. The important thing to note is that each separate object always has a unique ID, so when an ID is repeated, it indicates repeated references to the same object.

ints_and_symbols .rb

```
# These three symbols have the same object_id
puts( :ten.object_id )   #=> 20712
puts( :ten.object_id )   #=> 20712
puts( :ten.object_id )   #=> 20712

# These three integers have the same object_id
puts( 10.object_id )     #=> 21
puts( 10.object_id )     #=> 21
puts( 10.object_id )     #=> 21
```

You can also test for equality using the equal? method:

symbols_strings.rb

```
puts( :helloworld.equal?( :helloworld ) )      #=> true
puts( "helloworld".equal?( "helloworld" ) )    #=> false
puts( 1.equal?( 1 ) )                          #=> true
```

Being unique, a symbol provides an unambiguous identifier. You can pass symbols as arguments to methods, like this:

```
amethod( :deletefiles )
```

A method might contain code to test the value of the incoming argument:

symbols_1.rb

```
def amethod( doThis )
    if (doThis == :deletefiles) then
        puts( 'Now deleting files...')
    elsif (doThis == :formatdisk) then
        puts( 'Now formatting disk...')
    else
        puts( "Sorry, command not understood." )
    end
end
```

Symbols can also be used in case statements where they provide both the readability of strings and the uniqueness of integers:

```
case doThis
    when :deletefiles then puts( 'Now deleting files...')
    when :formatdisk then puts( 'Now formatting disk...')
    else  puts( "Sorry, command not understood." )
end
```

The scope in which a symbol is declared does not affect its uniqueness. Consider the following:

symbol_ref.rb

```
module One
    class Fred
    end
    $f1 = :Fred
end

module Two
    Fred = 1
    $f2 = :Fred
end

def Fred()
end

$f3 = :Fred
```

Here, the variables $f1, $f2, and $f3 are assigned the symbol :Fred in three different scopes: module One, module Two, and the "main" scope. Variables starting with $ are global, so once created, they can be referenced anywhere. I'll have more to say on modules in Chapter 12. For now, just think of them as "namespaces" that define different scopes. And yet each variable refers to the same symbol, :Fred, and has the same object_id.

```
# All three display the same id!
puts( $f1.object_id )   #=> 208868
puts( $f2.object_id )   #=> 208868
puts( $f3.object_id )   #=> 208868
```

Even so, the "meaning" of the symbol changes according to its scope. In module One, :Fred refers to the class Fred; in module Two, it refers to the constant Fred = 1; and in the main scope, it refers to the method Fred.

A rewritten version of the previous program demonstrates this:

symbol_ref2.rb

```
module One
    class Fred
    end
    $f1 = :Fred
    def self.evalFred( aSymbol )
        puts( eval( aSymbol.id2name ) )
    end
end

module Two
    Fred = 1
    $f2 = :Fred
    def self.evalFred( aSymbol )
        puts( eval( aSymbol.id2name ) )
    end
end
```

```
def Fred()
    puts( "hello from the Fred method" )
end

$f3 = :Fred
```

First I access the `evalFred` method inside the module named `One` using two colons (`::`), which is the Ruby "scope resolution operator." I then pass `$f1` to that method:

```
One::evalFred( $f1 )
```

In this context, `Fred` is the name of a class defined inside module `One`, so when the `:Fred` symbol is evaluated, the module and class names are displayed:

```
One::Fred
```

Next I pass `$f2` to the `evalFred` method of module `Two`:

```
Two::evalFred( $f2 )
```

In this context, `Fred` is the name of a constant that is assigned the integer 1, so that is what is displayed: 1. And finally, I call a special method called simply `method`. This is a method of Object. It tries to find a method with the same name as the symbol passed to it as an argument and, if found, returns that method as an object that can then be called:

```
method($f3).call
```

The `Fred` method exists in the main scope, and when called, its output is this string:

```
"hello from the Fred method"
```

Naturally, since the variables `$f1`, `$f2`, and `$f3` reference the same symbol, it doesn't matter which variable you use at any given point. Any variable to which a symbol is assigned, or, indeed, the symbol itself, will produce the same results. The following are equivalent:

```
One::evalFred( $f1 )    #=> One::Fred
Two::evalFred( $f2 )    #=> 1
method($f3).call         #=> hello from the Fred method

One::evalFred( $f3 )    #=> One::Fred
Two::evalFred( $f1 )    #=> 1
method($f2).call         #=> hello from the Fred method
```

```
One::evalFred( :Fred )   #=> One::Fred
Two::evalFred( :Fred )   #=> 1
method(:Fred).call       #=> hello from the Fred method
```

Symbols and Variables

To understand the relationship between a symbol and an identifier such as a variable name, take a look at the *symbols_2.rb* program. It begins by assigning the value 1 to a local variable, x. It then assigns the symbol :x to a local variable, xsymbol:

symbols_2.rb

```
x = 1
xsymbol = :x
```

At this point, there is no obvious connection between the variable x and the symbol :x. I have declared a method that simply takes some incoming argument and inspects and displays it using the p method. I can call this method with the variable and the symbol:

```
def amethod( somearg )
    p( somearg )
end

# Test 1
amethod( x )
amethod( :x )
```

This is the data that the method prints as a result:

```
1
:x
```

In other words, the value of the x variable is 1, since that's the value assigned to it and the value of :x is :x. But the interesting question that arises is this: If the value of :x is :x and this is also the symbolic name of the variable x, would it be possible to use the symbol :x to find the value of the variable x? Confused? I hope the next line of code will make this clearer:

```
# Test 2
amethod( eval(:x.id2name))
```

Here, id2name is a method of the Symbol class. It returns the name or string corresponding to the symbol (the to_s method would perform the same function); the end result is that, when given the symbol :x as an argument, id2name returns the string "x." Ruby's eval method (which is defined in the Kernel class) is able to evaluate expressions within strings. In the present case, that means it finds the string "x" and tries to evaluate it as though it were executable code. It finds that x is the name of a variable and that the value of x is 1. So, the value 1 is passed to amethod. You can verify this by running *symbols2.rb*.

NOTE *Evaluating data as code is explained in more detail in Chapter 20.*

Things can get even trickier. Remember that the variable xsymbol has been assigned the symbol :x.

```
x = 1
xsymbol = :x
```

That means that if you eval :xsymbol, you can obtain the name assigned to it—that is, the symbol :x. Having obtained :x, you can go on to evaluate this also, giving the value of x, namely, 1:

```
# Test 3
amethod( xsymbol )                                        #=> :x
amethod( :xsymbol )                                       #=> :xsymbol
amethod( eval(:xsymbol.id2name))                          #=> :x
amethod( eval( ( eval(:xsymbol.id2name)).id2name ) )      #=> 1
```

As you've seen, when used to create attribute accessors, symbols can refer to method names. You can make use of this by passing a method name as a symbol to the method method and then calling the specified method using the call method:

```
#Test 4
method(:amethod).call("")
```

The call method lets you pass arguments, so, just for the heck of it, you could pass an argument by evaluating a symbol:

```
method(:amethod).call(eval(:x.id2name))
```

If this seems complicated, take a look at a simpler example in *symbols_3.rb*. This begins with this assignment:

symbols_3.rb
```
def mymethod( somearg )
    print( "I say: " << somearg )
end

this_is_a_method_name = method(:mymethod)
```

Here `method(:mymethod)` looks for a method with the name specified by the symbol passed as an argument (`:mymethod`), and if one is found, it returns the Method object with the corresponding name. In my code I have a method called `mymethod`, and this is now assigned to the variable `this_is_a_method_name`.

When you run this program, you will see that the first line of output prints the value of the variable:

```
puts( this_is_a_method_name )  #=> #<Method: Object#mymethod>
```

This shows that the variable `this_is_a_method_name` has been assigned the method, `mymethod`, which is bound to the Object class (as are all methods that are entered as "freestanding" functions). To double-check that the variable really is an instance of the Method class, the next line of code prints out its class:

```
puts( "#{this_is_a_method_name.class}" )  #=> Method
```

Okay, so if it's really and truly a method, then you should be able to call it, shouldn't you? To do that, you need to use the `call` method. That is what the last line of code does:

```
this_is_a_method_name.call( "hello world" )  #=>I say: hello world
```

Why Use Symbols?

Some methods in the Ruby class library specify symbols as arguments. Naturally, if you need to call those methods, you are obliged to pass symbols to them. Other than in those cases, however, there is no absolute requirement to use symbols in your own programming. For many Ruby programmers, the "conventional" data types such as strings and integers are perfectly sufficient. However, many Ruby programmers do like to use symbols as the keys into hashes. When you look at the Rails framework in Chapter 19, for example, you will see examples similar to the following:

```
{ :text => "Hello world" }
```

Symbols do have a special place in "dynamic" programming, however. For example, a Ruby program is able to create a new method at runtime by calling, within the scope of a certain class, `define_method` with a symbol representing the method to be defined and a block representing the code of the method:

add_method.rb
```
class Array
    define_method( :aNewMethod, lambda{
        |*args| puts( args.inspect )
    } )
end
```

After the previous code executes, the Array class will have gained a method named `aNewMethod`. You can verify this by calling `method_defined?` with a symbol representing the method name:

```
Array.method_defined?( :aNewMethod )    #=> true
```

And, of course, you can call the method itself:

```
[].aNewMethod( 1,2,3     #=> [1,2,3]
```

You can remove an existing method at runtime in a similar way by calling `remove_method` inside a class with a symbol providing the name of the method to be removed:

```
class Array
    remove_method( :aNewMethod )
end
```

Dynamic programming is invaluable in applications that need to modify the behavior of the Ruby program while that program is still executing. Dynamic programming is widely used in the Rails framework, for example, and it is discussed in depth in the final chapter of this book.

DIGGING DEEPER

Symbols are fundamental to Ruby. Here you will learn why that is so and how you can display all the symbols available.

What Is a Symbol?

Previously, I said that a symbol is an identifier whose value is itself. That describes, in a broad sense, the way that symbols behave from the point of view of the Ruby programmer. But it doesn't tell you what symbols are *literally* from the point of view of the Ruby interpreter. A symbol is, in fact, a pointer into the symbol table. The symbol table is Ruby's internal list of known identifiers—such as variable and method names.

If you want to take a peek deep inside Ruby, you can display all the symbols that Ruby knows about like this:

allsymbols.rb

```
p( Symbol.all_symbols )
```

This will shows thousands of symbols including method names such as :to_s and :reverse, global variables such as :$/ and :$DEBUG, and class names such as :Array and :Symbol. You may restrict the number of symbols displayed using array indexes like this:

```
p( Symbol.all_symbols[0,10] )
```

In Ruby 1.8, you can't sort symbols since symbols are not considered to be inherently sequential. In Ruby 1.9, sorting is possible, and the symbol characters are sorted as though they were strings:

```
# In Ruby 1.9
p [:a,:c,:b].sort        #=> [:a,:b,:c]

# In Ruby 1.8
p [:a,:c,:b].sort        #=> 'sort': undefined method '<=>' for :a:Symbol
```

The easiest way to display a sorted list of symbols in a way that avoids incompatibility problems related to Ruby versions is to convert the symbols to strings and sort those. In the following code, I pass all the symbols known to Ruby into a block, convert each symbol to a string, and collect the strings into a new array that is assigned to the str_array variable. Now I can sort this array and display the results:

```
str_arr = Symbol.all_symbols.collect{ |s| s.to_s }
puts( str_arr.sort )
```

12

MODULES AND MIXINS

In Ruby, each class has only one immediate "parent," though each parent class may have many "children." By restricting class hierarchies to a single line of descent, Ruby avoids some of the problems that may occur in those programming languages (such as C++) that permit multiple lines of descent. When classes have many parents as well as many children and when their parents and children also have other parents and children, you risk ending up with an impenetrable network (a knotwork?) rather than the neat, well-ordered hierarchy that you may have intended.

Nevertheless, sometimes it is useful for classes that are not closely related to implement some shared features. For example, a Sword might be a type of Weapon but also a type of Treasure; a PC might be a type of Computer but also a type of Investment; and so on. But, since the classes defining Weapons and Treasures or Computers and Investments descend from different ancestor classes, their class hierarchy gives them no obvious way of sharing data and methods. Ruby's solution to this problem is provided by modules.

A Module Is Like a Class . . .

The definition of a module looks very similar to the definition of a class. In fact, modules and classes are closely related; the Module class is the immediate ancestor of the Class class. Just like a class, a module can contain constants, methods, and classes. Here's a simple module:

simple_module.rb

```
module MyModule
    REWARD = 100

    def prize
        return "You've won #{REWARD} credits"
    end

end
```

As you can see, this contains a constant, REWARD, and an *instance method,* prize.

Module Methods

In addition to instance methods, a module may also have module methods. Just as class methods are prefixed with the name of the class, module methods are prefixed with the name of the module:

```
def MyModule.lose
    return "Sorry, you didn't win"
end
```

You can call a module's module methods just as you would call a class's class methods, using dot notation, like this:

```
MyModule.lose   #=> "Sorry, you didn't win"
```

But how do you call an instance method? Neither of the following attempts succeeds:

```
puts( prize )          # Error: undefined local variable or method
puts( MyModule.prize ) # Error: undefined method 'prize'
```

In spite of their similarities, classes possess two major features that modules do not: *instances* and *inheritance.* Classes can have instances (objects created from the class), superclasses (parents), and subclasses (children); modules can have none of these. It is not possible to call an instance method from an instance of a module (a "module object") for the simple reason that it is impossible to create instances of a module. This explains the errors when you try to call the prize method in the previous code.

NOTE *The Module class does have a superclass, namely, Object. However, any named modules that you create do not have superclasses. For a more detailed account of the relationship between modules and classes, see "Digging Deeper" on page 205.*

That leads me to the next question: If you can't create an object from a module, what are modules for? This can be answered in two words: *namespaces* and *mixins*. Ruby's mixins provide a way of dealing with the problem of multiple inheritance. You'll learn how mixins work shortly. First, though, let's look at namespaces.

Modules as Namespaces

You can think of a module as a sort of named "wrapper" around a set of methods, constants, and classes. The various bits of code inside the module share the same "namespace," so they are all visible to each other but are not visible to code outside the module.

The Ruby class library defines a number of modules such as Math and Kernel. The Math module contains mathematical methods such as sqrt to return a square route and constants such as PI. The Kernel module contains many of the methods you've been using from the outset such as print, puts, and gets.

Let's assume you have written this module:

modules1.rb

```ruby
module MyModule
    GOODMOOD = "happy"
    BADMOOD = "grumpy"

    def greet
        return "I'm #{GOODMOOD}. How are you?"
    end

    def MyModule.greet
        return "I'm #{BADMOOD}. How are you?"
    end
end
```

You've already seen how to use a module method such as MyModule.greet, and you can access the module constants just as you would access class constants, using the scope resolution operator, :: , like this:

```ruby
puts(MyModule::GOODMOOD)    #=> happy
```

But how can you access the instance method, greet? This is where mixins enter the picture.

Included Modules, or "Mixins"

An object can access the instance methods of a module by including that module using the include method. If you were to include MyModule in your program, everything inside that module would suddenly pop into existence within the current scope. So, the greet method of MyModule will now be accessible:

modules2.rb

```
include MyModule
```

Note that only instance methods are included. In the previous example, the greet (instance) method has been included, but the MyModule.greet (module) method has not. As it's included, the greet instance method can be used just as though it were a normal instance method within the current scope, whereas the module method, also named greet, is accessed using dot notation:

```
puts( greet )           #=> I'm happy. How are you?
puts( MyModule.greet )  #=> I'm grumpy. How are you?
```

The process of including a module is also called *mixing in*, which explains why included modules are often called mixins. When you mix modules into a class definition, any objects created from that class will be able to use the instance methods of the mixed-in module just as though they were defined in the class itself. Here the MyClass class mixes in the MyModule module:

modules3.rb

```
class MyClass
    include MyModule

    def sayHi
        puts( greet )
    end

end
```

Not only can the methods of this class access the greet method from MyModule, but so too can any objects created from the class:

```
ob = MyClass.new
ob.sayHi          #=> I'm happy. How are you?
puts(ob.greet)    #=> I'm happy. How are you?
```

You can think of modules as discrete code units that may simplify the creation of reusable code libraries. On the other hand, you might be more interested in using modules as an alternative to multiple inheritance.

Returning to an example that I mentioned at the start of this chapter, let's assume you have a Sword class that is not only a weapon but also a treasure. Maybe Sword is a descendant of the Weapon class (so it inherits the Weapon's deadliness attribute), but it also needs to have the attributes of a Treasure (such as value and owner). Moreover, since this happens to be an

Elvish Sword, it also requires the attributes of a MagicThing. If you define these attributes inside `Treasure` and `MagicThing` *modules* rather than Treasure and MagicThing *classes*, the Sword class would be able to include those modules in order to "mix in" their methods or attributes:

modules4.rb

```
module MagicThing
    attr_accessor :power
end

module Treasure
    attr_accessor :value
    attr_accessor :owner
end

class Weapon
    attr_accessor :deadliness
end

class Sword < Weapon        # descend from Weapon
    include Treasure        # mix in Treasure
    include MagicThing      # mix in MagicThing
    attr_accessor :name
end
```

The Sword object now has access to the methods and attributes of the Sword class, of its ancestor class, Weapon, and also of its mixed-in modules, `Treasure` and `MagicThing`:

```
s = Sword.new
s.name = "Excalibur"
s.deadliness = "fatal"
s.value = 1000
s.owner = "Gribbit The Dragon"
s.power = "Glows when Orcs appear"
puts(s.name)              #=> Excalibur
puts(s.deadliness)        #=> fatal
puts(s.value)             #=> 1000
puts(s.owner)             #=> Gribbit The Dragon
puts(s.power)             #=> Glows when Orcs appear
```

Note, incidentally, that any variables that are *local* to the module cannot be accessed from outside the module. This is the case even if a method inside the module tries to access a local variable and that method is invoked by code from outside the module, such as when the module is mixed in through inclusion:

mod_vars.rb

```
x = 1            # local to this program

module Foo
    x = 50       # local to module Foo

             # this can be mixed in but the variable x won't be visible
```

```
    def no_bar
        return x
    end

    def bar
        @x = 1000
        return  @x
    end
    puts( "In Foo: x = #{x}" )   # this can access the module-local x
end

include Foo                      # mix in the Foo module
```

When you run this program, the puts method executes when the module is initialized, and it displays the value of the module-local variable x:

```
In Foo: x = 50
```

If you display the x variable within the main scope of the program, the value of the variable x local to the main scope of the program is used, *not* the value of the variable x local to the module:

```
puts(x)              #=> 1
```

But any attempt to execute the no_bar method will fail:

```
puts( no_bar )    # Error: undefined local variable or method 'x'
```

Here the no_bar method is unable to access either of the local variables named x even though x is declared both in the scope of the module (x = 50) and in the current or "main" scope (x = 1). But there is no such problem with instance variables. The bar method is able to return the value of the instance variable @x:

```
puts(bar)            #=> 1000
```

A module may have its own instance variables that belong exclusively to the module "object." These instance variables will be in scope to a module method:

inst_class_vars.rb
```
module X
    @instvar = "X's @instvar"

    def self.aaa
        puts(@instvar)
    end
end

X.aaa #=> X's @instvar
```

But instance variables that are referenced in instance objects "belong" to the scope into which that module is included:

```ruby
module X
    @instvar = "X's @instvar"
    @anotherinstvar = "X's 2nd @instvar"

        def amethod
            @instvar = 10          # creates @instvar in current scope
            puts(@instvar)
        end
end

include X
p( @instvar )                    #=> nil
amethod                          #=> 10
puts( @instvar )                 #=> 10
@instvar = "hello world"
puts( @instvar )                 #=> "hello world"
```

Class variables are also mixed in, and like instance variables, their values may be reassigned within the current scope:

```ruby
module X
    @@classvar = "X's @@classvar"
end

include X

puts( @@classvar )      #=> X's @classvar
@@classvar = "bye bye"
puts( @@classvar )      #=> "bye bye"
```

You may obtain an array of instance variable names using the instance_variables method:

```ruby
p( X.instance_variables )       #=> [:@instvar, @anotherinstvar]
p( self.instance_variables )    #=> [:@instvar]
```

Here, X.instance_variables returns a list of the instance variables belonging to the X class, while self.instance_variables returns the instance variables of the current, main, object. The @instvar variable is different in each case.

NOTE *In Ruby 1.9, the instance_variables method returns an array of symbols. In Ruby 1.8, it returns an array of strings.*

Name Conflicts

Module methods (those methods specifically preceded by the module name) can help protect your code from accidental name conflicts. However, no such protection is given by instance methods within modules. Let's suppose you have two modules—one called Happy and the other called Sad. They each contain a module method called mood and an instance method called expression.

happy_sad.rb

```
module Happy
    def Happy.mood          # module method
        return "happy"
    end

    def expression          # instance method
        return "smiling"
    end
end
module Sad
    def Sad.mood            # module method
        return "sad"
    end

    def expression          # instance method
        return "frowning"
    end
end
```

Now a class, Person, includes both these modules:

```
class Person
    include Happy
    include Sad
    attr_accessor :mood

    def initialize
        @mood = Happy.mood
    end
end
```

The initialize method of the Person class needs to set the value of its @mood variable using the mood method from one of the included modules. The fact that they both have a mood method is no problem; being a module method, mood must be preceded by the module name so Happy.mood won't be confused with Sad.mood.

But both the `Happy` and `Sad` modules also contain a method called expression. This is an *instance* method, and when both the modules are included in the Person class, the expression method can be called without any qualification:

```
p1 = Person.new
puts(p1.expression)
```

Which expression method is object `p1` using here? It turns out that it uses the method last defined. In the example case, that happens to be the method defined in the `Sad` module for the simple reason that `Sad` is included after `Happy`. So, `p1.expression` returns "frowning." If you change the order of inclusion so that `Happy` is included after `Sad`, the `p1` object will use the version of the expression method defined in the Happy module and will display "smiling."

Before getting carried away with the possibilities of creating big, complex modules and mixing them into your classes on a regular basis, bear this potential problem in mind: *Included instance methods with the same name will "overwrite" one another.* The problem may be obvious to spot in my little program here. But it may not be so obvious in a huge application!

Alias Methods

One way of avoiding ambiguity when you use similarly named methods from multiple modules is to *alias* those methods. An alias is a copy of an existing method with a new name. You use the alias keyword followed by the new name and then the old name:

```
alias  happyexpression expression
```

You can also use alias to make copies of methods that have been overridden so that you can specifically refer to a version prior to its overridden definition:

alias_methods.rb

```
module Happy
    def Happy.mood
        return "happy"
    end

    def expression
        return "smiling"
    end
    alias happyexpression expression
end
```

```
module Sad
    def Sad.mood
        return "sad"
    end

    def expression
        return "frowning"
    end
    alias sadexpression expression
end

class Person
    include Happy
    include Sad
    attr_accessor :mood
    def initialize
        @mood = Happy.mood
    end
end

p2 = Person.new
puts(p2.mood)                   #=> happy
puts(p2.expression)             #=> frowning
puts(p2.happyexpression)        #=> smiling
puts(p2.sadexpression)          #=> frowning
```

Mix In with Care!

Although each class can descend from only one superclass, it can mix in numerous modules. In fact, it is perfectly permissible to mix one lot of modules into another lot of modules, then mix those other modules into classes, then place those classes into yet more modules, and so on.

The following is an example of some code that subclasses some classes, mixes in some modules, and even subclasses classes from within mixed-in modules. I've deliberately simplified the following code to help you see what is happening. For the full horror of a working example, see the sample program, *multimods.rb*, which is supplied in the code archive for this chapter:

multimods.rb
```
# This is an example of how NOT to use modules!
module MagicThing                       # module
    class MagicClass                    # class inside module
    end
end

module Treasure                         # module
end
```

```
module MetalThing
    include MagicThing                  # mixin
    class Attributes < MagicClass       # subclasses class from mixin
    end
end

include MetalThing                      # mixin
class Weapon < MagicClass               # subclass class from mixin
    class WeaponAttributes < Attributes # subclass
    end
end

class Sword < Weapon                    # subclass
    include Treasure                    # mixin
    include MagicThing                  # mixin
end
```

Let me emphasize that the code shown previously and included in the archive is *not* intended as a model to be emulated. Far from it! It is included purely to demonstrate how rapidly a program that makes overenthusiastic use of modules may become difficult to understand and nearly impossible to debug.

In brief, although modules may, when used with care, help avoid some of the complexities associated with the C++ type of multiple inheritance, they are nonetheless open to misuse. If programmers really want to create convoluted hierarchies of classes with inscrutable dependencies on multiple levels of mixed-in modules, then they can certainly do so. The code in *multimods.rb* shows how easy it is to write an impenetrable program in just a few lines. Imagine what you could do over many thousands of lines of code spread over dozens of code files! Think carefully before mixing in modules.

Including Modules from Files

So far, I've mixed in modules that have been defined within a single source file. Often it is more useful to define modules in separate files and mix them in as needed. The first thing you have to do in order to use code from another file is to load that file using the require method, like this:

require_module.rb
```
require( "./testmod.rb" )
```

Optionally, you may omit the file extension:

```
require( "./testmod" )  # this works too
```

If no path is given, the required file must be in the current directory, on the search path, or in a folder listed in the predefined array variable $:. You can add a directory to this array variable using the usual array-append method, <<, in this way:

```
$: << "C:/mydir"
```

NOTE *The global variable, $: (a dollar sign and a colon), contains an array of strings representing the directories that Ruby searches when looking for a loaded or required file.*

There is one documented difference in the way require works in Ruby 1.8 and Ruby 1.9. In Ruby 1.8, the filename is *not* converted to an absolute path, so require "a"; require "./a" will load *a.rb* twice. In Ruby 1.9, the filename *is* converted to an absolute path, so require "a"; require "./a" will not load *a.rb* twice.

In addition, I've found that require may, in at least some versions of Ruby 1.9, fail to load a file from the current directory if you use an unqualified filename as in require("testmod"). In such cases, a LoadError is thrown. This occurs when the array of searchable directories stored in the global variable, $:, does not contain the current directory. You can verify whether this is the case by running this code:

search_dirs.rb
```
puts( $: )
```

The search paths will be displayed one per line. There should be a line that displays a single dot (.) representing the current directory. If that dot is missing, then files in the current directory are not on the search path and cannot be loaded using an unqualified filename.

To ensure that the file is loaded, I have preceded the filename with a dot to specify the current directory, and this now succeeds: require("./testmod"). Alternatively, you could use the require_relative method, though this is new to Ruby 1.9 and cannot be used in earlier versions:

```
require_relative( "testmod.rb" )    # Ruby 1.9 only
```

Alternatively, if $: doesn't contain the current directory, you could add it. Once this is done, require will work with the unqualified names of files in the current directory:

```
$: << "."                # add current directory to array of search paths
require( "testmod.rb" )
```

The require method returns a true value if the specified file is successfully loaded; otherwise, it returns false. If the file does not exist, it returns a LoadError. If in doubt, you can simply display the result.

```
puts(require( "testmod.rb" )) #=> true, false or LoadError
```

Any code that would normally be executed when a file is run will be executed when that file is required. So, if the file, *testmod.rb*, contains this code:

```
def sing
    puts( "Tra-la-la-la-la....")
end

puts( "module loaded")
sing
```

when the *require_module.rb* program is run and it requires *testmod.rb*, this will be displayed:

```
module loaded
Tra-la-la-la-la....
```

When a module is declared in the required file, it can be mixed in:

```
require_module2.rb
require( "testmod.rb")
include MyModule        #mix in MyModule declared in testmod.rb
```

Ruby also lets you load a file using the load method. In most respects, require and load can be regarded as interchangeable. But there are a few subtle differences. In particular, load can take an optional second argument, which, if this is true, loads and executes the code as an unnamed or anonymous module:

```
load( "testmod.rb", true)
```

When the second argument is true, the file loaded does not introduce the new namespace into the main program, and you will not have access to the module(s) in the loaded file. In that case, the Module methods, constants, and instance methods will *not* be available to your code:

```
load( "testmod.rb", true)

puts( MyModule.greet )     #=>Error:uninitialized constant Object::MyModule
puts(MyModule::GOODMOOD)   #=>Error:uninitialized constant Object::MyModule
include MyModule           #=>Error:uninitialized constant Object::MyModule
puts( greet )              #=>Error:undefined local variable or method 'greet'
```

When the second argument to load is false or when there is no second argument, however, you *will* have access to modules in the loaded file:

```
load( "testmod.rb", false)

puts( MyModule.greet )   #=> I'm grumpy. How are you?
puts(MyModule::GOODMOOD) #=> happy
```

```
include MyModule           #=> [success]
puts( greet )              #=> I'm happy. How are you?
```

Note that you must enter the full filename with load (*testmod* minus the
.rb extension will not suffice). Another difference between load and require is
that require loads a file once only (even if your code requires that file many
times), whereas load causes the specified file to be reloaded each time load is
called. Let's suppose you have a file, *test.rb*, containing this code:

test.rb
```
MyConst = 1
if @a == nil then
    @a = 1
else
    @a += MyConst
end

puts @a
```

You now *require* this file three times:

require_again.rb
```
require "./test"
require "./test"
require "./test"
```

This will be the output:

```
1
```

But if you *load* the file three times . . .

load_again.rb
```
load "test.rb"
load "test.rb"
load "test.rb"
```

then this will be the output:

```
1
./test.rb:1: warning: already initialized constant MyConst
2
./test.rb:1: warning: already initialized constant MyConst
3
```

DIGGING DEEPER

How exactly is a module related to a class? Here we answer that question, examine some important Ruby modules and find out how to use modules to extend objects.

Modules and Classes

In this chapter, I've discussed the *behavior* of a module. Let's now find out what a module really *is*. It turns out that, as with most other things in Ruby, a module is an object. Each named module is, in fact, an instance of the Module class:

module_inst.rb

```
module MyMod
end

puts( MyMod.class )          #=> Module
```

You cannot create descendants of *named modules*, so this is not allowed:

```
module MyMod
end

module MyOtherMod < MyMod      # You can't do this!
end
```

However, as with other classes, it is permissible to create a descendant of the Module *class*:

```
class X < Module              # But you can do this
end
```

Indeed, the Class class is itself a descendant of the Module class. It inherits the behavior of Module and adds some important new behavior, notably the ability to create objects. You can verify that Module is the superclass of Class by running the *modules_classes.rb* program, which shows this hierarchy:

*modules_classes
.rb*

```
Class
Module        #=> is the superclass of Class
Object        #=> is the superclass of Module
BasicObject   #=> (in Ruby 1.9) is the superclass of Module
```

Predefined Modules

The following modules are built into the Ruby interpreter: Comparable, Enumerable, FileTest, GC, Kernel, Math, ObjectSpace, Precision, Process, and Signal.

Comparable is a mixin module that permits the including class to implement comparison operators. The including class must define the <=> operator, which compares the receiver against another object, returning -1, 0, or +1 depending on whether the receiver is less than, equal to, or greater than the other object.

- Comparable uses <=> to implement the conventional comparison operators (<, <=, ==, >=, and >) and the method between?.

- Enumerable is a mixin module for enumeration. The including class must provide the method each.

- FileTest is a module containing file test functions; its methods can also be accessed from the File class.

- The GC module provides an interface to Ruby's mark and sweep garbage collection mechanism. Some of the underlying methods are also available via the ObjectSpace module.

- Kernel is a module included by the Object class; it defines Ruby's "built-in" methods.

- Math is a module containing module functions for basic trigonometric and transcendental functions. It has both "instance methods" and module methods of the same definitions and names.

- ObjectSpace is a module that contains routines that interact with the garbage collection facility and allow you to traverse all living objects with an iterator.

- Precision is a mixin for concrete numeric classes with precision. Here, "precision" means the fineness of approximation of a real number, so this module should not be included into anything that is not a subset of Real (so it should not be included in classes such as Complex or Matrix).

- Process is the module for manipulating processes. All its methods are module methods.

- Signal is the module for handling signals sent to running processes. The list of available signal names and their interpretation is system dependent.

The following is a brief overview of three of the most commonly used Ruby modules.

Kernel

The most important of the predefined modules is Kernel, which provides many of the "standard" Ruby methods such as gets, puts, print, and require. In common with much of the Ruby class library, Kernel is written in the C language. Although Kernel is, in fact, "built into" the Ruby interpreter, conceptually it can be regarded as a mixed-in module that, just like a normal Ruby mixin, makes its methods directly available to any class that requires it. Since it is mixed into the Object class from which all other Ruby classes descend, the methods of Kernel are universally accessible.

Math

The Math module's methods are provided as both "module" and "instance" methods and can therefore be accessed either by mixing Math into a class or by accessing the module methods "from the outside" by using the module name, a dot, and the method name; you can access constants using a double colon:

math.rb

```
puts( Math.sqrt(144) )   #=> 12.0
puts( Math::PI )         #=> 3.141592653589793
```

Comparable

The Comparable module provides the neat ability to define your own comparison "operators" as in <, <=, ==, >=, and > (strictly speaking, these are methods, but they can be used like the comparison operators in other languages). This is done by mixing the module into your class and defining the <=> method. You can then specify the criteria for comparing some value from the current object with some other value. You might, for example, compare two integers, the length of two strings, or some more eccentric value such as the position of a string in an array. I've opted for this eccentric type of comparison in my example program, *compare.rb*. This uses the index of a string in an array of mythical beings in order to compare the name of one being with that of another. A low index such as hobbit at index 0 is considered to be "less than" a high index such as dragon at index 6:

compare.rb

```
class Being
        include Comparable

        BEINGS = ['hobbit','dwarf','elf','orc','giant','oliphant','dragon']

        attr_accessor :name

        def <=> (anOtherName)
                BEINGS.index(@name)<=>BEINGS.index(anOtherName.name)
        end

        def initialize( aName )
                @name = aName
        end

end

elf =  Being.new('elf')
orc = Being.new('orc')
giant = Being.new('giant')

puts( elf < orc )      #=> true
puts( elf > giant )    #=> false
```

Scope Resolution

As with classes, you can use the double-colon scope resolution operator to access constants (including classes and other modules) declared inside modules. For example, let's suppose you have nested modules and classes, like this:

```
module OuterMod
    moduleInnerMod
        class Class1
        end
    end
end
```

You could use the :: operator to access Class1, like this:

```
OuterMod::InnerMod::Class1
```

NOTE   *See Chapter 2 for an introduction to scope resolution of constants within classes.*

Each module and class has its own scope, which means that a single constant name might be used in different scopes. This being so, you could use the :: operator to specify a constant within a precise scope:

```
Scope1::Scope2::Scope3         #...etc
```

If you use this operator at the very start of the constant name, this has the effect of breaking out of the current scope and accessing the "top-level" scope:

```
::ACONST                       # refers to ACONST at top-level scope
```

The following program provides some examples of the scope operator:

scope_resolution .rb

```
ACONST = "hello"                          # This is a top-level constant

module OuterMod
    module InnerMod
        ACONST=10                         # OuterMod::InnerMod::ACONST
        class Class1
            class Class2
                module XYZ
                    class ABC
                        ACONST=100        # Deeply nested ACONST
                        def xyz
                            puts( ::ACONST )  # <= This refers to top-level ACONST
                        end
                    end
                end
            end
        end
    end
end
```

```
puts(OuterMod::InnerMod::ACONST)                         #=> 10
puts(OuterMod::InnerMod::Class1::Class2::XYZ::ABC::ACONST)  #=> 100
ob = OuterMod::InnerMod::Class1::Class2::XYZ::ABC.new
ob.xyz                                                    #=> hello
```

Module Functions

If you want a function to be available both as an instance and as a module method, you can use the `module_function` method with a symbol matching the name of an instance method, like this:

module_func.rb
```ruby
module MyModule
    def sayHi
        return "hi!"
    end

    def sayGoodbye
        return "Goodbye"
  end

    module_function :sayHi
end
```

The `sayHi` method may now be mixed into a class and used as an instance method:

```ruby
class MyClass
    include MyModule
        def speak
            puts(sayHi)
            puts(sayGoodbye)
        end
end
```

It may be used as a module method, using dot notation:

```ruby
ob = MyClass.new
ob.speak              #=> hi!\nGoodbye
puts(MyModule.sayHi)  #=> hi!
```

Since the `sayGoodbye` method here is not a module function, it cannot be used in this way:

```ruby
puts(MyModule.sayGoodbye)  #=> Error: undefined method
```

Ruby uses `module_function` in some of its standard modules such as `Math` (in the Ruby library file, *complex.rb*) to create "matching pairs" of module and instance methods.

Extending Objects

You can add the methods of a module to a specific object (rather than to an entire class) using the extend method, like this:

extend.rb

```
module A
    def method_a
        puts( 'hello from a' )
    end
end

class MyClass
    def mymethod
        puts( 'hello from mymethod of class MyClass' )
    end
end

ob = MyClass.new
ob.mymethod        #=> hello from mymethod of class MyClass
ob.extend(A)
```

Now that the object ob is extended with the module A, it can access that module's instance method, method_a:

```
ob.method_a        #=> hello from a
```

You can, in fact, extend an object with several modules all at once. Here, the modules B and C extend the object, ob:

```
module B
    def method_b
        puts( 'hello from b' )
    end
end

module C
    def mymethod
        puts( 'hello from mymethod of module C' )
    end
end

ob.extend(B, C)
ob.method_b        #=> hello from b
ob.mymethod        #=> hello from mymethod of module C
```

When an object is extended with a module containing a method with the same name as a method in the object's class, the method from the module replaces the method from the class. So, when ob is extended with C and you call ob.mymethod, the string "hello from mymethod of module C" will be displayed rather than the "hello from mymethod of class MyClass" that was displayed before ob was extended with module C.

Freezing Objects

You can explicitly prevent an object from being extended it by "freezing" it using the freeze method:

```
ob.freeze
```

Any attempt to extend this object further would result in a runtime error:

```
module D
    def method_d
        puts( 'hello from d' )
    end
end
ob.extend( D ) #=> Error: can't modify frozen object (RuntimeError)
```

To avoid such an error, you can use the frozen? method to test whether an object has been frozen:

```
if !(ob.frozen?)
    ob.extend( D )
    ob.method_d
else
    puts( "Can't extend a frozen object" )
end
```

13

FILES AND IO

Ruby provides classes dedicated to handling input and output (IO). Chief among these is a class called, unsurprisingly, IO. The IO class lets you open and close IO *streams* (sequences of bytes) and read and write data to and from them.

For example, assuming you have a file called *textfile.txt*, containing some lines of text, this is how you might open the file and display each line on the screen:

io_test.rb

```
IO.foreach("testfile.txt") {|line| print( line ) }
```

Here foreach is a class method of IO, so you don't need to create a new IO object to use it; instead, you just specify the filename as an argument. The foreach method takes a block into which each line that is read from the file is passed as an argument. You don't have to open the file for reading and close it when you've finished (as you might expect from your experience with other languages) because Ruby's IO.foreach method does this for you.

IO has a number of other useful methods. For example, you could use the readlines method to read the file contents into an array for further processing. Here is a simple example that once again prints the lines to screen:

```
lines = IO.readlines("testfile.txt")
lines.each{|line| print( line )}
```

The File class is a subclass of IO, and the previous examples could be rewritten using the File class:

file_test.rb

```
File.foreach("testfile.txt") {|line| print( line ) }

lines = File.readlines("testfile.txt")
lines.each{|line| print( line )}
```

Opening and Closing Files

Although some standard methods open and close files automatically, often when processing the contents of a file, you will need to open and close the file explicitly. You can open a file using either the new or open method. You must pass two arguments to one of those methods—the filename and the file "mode"—and it returns a new File object. The File modes may be either integers that are defined by operating system–specific constants or strings. The mode generally indicates whether the file is be opened for reading ("r"), writing ("w"), or reading and writing ("rw"). Table 13-1 shows the list of available string modes.

Table 13-1: File Mode Strings

Mode	Meaning
"r"	Read-only, starts at beginning of file (default mode)
"r+"	Read-write, starts at beginning of file
"w"	Write-only, truncates existing file to zero length or creates a new file for writing
"w+"	Read-write, truncates existing file to zero length or creates a new file for reading and writing
"a"	Write-only, starts at end of file if file exists; otherwise, creates a new file for writing
"a+"	Read-write, starts at end of file if file exists; otherwise, creates a new file for reading and writing
"b"	(DOS/Windows only) Binary file mode (may appear with any of the key letters listed earlier)

Let's look at an actual example of opening, processing, and closing files. In *open_close.rb*, I first open a file, *myfile.txt*, for writing ("w"). When a file is opened for writing, a new file will be created if it doesn't already exist. I use puts() to write six strings to the file, one string on each of six lines. Finally, I close the file:

```
f = File.new("myfile.txt", "w")
f.puts( "I", "wandered", "lonely", "as", "a", "cloud" )
f.close
```

Closing a file not only releases the *file handle* (the pointer to the file data) but also "flushes" any data from memory to ensure that it is all saved into the file on disk.

Having written text into a file, let's see how to open that file and read the data back in. This time I'll read in the data one character at a time up to the end of the file (eof). As I do so, I'll keep a count of the characters that have been read. I'll also keep a count of the lines, which will be incremented whenever I read in a linefeed character (given by ASCII code 10). For the sake of clarity, I'll add a string to the end of each line that's been read, displaying its line number. I'll display the characters plus my line-end strings on the screen, and when everything has been read from the file, I'll close it and display the statistics that I've calculated. Here is the complete code:

open_close.rb
```
f = File.new("myfile.txt", "w")
f.puts( "I", "wandered", "lonely", "as", "a", "cloud" )
f.close                          # Try commenting this out!

charcount = 0
linecount = 0
f = File.new("myfile.txt", "r")
while !( f.eof ) do              # while not at end of file...
    c = f.getc()                 # get a single character
    if ( c.ord == 10 ) then      # test ASCII code (Ruby 1.9)
        linecount += 1
        puts( " <End Of Line #{linecount}>" )
    else
        putc( c )                # put the char to screen
        charcount += 1
    end
end
if f.eof then
    puts( "<End Of File>" )
end
f.close
puts("This file contains #{linecount} lines and #{charcount} characters." )
```

This code is written for Ruby 1.9 and won't run in Ruby 1.8. See the following section for more details.

When manipulating files in this way, it is the programmer's responsibility to ensure that the file is closed after data is written to or read from it. Failing to close a file may result in unpredictable side effects. For example, try commenting out the first f.close (on the third line in the previous code) to see for yourself! You'll find that when the program subsequently tries to read back the contents of the file, no data is found, and a count of zero lines and characters is returned!

Characters and Compatibility

The *open_close.rb* program is written for Ruby 1.9 and cannot be run in Ruby 1.8. This is because when a single character is returned by Ruby 1.8, it is treated as an integer ASCII value, whereas in Ruby 1.9 it is treated as a one-character string. So, when getc() returns the character, c, Ruby 1.8 is able to test its ASCII value (c == 10), whereas Ruby 1.9 must either test it as a string (c == "\n") or convert the character to an integer using the ord method: (c.ord == 10). The ord method does not exist in Ruby 1.8.

As a general principle, if you want to write programs that work in different versions of Ruby, you may code around incompatibility issues by testing the value of the RUBY_VERSION constant. This constant returns a string giving a version number such as 1.9.2. You could simply convert the string to a floating-point number using the to_f method and then take different actions if the value is greater than 1.8:

```
if (RUBY_VERSION.to_f > 1.8) then
    c = c.ord
end
```

Alternatively, you could analyze the string to determine the minor and major version numbers. Here, for example, is a very simple method that indexes into the RUBY_VERSION string to obtain the first character as the major version (1 or 2) and the second character as the minor version (for example, 8 or 9). It returns true if the Ruby version is 1.9 or higher and false otherwise:

open_close2.rb
```
def isNewRuby
    newR = false # is this > Ruby version 1.8?
    majorNum = RUBY_VERSION[0,1]
    minorNum = RUBY_VERSION[2,1]
    if ( majorNum == "2" ) || (minorNum  == "9" ) then
        newR = true
    else
        newR == false
    end
    return newR
end
```

You can use this test in your code to deal with compatibility issues. Here the ord method is applied to the character, c, only if the Ruby version is 1.9 or greater:

```
if (isNewRuby) then
    c = c.ord
end
```

Files and Directories

You can also use the File class to manipulate files and directories on disk. Before attempting to perform some operation on a file, you must naturally make sure that the file exists. It might, after all, have been renamed or deleted after the program started—or the user may have incorrectly entered a file or directory name.

You can verify the existence of a file using the File.exist? method. This is one of several testing methods that are provided to the File class by the FileTest module. As far as the File.exist? method is concerned, a directory counts as a file, so you could use the following code to test for the presence of a C:\drive (note that you must use double file separator "\\" characters in strings, because a single "\" will be treated as an escape character):

file_ops.rb
```
if File.exist?( "C:\\" ) then
    puts( "Yup, you have a C:\\ directory" )
else
    puts( "Eeek! Can't find the C:\\ drive!" )
end
```

If you want to distinguish between a directory and a data file, use the directory? method:

```
def dirOrFile( aName )
    if File.directory?( aName ) then
        puts( "#{aName} is a directory" )
    else
        puts( "#{aName} is a file" )
    end
end
```

Copying Files

Let's put the File class to some practical use by writing a simple file backup program. When you run *copy_files.rb*, you will be asked to choose a directory to copy from (the source directory) and another directory to copy to (the target directory). Assuming both directories exist, the program will then copy all the files from the source directory to the target directory. If the target directory does not exist, it will ask you whether you would like to create it, in which case you should enter *Y* to accept. I've supplied a source directory for you; just enter the name *srcdir* when prompted. When asked for a target directory, enter *targetdir* in order to create a subdirectory of that name beneath the current directory.

The program initializes the variable sourcedir with the path of the source directory, and it initializes targetdir with the name of the target directory. This is the code that does the file copying:

```
Dir.foreach( sourcedir ){
    |f|
    filepath = "#{sourcedir}\\#{f}"
        if !(File.directory?(filepath) ) then
            if File.exist?("#{targetdir}\\#{f}") then
                puts("#{f} already exists in target directory" )
            else
                FileUtils.cp( filepath, targetdir )
                puts("Copying... #{filepath}" )
            end
        end
}
```

Here I've used the foreach method of the Dir class, which passes into a block the filename, f, of each file in the specified directory. I'll have more to say about the Dir class shortly. The code constructs a qualified path to the file, filepath, by appending the filename to the directory name given by the sourcedir variable. I only want to copy data files but not directories, so I test that filepath is a file and not a directory:

```
if !(File.directory?(filepath) )
```

I don't want this program to copy over files that already exist, so it first checks to see whether a file with the name f already exists in the target directory, targetdir:

```
if File.exist?("#{targetdir}\\#{f}")
```

Finally, assuming all the specified conditions are met, the source file, filepath, is copied to targetdir:

```
FileUtils.cp( filepath, targetdir )
```

Here cp is a file-copy method found in the FileUtils module. This module also contains a number of other useful file-handling routines such as mv(source, target) to move a file from source to target, rm(files) to delete one or more files listed in the files parameter, and mkdir to create a directory as I have done when creating targetdir in the current program:

```
FileUtils.mkdir( targetdir )
```

Directory Inquiries

My backup program deals with just one directory level at a time, which is why it tests to see that a file, f, is not a directory before attempting to copy it. There are many times, however, when you may want to traverse the subdirectories. For an example of this, let's write a program that calculates the sizes of all the subdirectories beneath a specified root directory. This might be useful if, for example, you wanted to locate the biggest files and directories in order to free up disk space by archiving or deleting them.

Navigating through subdirectories creates an interesting programming problem. When you begin searching for the presence of subdirectories, you have no idea whether you will find one, none, or many. Moreover, any subdirectory you find may contain yet another level of subdirectories, each of which may contain other subdirectories and so on through many possible levels.

A Discursion into Recursion

This program needs to be able to navigate down the entire subdirectory tree to any number of levels. To be able to do this, you have to use *recursion*. Put simply, a recursive method is one that calls itself. If you aren't familiar with recursive programming, see "Recursion Made Simple" on page 224.

In the program *file_info.rb*, the processfiles method is recursive:

file_info.rb

```
def processfiles( aDir )
    totalbytes = 0
    Dir.foreach( aDir ){
    |f|
    mypath = "#{aDir}\\#{f}"
    s = ""
    if File.directory?(mypath) then
        if f != '.' and f != '..' then
        bytes_in_dir = processfiles(mypath)      # <==== recurse!
        puts( "<DIR> --->
            #{mypath} contains [#{bytes_in_dir/1024}] KB" )
    end
    else
        filesize = File.size(mypath)
        totalbytes += filesize
        puts ( "#{mypath} : #{filesize/1024}K" )
    end
    }
    $dirsize += totalbytes
    return totalbytes
end
```

You will see that when the method is first called, toward the bottom of the source code, it is passed the name of a directory in the variable dirname:

```
processfiles( dirname )
```

I've already assigned the parent of the current directory, given by two dots:

```
dirname = ".."
```

If you are running this program in its original location (that is, the location to which it is extracted from this book's source code archive), this will reference the directory containing the subdirectories of all the sample code files. Alternatively, you could assign the name of some directory on your hard disk to the variable, dirname. If you do this, don't specify a directory containing huge numbers of files and directories (on Windows, *C:\Program Files* would not be a good choice, and *C:* would be even worse!) because the program would then take quite some time to execute.

Let's take a closer look at the code in the processfiles method. Once again, I use Dir.foreach to find all the files in the current directory and pass each file, f, one at a time, to be handled by the code in a block between curly brackets. If f is a directory and is not the current one ('.') or its parent directory ('..'), then I pass the full path of the directory back to the processfiles method:

```
if File.directory?(mypath) then
    if f != '.' and f != '..' then
        bytes_in_dir = processfiles(mypath)
```

If f is not a directory but just an ordinary data file, I find its size in bytes with File.size and assign this to the variable filesize:

```
filesize = File.size(mypath)
```

As each successive file, f, is processed by the block of code, its size is calculated, and this value is added to the variable totalbytes:

```
totalbytes += filesize
```

Once every file in the current directory has been passed into the block, totalbytes will be equal to the total size of all the files in the directory.

However, I need to calculate the bytes in all the subdirectories too. Because the method is recursive, this is done automatically. Remember that when the code between curly brackets in the processfiles method determines that the current file, f, is a directory, it passes this directory name back to *itself*—the processfiles method.

Let's imagine that you first call processfiles with the *C:\test* directory. At some point, the variable f is assigned the name of one of its subdirectories, say, *C:\test\dir_a*. Now this subdirectory is passed back to processfiles. No further directories are found in *C:\test\dir_a*, so processfiles simply calculates the sizes of all the files in this subdirectory. When it finishes calculating these files, the processfiles method comes to an end and returns the number of bytes in the current directory, totalbytes, to whichever bit of code called the method in the first place:

```
return totalbytes
```

In this case, it was this bit of code inside the processfiles method that recursively called the processfiles method:

```
bytes_in_dir = processfiles(mypath)
```

So, when processfiles finishes processing the files in the subdirectory, *C:\test\dir_a*, it returns the total size of all the files found there, and this is assigned to the bytes_in_dir variable. The processfiles method now carries on where it left off (that is, it continues from the point at which it called itself to deal with the subdirectory) by processing the files in the original directory, *C:\test*.

No matter how many levels of subdirectories this method encounters, the fact that it calls itself whenever it finds a directory ensures that it automatically travels down every directory pathway it finds, calculating the total bytes in each.

One final thing to note is that the values assigned to variables declared inside the processfiles method will change back to their "previous" values as each level of recursion completes. So, the totalbytes variable will first contain the size of *C:\test\test_a\test_b*, then of *C:\test\test_a*, and finally of *C:\test*. To keep a running total of the combined sizes of all the directories, you need to assign values to a variable declared *outside* the method. Here I use the global variable $dirsize for this purpose, adding to it the value of totalbytes calculated for each subdirectory processed:

```
$dirsize += totalbytes
```

Incidentally, although a byte may be a convenient unit of measurement for very small files, it is generally better to describe larger files in kilobyte sizes and very large files or directories in megabytes. To change bytes to kilobytes or to change kilobytes to megabytes, you need to divide by 1,024. To change bytes to megabytes, divide by 1,048,576. The last line of code in my program does these calculations and displays the results in a formatted string using Ruby's printf method:

```
printf( "Size of this directory and subdirectories is
    #{$dirsize} bytes,
    #{$dirsize/1024}K, %0.02fMB",
    "#{$dirsize/1048576.0}" )
```

Notice that I have embedded the formatting placeholder `"%0.02fMB"` in the first string, and I have added a second string following a comma: `"#{$dirsize/1048576.0}"`. The second string calculates the directory size in megabytes, and this value is then substituted for the placeholder in the first string. The placeholder's formatting option `"%0.02f"` ensures that the megabyte value is shown as a floating-point number, `"f"`, with two decimal places, `"0.02"`.

Sorting by Size

Currently this program prints the file and directory names and their sizes in alphabetical order. But I am more interested in their *relative* sizes. It would, therefore, be more useful if the files were sorted by size rather than by name.

To be able to sort the files, you need some way of storing a complete list of all file sizes. One obvious way of doing this would be to add the file sizes to an array. In *file_info2.rb*, I create an empty array, $files, and each time a file is processed, I append its size to the array:

file_info2.rb

```
$files << fsize
```

I can then sort the file sizes to display low to high values or (by sorting and then reversing the array) to display from high to low values:

```
$files.sort          # sort low to high
$files.sort.reverse  # sort high to low
```

The only trouble with this is that I now end up with an array of file sizes without the associated filenames. A better solution would be to use a Hash instead of an Array. I've done this in *file_info3.rb*. First, I create two empty Hashes:

file_info3.rb

```
$dirs = {}
$files = {}
```

Now, when the processfiles method encounters a directory, it adds a new entry to the $dirs Hash using the full directory path, mypath, as the key and using the directory size, dsize, as the value:

```
$dirs[mypath] = dsize
```

Key-value pairs are similarly added to the $files hash. When the entire structure of subdirectories and files has been processed by recursive calls to the processfiles method, the $dirs hash variable will contain key-value pairs of directory names and sizes, and the $files hash will contain key-value pairs of file names and sizes.

All that remains now is for these hashes to be sorted and displayed. The standard sort method for a Hash sorts the keys, not the values. I want to sort the values (sizes), not the keys (names). To do this, I have defined a custom sort method (refer to Chapters 4 and 5 for guidance on defining custom comparisons using <=>):

```
$files.sort{|a,b| a[1]<=>b[1]}
```

Here the sort method converts the $files Hash into nested arrays of [key,value] pairs and passes two of these, a and b, into the block between curly brackets. The second item (at index [1]) of each [key,value] pair provides the value. The sorting itself is done on the value using Ruby's <=> comparison method. The end result is that this program now displays first a list of files in ascending order (by size) and then a similarly sorted list of directories. This is an example of its output:

```
..\ch19\blog\app\models\post.rb : 36 bytes
..\ch19\say_hello.html.erb : 41 bytes
..\ch13\testfile.txt : 57 bytes
..\ch01\2helloname.rb : 67 bytes
..\ch9\div_by_zero.rb : 71 bytes
..\ch12\test.rb : 79 bytes
..\ch4\dir_array.rb : 81 bytes
..\ch3\for_to.rb : 89 bytes
```

DIGGING DEEPER

Recursion is an important programming technique that can, however, be quite difficult to understand. Here I will explain recursion one step at a time.

Recursion Made Simple

If you've never used recursion before, the recursive "directory-walking" methods in this chapter may need a little explanation. To clarify how recursion works, let's look at a much simpler example. Load the *recursion.rb* program:

recursion.rb

```
$outercount = 0

def addup( aNum )
    aNum += 1
    $outercount +=1
    puts( "aNum is #{aNum}, $outercount is #{$outercount}" )
    if $outercount < 3 then
        addup( aNum )            #<= recursive call to addup method
    end
    puts("At END: aNum is #{aNum},outercount is #{$outercount}")
end

addup( 0 )                       #<= This is where it all begins
```

This contains the recursive method, addup, whose sole purpose in life is to count from 1 to 3. The addup method receives an integer value as an incoming argument, aNum.

```
addup( aNum )
```

There is also global variable, $outercount, which lives "outside" the addup method. Whenever the addup method executes, 1 is added to aNum, and 1 is also added to $outercount. Then, just so long as $outercount is less than 3, the code inside the addup method calls the same method (addup) all over again, passing to it the new value of aNum:

```
if $outercount < 3 then
    addup( aNum )
end
```

Let's follow what happens. The process is started off by calling addup with the value 0:

```
addup( 0 )
```

The addup method adds 1 to both aNum and $outercount, so both variables now have the value 1. The test ($outercount < 3) evaluates to true, so aNum is passed as an argument to addup. Once again, 1 is added to both variables, so aNum is now 2, and $outercount is also 2. Now aNum is once more passed to addup. Yet again 1 is added to both variables, giving each the value 3. This time, however, the test condition fails since $outercount is no longer less than 3. So, the code that calls addup is skipped, and you arrive at the last line in the method:

```
puts( "At END: aNum is #{aNum}, outercount is #{$outercount}" )
```

This prints out the values of aNum and $outercount, which, as you expect, are both 3. Having arrived at the end of this method, the "flow of control" moves back to the line of code immediately following the code that originally called the method. Here, the line of code that called the addup method happens to be inside the method itself. Here it is:

```
addup( aNum )
```

And the first executable line that follows this is (once again) the final line of the method that prints out the values of the two variables:

```
puts( "At END: aNum is #{aNum}, outercount is #{$outercount}" )
```

So, you have gone back to an earlier "point of execution"—the point at which you recursively called the addup method. At that time, the value of aNum was 2, and that is its value *now*. If this seems confusing, just try to think what would have happened if aNum had been 2 and then you called some other, unrelated method. On returning from that other method, aNum would, of course, still have had the value 2. That's all that's happened here. The only difference is that this method happened to call *itself* rather than some other method.

Once again, the method exits, and control returns to the next executable line following the code that called the method, and aNum's value has taken another step back into its own history—it now has the value 1. The $outercount variable, however, lives *outside* the method and is unaffected by recursion, so it is still 3.

If you have access to a visual debugger, this entire process will become much clearer: You can place a breakpoint on line 9 (if $outercount < 3 then), add aNum and $outercount to the Watch window, and repeatedly step into the code after you hit the breakpoint.

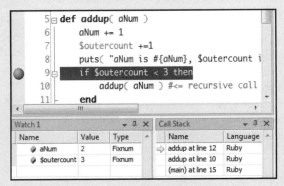

This screenshot shows the recursion program being debugged visually in the IDE Ruby In Steel. I can step through the source code, use the call stack to keep track of the current "level" of recursion (how many times the addup method has been called), and use the Watch window to monitor the current values of the variables.

14

YAML

At some point, most desktop applications are going to want to save and read structured data to and from disk. You've already seen how to read and write data using simple IO routines such as `gets` and `puts`. But how would you go about saving and restoring data from, say, lists of mixed object types? One simple way of doing this with Ruby is by using YAML.

NOTE *YAML is an acronym that is (debatably) either short for Yet Another Markup Language or (recursively) for YAML Ain't Markup Language.*

Converting to YAML

YAML defines a serialization (data-saving) format that stores information as human-readable text. YAML can be used with a variety of programming languages; in order to use it in Ruby, your code needs access to routines from Ruby's *yaml.rb* file. Generally, this would be done by loading or "requiring" the file at the top of a code unit like this:

```
require "yaml"
```

Having done this, you will have access to a variety of methods to convert Ruby objects to the YAML format so that they can write their data to a file. Subsequently, you will be able to read back this saved data and use it to reconstruct Ruby objects. To convert an object to YAML format, you can use the to_yaml method. This will convert standard object types such as strings, integers, arrays, hashes, and so on. For example, this is how you would convert a string:

to_yaml1.rb
```
"hello world".to_yaml
```

And this is how you would convert an array:

```
["a1", "a2" ].to_yaml
```

This is the YAML format that you would obtain as a result of this array conversion:

```
---
- a1
- a2
```

Notice the three dashes that define the start of a new YAML "document" and the single dash that defines each new element in a list. In YAML terms, a document is not a separate file on disk but a separate YAML definition; one disk file may contain many YAML documents. For more information on the YAML format, refer to "Digging Deeper" on page 237.

You can also convert objects of nonstandard types to YAML. For example, let's suppose you create this class and object:

to_yaml2.rb
```
class MyClass
    def initialize( anInt, aString )
        @myint = anInt
        @mystring =aString
    end
end

ob1 = MyClass.new( 100, "hello world" ).to_yaml
```

The YAML representation of this object will be preceded by the text !ruby/object: followed by the class name, the names of variables with a colon appended (but minus the @), and their values, one per line:

```
--- !ruby/object:MyClass
myint: 100
mystring: hello world
```

If you want to print out the YAML representation of an object, you can use the method y(), which is a sort of YAML equivalent of the familiar p() method used to inspect and print normal Ruby objects:

yaml_test1.rb

```
y( ['Bert', 'Fred', 'Mary'] )
```

This displays the following:

```
---
- Bert
- Fred
- Mary
```

You could similarly display a hash:

```
y({ 'fruit' => 'banana', :vegetable => 'cabbage', 'number' => 3 })
```

in which case each key-value pair is placed onto a new line:

```
---
fruit: banana
:vegetable: cabbage
number: 3
```

NOTE *The ordering of hash elements may differ according to which version of Ruby you are using (see Chapter 4). It is best to assume no intrinsic order when working with a hash.*

Or you could display your own "custom" objects:

```
t = Treasure.new( 'magic lamp', 500 )
y( t )
```

This displays data formatted, as in the earlier example where I used to_yaml, with the class name at the top and with pairs of variable names and values on successive lines. This is the YAML representation of a Treasure object containing the instance variables @name and @value:

```
--- !ruby/object:Treasure
name: magic lamp
value: 500
```

You can even use y() to display quite complex objects such as nested arrays:

yaml_test2.rb

```
arr1 =    [    ["The Groovesters", "Groovy Tunes", 12 ],
               [  "Dolly Parton", "Greatest Hits", 38 ]
          ]
y( arr1 )
```

This is the YAML representation of arr1:

```
---
- - The Groovesters
  - Groovy Tunes
  - 12
- - Dolly Parton
  - Greatest Hits
  - 38
```

Here is another example of an array containing objects of user-defined types:

```
class CD
    def initialize( anArtist, aName, theNumTracks )
        @artist = anArtist
        @name   = aName
        @numtracks    = theNumTracks
    end
end

arr2 = [CD.new("The Beasts", "Beastly Tunes", 22),
        CD.new("The Strolling Bones","Songs For Senior Citizens",38)
]

y( arr2 )
```

This outputs the following YAML:

```
---
- !ruby/object:CD
  artist: The Beasts
  name: Beastly Tunes
  numtracks: 22
- !ruby/object:CD
  artist: The Strolling Bones
  name: Songs For Senior Citizens
  numtracks: 38
```

Nested Sequences

When related sequences of data (such as arrays) are nested inside other sequences of data, this relationship is indicated by indentation. So, for example, let's suppose you have this array declared in Ruby:

nested_arrays.rb

```
arr = [1,[2,3,[4,5,6,[7,8,9,10],"end3"],"end2"],"end1"]
```

When rendered as YAML (for example, by y(arr)), this becomes as follows:

```
---
- 1
- - 2
  - 3
  - - 4
    - 5
    - 6
    - - 7
      - 8
      - 9
      - 10
    - end3
  - end2
- end1
```

Saving YAML Data

Another handy way of turning your Ruby objects into YAML format is provided by the dump method. At its simplest, this converts your Ruby data into YAML format and "dumps" it into a string:

yaml_dump1.rb

```
arr = ["fred", "bert", "mary"]
yaml_arr = YAML.dump( arr )
    # yaml_arr is now: "--- \n- fred\n- bert\n- mary\n"
```

More usefully, the dump method can take a second argument, which is some kind of IO object, typically a file. You can open a file and dump data to it:

yaml_dump2.rb

```
f = File.open( 'friends.yml', 'w' )
YAML.dump( ["fred", "bert", "mary"], f )
f.close
```

Or you can open the file (or some other type of IO object) and pass this into an associated block:

```
File.open( 'morefriends.yml', 'w' ){ |friendsfile|
    YAML.dump( ["sally", "agnes", "john" ], friendsfile )
}
```

In each case, the YAML representation of the data from the array will be saved, as plaintext, into the specified file. For example, when the previous code executes, it writes this text into the *morefriends.yml* file:

morefriends.yml

```
---
- sally
- agnes
- john
```

If you use a block, the file will be closed automatically on exiting the block; otherwise, you should explicitly close the file using the close method. You can also use a block in a similar way to open a file and read in YAML data:

```
File.open( 'morefriends.yml' ){ |f|
    $arr= YAML.load(f)
}
```

Assuming *morefriends.yml* contains the data saved earlier, once it is loaded and assigned to the global variable $arr in the block shown earlier, $arr will contain this array of strings:

```
["sally", "agnes", "john"]
```

Omitting Variables on Saving

If, for some reason, you want to omit some instance variables when serializing objects, you can do so by defining a method named to_yaml_properties. In the body of this method, place an array of strings. Each string should match the name of the instance variable to be saved. Any variables that are not specified will not be saved. Take a look at this example:

limit_y.rb

```
class Yclass
    def initialize(aNum, aStr, anArray)
        @num = aNum
        @str = aStr
        @arr = anArray
    end

    def to_yaml_properties
        ["@num", "@arr"]      #<= @str will not be saved!
    end
end
```

Here to_yaml_properties limits the variables that will be saved when you call YAML.dump to @num and @arr. The string variable, @str, will not be saved. If you want to reconstruct the objects based on the saved YAML data, it is your responsibility to ensure that any "missing" variables are either not needed (in which case they may be ignored) or, if they are needed, that they are initialized with some meaningful value.

```
ob = Yclass.new( 100, "fred", [1,2,3] )
    # ...creates object with @num=100, @str="fred", @arr=[1,2,3]

yaml_ob = YAML.dump( ob )
    #...dumps to YAML only the @num and @arr data (omits @str)

ob2 = YAML.load( yaml_ob )
    #...creates ob2 from dumped data with @num=100, @arr=[1,2,3]
    # but without @str
```

Multiple Documents, One File

Earlier, I mentioned that three dashes are used to mark the start of a new YAML section known as a *document*. For example, let's assume you want to save two arrays, arr1 and arr2, to a file, *multidoc.yml*. Here arr1 is an array containing two nested arrays, and arr2 is an array containing two CD objects:

multi_docs.rb

```
arr1 = [   ["The Groovesters", "Groovy Tunes", 12 ],
           [  "Dolly Parton", "Greatest Hits", 38 ]
       ]

arr2 = [ CD.new("Gribbit Mcluskey", "Fab Songs", 22),
         CD.new("Wayne Snodgrass", "Singalong-a-Snodgrass", 24)
       ]
```

This is my routine to dump these arrays to YAML and write them to a file (as explained in Chapter 13, the 'w' argument causes the file to be opened for writing):

```
File.open( 'multidoc.yml', 'w' ){ |f|
    YAML.dump( arr1, f )
    YAML.dump( arr2, f )
}
```

If you now look at the file *multidoc.yml*, you'll see that the data has been saved as two separate "documents," each one beginning with three dashes:

```
---
- - The Groovesters
  - Groovy Tunes
  - 12
- - Dolly Parton
  - Greatest Hits
  - 38
---
- !ruby/object:CD
  artist: Gribbit Mcluskey
  name: Fab Songs
  numtracks: 22
```

```
-  !ruby/object:CD
   artist: Wayne Snodgrass
   name: Singalong-a-Snodgrass
   numtracks: 24
```

Now, I need to find a way of reconstructing these arrays by reading in the data as two documents. This is where the `load_documents` method comes to the rescue. The `load_documents` method calls a block and passes to it each consecutive document. Here is an example of how to use this method in order to reconstruct two arrays (placed inside another array, `$new_arr`) from the two YAML documents:

```
File.open( 'multidoc.yml' ) {|f|
   YAML.load_documents( f ) { |doc|
     $new_arr << doc
   }
}
```

You can verify that `$new_arr` has been initialized with the two arrays by executing the following:

```
p( $new_arr )
```

This displays an array containing the loaded data in two nested arrays:

```
[[["The Groovesters", "Groovy Tunes", 12], ["Dolly Parton", "Greatest Hits",
38]], [#<CD:0x2c30e98 @artist="Gribbit Mcluskey", @name="Fab Songs",
@numtracks=22>, #<CD:0x2c30ad8 @artist="Wayne Snodgrass", @name="Singalong-a-
Snodgrass", @numtracks=24>]]
```

Because this is a bit unmanageable, you might prefer to display each of the nested arrays individually using an index into the outer array:

```
p( $new_arr[0] )
p( $new_arr[1] )
```

The previous assumes that you know, in advance, the number of nested arrays available. Alternatively, here's a more generic way of doing the same thing, using the each method to pass all available items into a block; this works with any number of arrays:

```
$new_arr.each{ |arr| p( arr ) }
```

A YAML Database

For an example of a slightly more complicated application that saves and loads data in YAML format, take a look at the *cd_db.rb* sample program. This implements a simple CD database. It defines three types of CD objects: a basic CD that contains data on the name, artist, and number of tracks; and two more specialized descendants, PopCD, which adds data on the genre (for example, rock or country), and ClassicalCD, which adds data on the conductor and composer:

cd_db.rb

```ruby
class CD
    def initialize( arr )
        @name      = arr[0]
        @artist    = arr[1]
        @numtracks = arr[2]
    end

    def getdetails
        return[@name, @artist, @numtracks]
    end
end

class PopCD < CD

    def initialize( arr )
        super( arr   )
        @genre = arr[3]
    end

    def getdetails
        return( super << @genre )
    end
end

class ClassicalCD < CD
    def initialize( arr )
        super( arr )
        @conductor = arr[3]
        @composer  = arr[4]
    end

    def getdetails
        return( super << @conductor << @composer )
    end
end
```

When the program is run, the user can enter data to create new CD objects of any of these three types. There is also an option to save data to disk. When the application is run subsequently, the existing data is reloaded.

The data itself is organized very simply (trivially even) in the code, with the data for each object being read into an array before the object itself is created. The whole database of CD objects is saved into the global variable $cd_arr, and this is written to disk and reloaded into memory using YAML methods:

```ruby
def saveDB
    File.open( $fn, 'w' ) {
        |f|
        f.write($cd_arr.to_yaml)
    }
end
```

```
def loadDB
    input_data = File.read( $fn )
    $cd_arr = YAML::load( input_data )
end
```

Bear in mind that this program has been written for simplicity rather than beauty. In a real-world application, you would, I am sure, want to create somewhat more elegant data structures to manage your Dolly Parton collection!

Adventures in YAML

As one final example of using YAML, I've provided an elementary framework for an adventure game (*gamesave_y.rb*). This creates some Treasure objects and some Room objects. The Treasure objects are put "into" the Room objects (that is, they are placed into arrays contained by the Rooms), and the Room objects are then put into a Map object. This has the effect of constructing a moderately complex data structure in which an object of one type (a Map) contains an arbitrary number of objects of another type (Rooms), each of which may contain zero or more objects of yet other types (Treasures).

At first sight, finding a way of storing this entire network of mixed object types to disk and reconstructing that network at a later stage might look like a programming nightmare. In fact, thanks to the serialization capabilities supplied by Ruby's YAML library, saving and restoring this data could hardly be easier. This is because serialization relieves you of the chore of saving each object one by one. Instead, you have to "dump" only the top-level object; here, that is the Map object, mymap.

When this is done, any objects that the top-level object "contains" (such as Rooms) or that the *contained* objects themselves contain (such as Treasures) are automatically saved for you. They can then be reconstructed just by loading all the saved data in a single operation and assigning it to the "top-level" object (here the map):

gamesave_y.rb
```
# Save mymap
File.open( 'game.yml', 'w' ){ |f|
    YAML.dump( mymap, f )
}

# Reload mymap
File.open( 'game.yml' ){ |f|
    mymap = YAML.load(f)
}
```

The full code of this program is too long to show here, so I suggest you try the program supplied in the source code archive in order to appreciate how simple it is to save and load a fairly complex data structure with YAML.

DIGGING DEEPER

This section summarizes the structure of a YAML datafile and explains how to save nested hashes in YAML format.

A Brief Guide to YAML

As I mentioned earlier, YAML stores information in the form of chunks of text known as *documents* containing *sequences* of data. Each document begins with three hyphens (---), and each individual element in a list begins with a single hyphen (-) character. Here, for example, is a YAML datafile comprising one document and two list items:

```
---
- artist: The Groovesters
  name: Groovy Tunes
  numtracks: 12
- artist: Dolly Parton
  name: Greatest Hits
  numtracks: 38
```

In the previous example, you can see that each list item consists of two parts: a name such as artist: (which is the same in each list item) and a piece of data to its right, such as Dolly Parton, which may vary for each list item. These items are like the key-value pairs in a Ruby hash. YAML refers to key-value lists as *maps*.

The following is a YAML document containing a list of two items, each of which contains three items; in other words, it is the YAML representation of an array containing two three-item "nested" arrays:

```
---
- - The Groovesters
  - Groovy Tunes
  - 12
- - Dolly Parton
  - Greatest Hits
  - 38
```

Now let's see how YAML would deal with nested hashes. Consider this hash:

hash_to_yaml.rb
```
hsh = { :friend1 => 'mary',
        :friend2 => 'sally',
        :friend3 => 'gary',
        :morefriends => { :chap_i_met_in_a_bar => 'simon',
                          :girl_next_door => 'wanda'
                        }
}
```

As you've already seen, a hash is quite naturally represented in YAML as a list of key-value pairs. However, in the example shown previously, the *key* :morefriends is associated with a nested hash as its *value*. How does YAML represent that? It turns out that, as with arrays (see "Nested Sequences" on page 231), it simply indents the nested hash:

```
:friend1: mary
:friend2: sally
:friend3: gary
:morefriends:
    :chap_i_met_in_a_bar: simon
    :girl_next_door: wanda
```

NOTE   *For in-depth information on YAML, see* http://www.yaml.org/.

The YAML libraries supplied with Ruby are quite large and complex, and many more methods are available than have been described in this chapter. However, you should now have enough of an understanding of YAML to use it to good effect in your own programs. You may explore the outer reaches of the YAML libraries at your leisure. It turns out, though, that YAML is not the only way of serializing data in Ruby. You'll be looking at another way in the next chapter.

15

MARSHAL

An alternative way of saving and loading data is provided by Ruby's Marshal library. This has a similar set of methods to YAML to enable you to save and load data to and from disk.

Saving and Loading Data

Compare the following program with *yaml_dump2.rb* from the previous chapter:

marshal1.rb

```
f = File.open( 'friends.sav', 'w' )
Marshal.dump( ["fred", "bert", "mary"], f )
f.close

File.open( 'morefriends.sav', 'w' ){ |friendsfile|
    Marshal.dump( ["sally", "agnes", "john" ], friendsfile )
}

File.open( 'morefriends.sav' ){ |f|
    $arr= Marshal.load(f)
}
```

```
myfriends = Marshal.load(File.open( 'friends.sav' ))
morefriends = Marshal.load(File.open( 'morefriends.sav' ))

p( myfriends )      #=> ["fred", "bert", "mary"]
p( morefriends )    #=> ["sally", "agnes", "john"]
p( $arr )           #=> ["sally", "agnes", "john"]
```

The two programs are pretty much identical except that each occurrence of YAML (as in YAML.dump and YAML.load) has been replaced with Marshal. Moreover, Marshal is "built in" to Ruby as standard, so you don't have to require any extra files in order to use it.

If you look at the data files produced (such as *friends.sav*), you will immediately see that there is a major difference, however. Whereas YAML files are in plaintext format, Marshal files are in binary format. So although you may be able to read *some* characters, such as those in the strings, you won't simply be able to load the saved data and modify it in a text editor.

As with YAML, most data structures can be automatically serialized using Marshal just by dumping the top-level object and loading it when you want to reconstruct all the objects beneath it. For an example, take a look at my little adventure game program. In the previous chapter, I explained how to save and restore a Map containing Rooms containing Treasures just by dumping and loading the Map object, mymap (see *gamesave_y.rb* on page 236). You can do the same using Marshal instead of YAML:

gamesave_m.rb
```
File.open( 'game.sav', 'w' ){ |f|
    Marshal.dump( mymap, f )    # save data to file
}

File.open( 'game.sav' ){ |f|
    mymap = Marshal.load(f)     # reload saved data from file
}
```

Objects cannot be so easily serialized in a few special circumstances. These exceptions are documented in the code of Ruby's Marshal module (*marshal.c*), which states, "If the objects to be dumped include bindings, procedure or method objects, instances of class IO, or singleton objects, a TypeError will be raised." I'll show an example of this while discussing how you might go about saving singletons with marshaling.

Omitting Variables on Saving

As with YAML serialization, it is possible to limit the variables that are saved when serializing using Marshal. In YAML, you did this by writing a method called to_yaml_properties. With Marshal, you need to write a method named marshal_dump. In the code of this method you should create an array containing the *actual variables* to be saved (in YAML, you created an array of *strings* containing the variable *names*).

This is an example:

```
def marshal_dump
    [@variable_a, @variable_b]
end
```

Another difference is that, with YAML, you were able simply to load the data in order to re-create an object. With Marshal, you need to add a special method called marshal_load to which any loaded data is passed as an argument. This will be invoked automatically when you call Marshal.load, and it will be passed the data in the form of an array. The previously saved objects can be parsed from this array. You can also assign values to any variables that were omitted (such as @some_other_variable here) when the data was saved:

```
def marshal_load(data)
    @variable_a = data[0]
    @variable_b = data[1]
    @some_other_variable = "a default value"
end
```

Here is a complete program that saves and restores the variables @num and @arr but omits @str:

limit_m.rb

```
class Mclass
    def initialize(aNum, aStr, anArray)
        @num = aNum
        @str = aStr
        @arr = anArray
    end

    def marshal_dump
        [@num, @arr]
    end

    def marshal_load(data)
        @num = data[0]
        @arr = data[1]
        @str = "default"
    end
end

ob = Mclass.new( 100, "fred", [1,2,3] )
p( ob )
#=> #<Mclass:0x2be7278 @num=100, @str="fred", @arr=[1, 2, 3]>

marshal_data = Marshal.dump( ob )
ob2 = Marshal.load( marshal_data )
p( ob2 )
#=> #<Mclass:0x2be70e0 @num=100, @str="default", @arr=[1, 2, 3]>
```

Note that although the serialization is done here in memory, the same techniques can be used when using Marshal to save and load objects to and from disk.

Saving Singletons

Let's take a look at a concrete example of a problem mentioned earlier, namely, the inability to use marshaling to save and load a singleton. In *singleton_m.rb* I have created an instance of Object, ob, and then extended it in the form of a singleton class that is given the additional method, xxx:

singleton_m.rb
```
ob = Object.new

class << ob
    def xxx( aStr )
        @x = aStr
    end
end
```

The problem arises when I try to save this data to disk using `Marshal.dump`. Ruby displays an error message: "singleton can't be dumped (TypeError)."

YAML and Singletons

Before considering how you might deal with this, let's briefly take a look at how YAML would cope in this situation. The program *singleton_y.rb* tries to save the singleton that I created a moment ago using `YAML.dump`, and, unlike `Marshal.dump`, it succeeds—well, sort of:

singleton_y.rb
```
# YAML version of singleton-save
ob.xxx( "hello world" )

File.open( 'test.yml', 'w' ){ |f|
    YAML.dump( ob, f )
}

ob.xxx( "new string" )

File.open( 'test.yml' ){ |f|
    ob = YAML.load(f)
}
```

If you look at the YAML file that is saved, *test.yml*, you'll find that it defines an instance of a plain-vanilla Object to which a variable named x is appended that has the string value `hello world`:

```
--- !ruby/object
x: hello world
```

That's all well and good. However, when you reconstruct the object by loading the saved data, the new ob will be a standard instance of Object, which happens to contain an additional instance variable, @x. Since it is no longer the original singleton, this ob will not have access to any of the methods (here the xxx method) defined in that singleton. So, although YAML serialization is more permissive about saving and loading data items that were created in a singleton, it does not automatically re-create the singleton itself when the saved data is reloaded.

Marshal and Singletons

Let's now return to the Marshal version of this program. The first thing I need to do is find a way of at least making it save and load data items. Once I've done that, I'll try to figure out how to reconstruct singletons on reloading.

To save specific data items, I can define the marshal_dump and marshal_load methods as explained earlier (see *limit_m.rb*). These should normally be defined in a class from which the singleton derives, *not* in the singleton itself. This is because, as already explained, when the data is saved, it will be stored as a representation of the class from which the singleton derives. This means that although you could indeed add marshal_dump to a singleton derived from class X, when you reconstruct the object, you will be loading data for an object of the generic type X, not of the specific singleton instance.

This code creates a singleton, ob, of class X, saves its data, and then re-creates a generic object of class X:

singleton_m2.rb
```
class X
    def marshal_dump
        [@x]
    end

    def marshal_load(data)
        @x = data[0]
    end
end

ob = X.new

class << ob
    def xxx( aStr )
        @x = aStr
    end
end

ob.xxx( "hello" )
p( ob )

File.open( 'test2.sav', 'w' ){ |f|
    Marshal.dump( ob, f )
}

ob.xxx( "new string" )
p( ob )
```

```
File.open( 'test2.sav' ){ |f|
    ob = Marshal.load(f)
}

p( ob )
```

The code here uses `Marshal.dump` to save an object, `ob`, of class X and then calls the singleton method, `xxx`, to assign a different string to the `@x` variable before reloading the saved data using `Marshal.load` and using this data to re-create the object. The contents of `ob` are displayed using `p()` before it is saved, then again after a new string is assigned to it, and finally once again when it is reloaded. This lets you verify that `@x` is assigned the value that was saved when the reloaded object is reconstructed:

```
#<X:0x2b86cc0 @x="hello">         # value when saved
#<X:0x2b86cc0 @x="new string">    # new value then assigned
#<X:0x2b869f0 @x="hello">         # value after saved data loaded
```

In terms of the data it contains, the object saved and the object reloaded are identical. However, the object that is reloaded knows nothing about the singleton class. The method `xxx` that the singleton class contains forms no part of the reconstructed object. The following, then, would fail:

```
ob.xxx( "this fails" )
```

This Marshal version of the code is equivalent to the YAML version given earlier. It saves and restores the data correctly, but it does not reconstruct the singleton. How, then, is it possible to reconstruct a singleton from saved data? There are, no doubt, many clever and subtle ways in which this might be accomplished. I shall, however, opt for a very simple technique:

singleton_m3.rb
```
FILENAME = 'test2.sav'

class X
    def marshal_dump
        [@x]
    end

    def marshal_load(data)
        @x = data[0]
    end
end

ob = X.new

# a) if File exists, load data into ob - a generic X object
if File.exists?(FILENAME) then
    File.open(FILENAME){ |f|
        ob = Marshal.load(f)
    }
else
    puts( "Saved data can't be found" )
end
```

```
# b) Now transform ob in a singleton
class << ob
    def xxx=( aStr )
        @x = aStr
    end

    def xxx
        return @x
    end
end
```

This code first checks whether a file containing the saved data can be found. (This sample has been kept deliberately simple—in a real application you would of course need to write some exception-handling code to deal with the possibility of reading in invalid data.) If the file is found, the data is loaded into an object of the generic X type.

Only when this has been done is this object "transformed" into a singleton in the usual way. In other words, the object is loaded, and then the code beginning class << ob executes (simply because the singleton-creation code occurs after the loading code and so is executed in sequence by the Ruby interpreter). This provides the object with the additional xxx singleton method. You can then save the new data back to disk and reload and re-create the modified singleton, as explained earlier, at a later stage:

```
if ob.xxx == "hello" then
    ob.xxx = "goodbye"
else
    ob.xxx = "hello"
end

File.open( FILENAME, 'w' ){ |f|
    Marshal.dump( ob, f )
}
```

If you wanted to save and load singletons in a real application, the singleton "reconstruction" code could, naturally, be given its own method so that you don't have to rely upon its position in your code as in the previous example.

singleton_m4.rb
```
def makeIntoSingleton( someOb )
    class << someOb
        def xxx=( aStr )
            @x = aStr
        end

        def xxx
            return @x
        end
    end
    return someOb
end
```

DIGGING DEEPER

If you attempt to load data that was saved with a different version of the Marshal library you may run into problems. Here you will learn how to verify the version of Marshal.

Marshal Version Numbers

The embedded documentation of the Marshal library (a C language file named *marshal.c*) states the following: "Marshaled data has major and minor version numbers stored along with the object information. In normal use, marshaling can only load data written with the same major version number and an equal or lower minor version number."

This clearly raises the potential problem that the format of data files created by marshaling may be incompatible with the current Ruby application. The Marshal version number, incidentally, is not dependent on the Ruby version number, so it is not safe to make assumptions of compatibility based solely on the Ruby version.

This possibility of incompatibility means you should always check the version number of the saved data before attempting to load it. But how do you get hold of the version number? Once again, the embedded documentation provides a clue. It states, "You can extract the version by reading the first two bytes of marshaled data."

Ruby 1.8 provides this example:

```
str = Marshal.dump("thing")
RUBY_VERSION        #=> "1.8.0"
str[0]              #=> 4
str[1]              #=> 8
```

Okay, so let's try this in a fully worked piece of code. Here goes:

version_m.rb
```
x = Marshal.dump( "hello world" )
print( "Marshal version: #{x[0]}:#{x[1]}\n" )
```

In the previous code, x is a string, and its first two bytes are the major and minor version numbers. In Ruby 1.8, this prints out the following:

```
Marshal version: 4:8
```

In Ruby 1.9, however, no numbers are displayed. This is because the first two bytes are returned as integers in Ruby 1.8 but as strings in Ruby 1.9. These strings are not necessarily printable. You can see this quite simply by using the p() method to display the elements at index 0 and index 1 of the array x:

```
p( x[0] )   #=> 4 (Ruby 1.8)    "\x04" (Ruby 1.9)
p( x[1] )   #=> 8 (Ruby 1.8)    "\b"   (Ruby 1.9)
```

The strings returned by Ruby 1.9 may be shown either as hexadecimal values or as escape characters. Here you can see that, for Marshal version 4.8, the first value is \x04, which is the hexadecimal representation of 4, while the second value is \b, which is the escape character for the backspace that happens to have the ASCII value of 8. The ord method can be used to do the necessary conversion from string to integer. This is the Ruby 1.9 version:

```
print( "Marshal version: #{x[0].ord}:#{x[1].ord}\n" )
```

This now correctly displays the version number: 4:8. Of course, if you are using a different version of the Marshal library, the numbers displayed will be different. The Marshal library also declares two constants, MAJOR_VERSION and MINOR_VERSION, which store the version numbers of the Marshal library currently in use. So, at first sight, it looks as though it should be easy to compare the version number of saved data with the current version number.

There is just one problem: When you save data to a file on disk, the dump method takes an IO or File object, and it returns an IO (or File) object rather than a string:

version_error.rb
```
f = File.open( 'friends.sav', 'w' )
x = Marshal.dump( ["fred", "bert", "mary"], f )
f.close          #=> x is now: #<File:friends.sav (closed)>
```

If you now try to get the values of x[0] and x[1], you will receive an error message:

```
p( x[0] )
#=> Error: undefined method '[]' for #<File:friends.sav (closed)>
(NoMethodError)
```

Loading the data back from the file is no more instructive:

```
File.open( 'friends.sav' ){ |f|
    x = Marshal.load(f)
}

puts( x[0] )
puts( x[1] )
```

The two puts statements here don't (as I was naively hoping) print out the major and minor version numbers of the marshaled data; in fact, they print out the names "fred" and "bert"—that is, the two first items loaded into the array, x, from the data file, *friends.sav.*

So, how the heck can you get the version number from the saved data? I have to admit that I was forced to read my way through the C code (not my favorite activity!) in *marshal.c* and examine the hexadecimal data in a saved file to figure this out. It turns out that, just as the documentation says, "You can extract the version by reading the first two bytes of marshaled data."

However, this isn't done for you. You have to read this data explicitly, as shown here:

version_m2.rb

```
f = File.open('test2.sav')
if (RUBY_VERSION.to_f > 1.8) then
    vMajor = f.getc().ord
    vMinor = f.getc().ord
else
    vMajor = f.getc()
    vMinor = f.getc()
end
f.close
```

Here the getc method reads the next 8-bit byte from the input stream. Notice that I have once again written a test to make this compatible both with Ruby 1.8, in which getc returns a numeric character value, and with Ruby 1.9, in which getc returns a one-character string that has to be converted to an integer using ord.

My sample project, *version_m2.rb*, shows a simple way of comparing the version number of the saved data with that of the current Marshal library in order to establish whether the data formats are likely to be compatible before attempting to reload the data.

```
if vMajor == Marshal::MAJOR_VERSION then
   puts( "Major version number is compatible" )
   if vMinor == Marshal::MINOR_VERSION then
      puts( "Minor version number is compatible" )
   elsif vMinor < Marshal::MINOR_VERSION then
      puts( "Minor version is lower - old file format" )
   else
      puts( "Minor version is higher - newer file format" )
   end
else
   puts( "Major version number is incompatible" )
end
```

16

REGULAR EXPRESSIONS

Regular expressions provide you with powerful ways to find and modify patterns in text—not only short bits of text such as might be entered at a command prompt but also huge stores of text such as might be found in files on disk.

A regular expression takes the form of a pattern that is compared with a string. Regular expressions also provide the means by which you can modify strings so that, for example, you might change specific characters by putting them into uppercase, you might replace every occurrence of "Diamond" with "Ruby," or you might read in a file of programming code, extract all the comments, and write out a new documentation file containing all the comments but none of the code. You'll find out how to write a comment-extraction tool shortly. First, though, let's take a look at some very simple regular expressions.

Making Matches

Just about the simplest regular expression is a sequence of characters (such as "abc") that you want to find in a string. A regular expression to match "abc" can be created by placing those letters between two forward slash delimiters, like this: /abc/. You can test for a match using the =~ operator method like this:

regex0.rb

```
p( /abc/ =~ 'abc' )                    #=> 0
```

If a match is made, an integer representing the character position in the string is returned. If no match is made, nil is returned.

```
p( /abc/ =~ 'xyzabcxyzabc' )           #=> 3
p( /abc/ =~ 'xycab' )                  #=> nil
```

You can also specify a group of characters, between square brackets, in which case a match will be made with any one of those characters in the string. Here, for example, the first match is made with "c"; then that character's position in the string is returned:

```
p( /[abc]/ =~ 'xycba' )                #=> 2
```

Although I've used forward-slash delimiters in the previous examples, there are alternative ways of defining regular expressions: You can specifically create a new Regexp object initialized with a string, or you can precede the regular expression with %r and use custom delimiters—nonalphanumeric characters—as you can with strings (see Chapter 3). In the following example, I use curly bracket delimiters:

regex1.rb

```
regex1 = Regexp.new('^[a-z]*$')
regex2 = /^[a-z]*$/
regex3 = %r{^[a-z]*$}
```

Each of the previous examples defines a regular expression that matches an all-lowercase string (I'll explain the details of the expressions shortly). These expressions can be used to test strings like this:

```
def test( aStr, aRegEx )
    if aRegEx =~ aStr then
        puts( "All lowercase" )
    else
        puts( "Not all lowercase" )
    end
end

test( "hello", regex1 )        #=> matches: "All lowercase"
test( "hello", regex2 )        #=> matches: "All lowercase"
test( "Hello", regex3 )        #=> no match: "Not all lowercase"
```

To test for a match, you can use `if` and the `=~` operator:

```
if /def/ =~ 'abcdef'
```

The previous expression evaluates to true if a match is made (and an integer is returned); it would evaluate to false if no match were made (and nil were returned):

if_test.rb

```
RegEx = /def/
Str1  = 'abcdef'
Str2  = 'ghijkl'

if RegEx =~ Str1 then
    puts( 'true' )
else
    puts( 'false' )
end                     #=> displays: true

if RegEx =~ Str2 then
    puts( 'true' )
else
    puts( 'false' )
end                     #=> displays: false
```

Frequently, it is useful to attempt to match some expression from the very start of a string; you can use the character ^ followed by a match term to specify this. It may also be useful to make a match from the end of the string; you use the character $ preceded by a match term to specify that.

start_end1.rb

```
puts( /^a/ =~ 'abc' )       #=> 0
puts( /^b/ =~ 'abc' )       #=> nil
puts( /c$/ =~ 'abc' )       #=> 2
puts( /b$/ =~ 'abc' )       #=> nil
```

NOTE   *As mentioned previously, when a nil value is passed to print or puts in Ruby 1.9, nothing is displayed. In Ruby 1.8, nil is displayed. To be sure that nil is displayed in Ruby 1.9, use p instead of puts.*

Matching from the start or end of a string becomes more useful when it forms part of a more complex expression. Often such an expression tries to match zero or more instances of a specified pattern. The * character is used to indicate zero or more matches of the pattern that it follows. Formally, this is known as a *quantifier*. Consider this example:

start_end2.rb

```
p( /^[a-z 0-9]*$/ =~ 'well hello 123' )
```

Here, the regular expression specifies a range of characters between square brackets. This range includes all lowercase characters (a–z), all digits (0–9), and the space character (that's the space between the z and the 0 in the expression shown earlier). The ^ character means the match must be made from the start of the string, the * character after the range means that zero or more matches with the characters in the range must be made, and the $ character means that the matches must be made right up to the end of the string. In other words, this pattern will only match a string containing lowercase characters, digits, and spaces from the start right to the end of the string:

```
puts( /^[a-z 0-9]*$/ =~ 'well hello 123' ) # match at 0
puts( /^[a-z 0-9]*$/ =~ 'Well hello 123' ) # no match due to ^ and upcase W
```

Actually, this pattern will also match an empty string, since * indicates that *zero or more* matches are acceptable:

```
puts( /^[a-z 0-9]*$/ =~ '' )          # this matches!
```

If you want to exclude empty strings, use + (to match *one or more* occurrences of the pattern):

```
puts( /^[a-z 0-9]+$/ =~ '' )          # no match
```

Try the code in *start_end2.rb* for more examples of ways in which ^, $, * and + may be combined with ranges to create a variety of different match patterns.

You could use these techniques to determine specific characteristics of strings, such as whether a given string is uppercase, lowercase, or mixed case:

regex2.rb

```
aStr = "HELLO WORLD"

case aStr
    when /^[a-z 0-9]*$/
        puts( "Lowercase" )
    when /^[A-Z 0-9]*$/
        puts( "Uppercase" )
    else
        puts( "Mixed case\n" )
end
```

Since the string assigned to aStr is currently all uppercase, the previous code displays the "Uppercase" string. But if aStr were assigned hello world, it would display "Lowercase," and if aStr were assigned Hello World, it would display "Mixed case."

Often regular expressions are used to process the text in a file on disk. Let's suppose, for example, that you want to display all the full-line comments in a Ruby file but omit all the code and partial-line comments. You could do this by trying to match from the start of each line (^) zero or more whitespace characters (a whitespace character is represented by \s) up to a comment character (#).

```
# displays all the full-line comments in a Ruby file
File.foreach( 'regex1.rb' ){ |line|
    if line =~ /^\s*#/ then
        puts( line )
    end
}
```

Match Groups

You can also use a regular expression to match one or more substrings. To do this, you should put part of the regular expression between parentheses. Here I have two groups (sometimes called *captures*): The first tries to match the string "hi", and the second tries to match a string starting with "h" followed by any three characters (a dot means "match any single character," so the three dots here will match any three consecutive characters) and ending with "o":

```
/(hi).*(h...o)/ =~ "The word 'hi' is short for 'hello'."
```

After evaluating groups in a regular expression, a number of variables, equal to the number of groups, will be assigned the matched value of those groups. These variables take the form of a $ followed by a number: $1, $2, $3, and so on. After executing the previous code, I can access the variables $1 and $2 like this:

```
print( $1, " ", $2, "\n" )          #=> hi hello
```

Note that if the entire regular expression is unmatched, none of the group variables will be initialized. This would be the case if, for example, "hi" were in the string but "hello" was not. Both group variables would then be nil.

Here is another example, which returns three groups, indicated by pairs of parentheses (()), each of which contains a single character given by the dot: (.). Groups $1 and $3 are then displayed:

```
/(.)(.)(.)/ =~ "abcdef"
print( $1, " ", $3, "\n" )          #=> a c
```

Here is a new version of the comment-matching program that was given earlier (*regex3a.rb*); this has now been adapted to use the value of the group () containing a dot followed by an asterisk (.*) to return all the characters (zero or more) following the string matched by the preceding part of the regular expression (which here is ^\s*#). This new version reads the text from the specified file and matches zero or more whitespace (\s*) characters from the start of the current line (^) up to the first occurrence of a hash mark: #.

```
File.foreach( 'regex1.rb' ){ |line|
    if line =~ /^\s*#(.*)/ then
        puts( $1 )
    end
}
```

The end result of this is that only lines in which the first printable character is # are matched; $1 prints out the text of those lines minus the # character itself. As you will see shortly, this simple technique provides the basis of a useful tool for extracting documentation from a Ruby file.

You aren't limited merely to extracting and displaying characters verbatim; you can also modify text. This example displays the text from a Ruby file but changes all Ruby line-comment characters (#) preceding full-line comments to C-style line comments (//):

```
File.foreach( 'regex1.rb' ){ |line|
    line = line.sub(/(^\s*)#(.*)/, '\1//\2')
        puts( line )
}
```

In this example, the sub method of the String class has been used; this takes a regular expression as its first argument (/(^\s*)#(.*)/) and a replacement string as the second argument ('\1//\2'). The replacement string may contain numbered placeholders such as \1 and \2 to match any groups in the regular expression—here there are two groups between parentheses: (^\s*) and (.*). The sub method returns a new string in which the matches made by the regular expression are substituted into the replacement string, while any unmatched elements (here the # character) are omitted. So, for example, let's assume that the following comments are found in the input file:

```
# aStr = "hello world"
# aStr = "Hello World"
```

After substitution using our regular expression, the displayed output is as follows:

```
// aStr = "hello world"
// aStr = "Hello World"
```

MatchData

The =~ operator is not the only means of finding a match. The Regexp class also has a match method. This works in similar way to =~, but when a match is made, it returns a MatchData object rather than an integer. A MatchData object contains the result of a pattern match. At first sight, this may appear to be a string.

```
puts( /cde/ =~ 'abcdefg' )          #=> 2
puts( /cde/.match('abcdefg') )      #=> cde
```

In fact, it is an instance of the MatchData class that contains a string:

```
p( /cde/.match('abcdefg') )         #=> #<MatchData: "cde" >
```

A MatchData object may contain groups, or *captures*, and these can be
returned in an array using either the to_a or captures method, like this:

```
x = /(^.*)(#)(.*)/.match( 'def myMethod # This is a very nice method' )
x.captures.each{ |item| puts( item ) }
```

The previous displays the following:

```
def myMethod
#
 This is a very nice method
```

Note that there is a subtle difference between the captures and to_a methods. The first returns only the captures:

```
x.captures    #=>["def myMethod ","#"," This is a very nice method"]
```

The second returns the original string (at index 0) followed by the
captures:

```
x.to_a    #=>["def myMethod # This is a very nice method","def myMethod
","#"," This is a very nice method"]
```

Prematch and Postmatch

The MatchData class supplies the pre_match and post_match methods to return
the strings preceding or following a match. Here, for example, I am making
a match on the comment character, #:

```
x = /#/.match( 'def myMethod # This is a very nice method' )
puts( x.pre_match )      #=> def myMethod
puts( x.post_match )     #=>  This is a very nice method
```

Alternatively, you can use the special variables, $` (with a backquote) and
$' (with a normal quote), to access pre- and postmatches, respectively:

```
x = /#/.match( 'def myMethod # This is a very nice method' )
puts( $` )               #=> def myMethod
puts( $' )               #=>  This is a very nice method
```

When using match with groups, you can use array-style indexing to obtain specific items. Index 0 is the original string; higher indexes are the groups:

match_groups.rb

```
puts( /(.)(.)(.)/.match("abc")[2] )                          #=> "b"
```

You can use the special variable $~ to access the last MatchData object, and once again you can refer to groups using array-style indexing:

```
puts( $~[0], $~[1], $~[3] )
```

However, to use the full range of methods of the Array class, you must use to_a or captures to return the match groups as an array:

```
puts( $~.sort )            # this doesn't work!
puts( $~.captures.sort )   # this does
```

Greedy Matching

When a string contains more than one potential match, you may sometimes want to return the string up to the *first* match (that is, as little of the string as possible consistent with the match pattern), and at other times you may want the string up to the *last* match (that is, as much of the string as possible).

In the latter case (getting as much of the string as possible), the match is said to be *greedy*. The * and + pattern quantifiers are greedy. However, you can put them on a diet, to make them return the least possible, by putting ? after them:

greedy1.rb

```
puts( /.*at/.match('The cat sat on the mat!') )  #=> The cat sat on the mat
puts( /.*?at/.match('The cat sat on the mat!') ) #=> The cat
```

You can control the greediness of pattern matching to do things such as process directory paths (here matching on the \ character):

greedy2.rb

```
puts( /.+\\/.match('C:\mydirectory\myfolder\myfile.txt') )
    #=> C:\mydirectory\myfolder\
puts( /.+?\\/.match('C:\mydirectory\myfolder\myfile.txt') )
    #=> C:\
```

String Methods

Up to now, I've used methods of the Regexp class when processing strings. In fact, pattern matching can go both ways because the String class has a few regular expression methods of its own. These include =~ and match (so you can switch the order of the String and Regexp objects when matching), plus the scan method that iterates through a string looking for as many matches as possible. Each match is added to an array. Here, for example, I am looking for matches on the letters *a*, *b*, or *c*. The match method returns the first match ("a") wrapped up in a MatchData object, but the scan method keeps scanning along the string and returns all the matches it finds as elements in an array:

```
TESTSTR = "abc is not cba"
puts( "\n--match--" )
b = /[abc]/.match( TESTSTR )        #=> "a" (MatchData)
puts( "--scan--" )
a = TESTSTR.scan(/[abc]/)           #=> ["a", "b", "c", "c", "b", "a"]
```

The scan method may optionally be passed a block so that the elements of the array created by scan can be processed in some way:

```
a = TESTSTR.scan(/[abc]/){|c| print( c.upcase ) }     #=> ABCCBA
```

A number of other String methods can be used with regular expressions. One version of the String.slice method takes a regular expression as an argument and returns any matched substring, leaving the original (*receiver*) string unmodified. The String.slice! method (note the ! at the end) deletes the matched substring from the receiver string and returns the substring:

```
s = "def myMethod # a comment "

puts( s.slice( /m.*d/ ) )        #=> myMethod
puts( s )                        #=> def myMethod # a comment
puts( s.slice!( /m.*d/ ) )       #=> myMethod
puts( s )                        #=> def  # a comment
```

The split method splits a string into substrings, based on a pattern. The results (minus the pattern) are returned as an array:

```
s = "def myMethod # a comment"

p( s.split( /m.*d/ ) )    #=> ["def ", " # a comment"]
p( s.split( /\s/ ) )      #=> ["def", "myMethod", "#", "a", "comment"]
```

You can also split on an empty pattern (//):

```
p( s.split( // ) )
```

In this case, an array of characters is returned:

```
["d", "e", "f", " ", "m", "y", "M", "e", "t", "h", "o", "d", " ", "#", " ",
"a", " ", "c", "o", "m", "m", "e", "n", "t"]
```

You can use the sub method to match a regular expression and replace its first occurrence with a string. If no match is made, the string is returned unchanged:

```
s = "def myMethod # a comment"
s2 = "The cat sat on the mat"
p( s.sub( /m.*d/, "yourFunction" ) )   #=> "def yourFunction # a comment"
p( s2.sub( /at/, "aterpillar" ) )      #=> "The caterpillar sat on the mat"
```

The sub! method works like sub but modifies the original (receiver) string. Alternatively, you can use the gsub method (or gsub! to modify the receiver) to substitute all occurrences of the pattern with a string:

```
p( s2.gsub( /at/, "aterpillar" ) )
        #=> "The caterpillar saterpillar on the materpillar"
```

File Operations

I said earlier that regular expressions are often used to process data stored in files on disk. In some earlier examples, I read in data from a disk file, did some pattern matching, and displayed the results on the screen. Here is one more example in which I count the words in a file. You do this by scanning each line in order to create an array of words (that is, sequences of alphanumeric characters) and then adding the size of each array to the variable, count:

wordcount.rb
```
count = 0
File.foreach( 'regex1.rb' ){ |line|
    count += line.scan( /[a-z0-9A-Z]+/ ).size
}
puts( "There are #{count} words in this file." )
```

If you want to verify that the word count is correct, you could display a numbered list of words read in from the file. This is what is do here:

wordcount2.rb
```
File.foreach( 'regex1.rb' ){ |line|
    line.scan( /[a-z0-9A-Z]+/ ).each{ |word|
        count +=1
        print( "[#{count}] #{word}\n" )
    }
}
```

Now let's see how to deal with two files at once—one for reading, another for writing. The next example opens the file *testfile1.txt* for writing and passes the file variable, f, into a block. I now open a second file, *regex1.rb*, for reading and use File.foreach to pass into a second block each line of text read from this file. I use a simple regular expression to create a new string to match

lines with Ruby-style comments; the code substitutes C-style comment characters (//) for the Ruby comment character (#) when that character is the first
nonwhitespace character on a line and writes each line to *testfile1.txt* with
code lines unmodified (because there are no matches on those) and with
comment lines changed to C-style comment lines:

regexp_file1.rb

```
File.open( 'testfile1.txt', 'w' ){ |f|
    File.foreach( 'regex1.rb' ){ |line|
        f.puts( line.sub(/(^\s*)#(.*)/, '\1//\2') )
    }
}
```

This illustrates just how much can be done with regular expressions
and very little coding. The next example shows how you might read in
one file (here the file *regex1.rb*) and write out two new files—one of which
(*comments.txt*) contains only line comments, while the other (*nocomments.txt*)
contains all the other lines.

regexp_file2.rb

```
file_out1 = File.open( 'comments.txt', 'w' )
file_out2 = File.open( 'nocomments.txt', 'w' )

File.foreach( 'regex1.rb' ){ |line|
    if line =~ /^\s*#/ then
        file_out1.puts( line )
    else
        file_out2.puts( line )
    end
}

file_out1.close
file_out2.close
```

DIGGING DEEPER

This section provides a handy summary of regular expressions followed by some short examples in ready-to-use Ruby code.

Regular Expression Elements

This is a list of some of the elements that can be used in regular expressions:

^	Beginning of a line or string
$	End of a line or string
.	Any character except newline
*	Zero or more previous regular expression
*?	Zero or more previous regular expression (nongreedy)
+	One or more previous regular expression
+?	One or more previous regular expression (nongreedy)
[]	Range specification (for example, [a-z] means a character in the range a–z)
\w	An alphanumeric character
\W	A nonalphanumeric character
\s	A whitespace character
\S	A nonwhitespace character
\d	A digit
\D	A nondigit character
\b	A backspace (when in a range specification)
\b	Word boundary (when not in a range specification)
\B	Nonword boundary
*	Zero or more repetitions of the preceding
+	One or more repetitions of the preceding
{m,n}	At least m and at most n repetitions of the preceding
?	At most one repetition of the preceding
|	Either the preceding or next expression may match
()	A group

Regular Expression Examples

Here are a few more sample regular expressions:

overview.rb

```
# match chars...
puts( 'abcdefgh'.match( /cdefg/ ) )          # literal chars
       #=> cdefg
puts( 'abcdefgh'.match( /cd..g/ ) )          # dot matches any char
       #=> cdefg
```

```
# list of chars in square brackets...
puts( 'cat'.match( /[fc]at/ )
        #=> cat
puts( "batman's father's cat".match( /[fc]at/ ) )
        #=> fat
p( 'bat'.match( /[fc]at/ ) )
        #=> nil

# match char in a range...
puts( 'ABC100x3Z'.match( /[A-Z][0-9][A-Z0-9]/ ) )
        #=> C10
puts( 'ABC100x3Z'.match( /[a-z][0-9][A-Z0-9]/ ) )
        #=> x3Z

# escape 'special' chars with \
puts( 'ask who?/what?'.match( /who\?\/w..t\?/ ) )
        #=> who?/what?
puts( 'ABC 100x3Z'.match( /\s\S\d\d\D/ ) )
        #=>  100x (note the leading space)

# scan for all occurrences of pattern 'abc' with at least 2 and
# no more than 3 occurrences of the letter 'c'
p( 'abcabccabcccabccccabcccccabcccccccc'.scan( /abc{2,3}/ ) )
        #=> ["abcc", "abccc", "abccc", "abccc", "abccc"]

# match either of two patterns
puts( 'my cat and my dog'.match(/cat|dog/ ) )            #=> cat

puts( 'my hamster and my dog'.match( /cat|dog/ ) )       #=> dog
```

Symbols and Regular Expressions

Ruby 1.9 permits you to use match with a symbol. The symbol is converted to a string, and the index of the match is returned. Symbols cannot be used in this manner with Ruby 1.8.

regexp_symbols
.rb

```
p( :abcdefgh.match( /cdefg/ ) )                    #=> 2
p( :abcdefgh.match( /cd..g/ ) )                    #=> 2
p( :cat.match( /[fc]at/ ) )                        #=> 0
p( :cat.match( /[xy]at/ ) )                        #=> nil
p( :ABC100x3Z.match( /[A-Z][0-9][A-Z0-9]/ ) )      #=> 2
p( :ABC100x3Z.match( /[a-z][0-9][A-Z0-9]/ ) )      #=> 6
```

17

THREADS

There may be times when your programs
need to perform more than one action at
a time. For example, maybe you want to do
some disk operations and simultaneously display
some feedback to the user. Or you might want to copy
or upload some files "in the background" while still
allowing the user to carry on with some other task "in
the foreground."

In Ruby, if you want to do more than one task at a time, you can run
each task in its own *thread*. A thread is like a program within a program. It
runs some particular piece of code independently of any other threads.

However, as you will see shortly, multiple threads may need to find ways
of cooperating with each other so that, for example, they can share the same
data and they don't hog all the processing time available, thereby preventing
other threads from running. When reading this chapter, you need to be aware
that the behavior of threads in Ruby 1.9 and newer is substantially different
from threads in 1.8 and older. I'll explain why that is shortly.

Creating Threads

Threads can be created like any other object, using the `new` method. When you do this, you must pass to the thread a block containing the code you want the thread to run.

What follows is my first attempt at creating two threads, one of which should print four strings while the other prints ten numbers:

threads1.rb

```
# This is a simple threading example that, however,
# doesn't work as anticipated!

words = ["hello", "world", "goodbye", "mars" ]
numbers = [1,2,3,4,5,6,7,8,9,10]

Thread.new{
    words.each{ |word| puts( word ) }
}

Thread.new{
    numbers.each{ |number| puts( number ) }
}
```

In all probability, when you run this, you may see nothing or, anyway, very little. It may display some strings and some numbers but not all of them and not in any easily predictable order. In the sample code in the archive, I've added a report of the time taken for the program to execute, which shows that the darn thing finishes before it has time to get started!

Running Threads

Here is a simple fix to the thread-running problem. Right at the end of the code, add this:

threads2.rb

```
sleep( 5 )
```

This inserts a five-second delay. Now when you run the code again, you should see all the strings and all the numbers, albeit a bit jumbled up, like this:

```
hello1

2world
3

4goodbye

5mars
6
7
8
9
```

This is, in fact, exactly what you want since it shows that time is now being divided between the two threads. That's why the words and numbers are jumbled, sometimes with even the carriage returns printed by the `puts` statements being mixed up, with either no carriage return or two at once being displayed. This happens because the threads are madly competing with one another for the available time—first one thread executes and displays a word, then the next thread executes and displays a number, then execution returns to the first thread, and so on, until the first thread ends (when all four words have been displayed), at which point the second thread can run without interruption.

Now compare this with the first version of the program. In that program, I created two threads, but just as Ruby was getting itself ready to run the code inside each thread—*bam!*—it arrived at the end of the program and shut everything down, including my two threads. So, in effect, the threads were killed off before they had time to do anything of any interest.

But when I add a call to `sleep( 5 )` to insert a five-second delay, Ruby has plenty of time to run the threads before the program exits. There is just one problem with this technique—and it's a *big* problem. Adding unnecessary delays to your programs in order to let threads run defeats the object of the exercise. The timer display now shows that the program takes all of five whole seconds to run, which is about 4.99 seconds or so longer than is strictly necessary! You'll be learning more civilized ways of handling threads shortly. First, however, I need to say a few words about an important difference between threads in Ruby 1.8 and threads in Ruby 1.9.

Going Native

In all versions of Ruby up to and including Ruby 1.8.*x*, there was no access to "native" threads (that is, threads handled by the operating system). In effect, Ruby 1.8 threads exist inside the closed world of a Ruby program, with multiple threads each being allocated time, using a procedure called *time-slicing*, within a single process. Ruby 1.9 (and newer) uses a new interpreter, YARV (Yet Another Ruby Virtual-machine). This allows Ruby 1.9 to make use of native threads, albeit with some limitations that I'll explain shortly.

In principle, native threads allow more efficient execution (using *preemptive multitasking*) whereby the operating system takes care of the execution of threads on one or more processors. Even though Ruby 1.9 uses native threads, it does not perform preemptive multitasking. For reasons of compatibility with existing Ruby programs, Ruby 1.9 native threads work in a similar fashion to Ruby 1.8 non-native (or *green*) threads. In other words, although Ruby 1.9 may in fact run a native thread, it is the Ruby virtual machine, rather than the operating system, that schedules the execution of threads. This means Ruby threads sacrifice efficiency; however, they do at least benefit from portability: Threads written on one operating system will also run on a different operating system.

The Main Thread

Even if you don't explicitly create any threads, there is always at least one thread executing—the main thread in which your Ruby program is running. You can verify this by entering the following:

thread_main.rb
```
p( Thread.main )
```

This will display something like this:

```
#<Thread:0x28955c8 run>
```

Here, Thread is the thread's class, 0x28955c8 (or some other number) is its hexadecimal object identifier, and run is the thread's current status.

Thread Status

Each thread has a status that may be one of the following:

run	When the thread is executing
sleep	When the thread is sleeping or waiting on I/O
aborting	When the thread is aborting
false	When the thread terminated normally
nil	When the thread terminated with an exception

You can obtain the status of a thread using the status method. The status is also shown when you inspect a thread, in which case either a nil or a false status is shown as dead.

thread_status.rb
```
puts( Thread.main.inspect )                #=> #<Thread:0x28955c8 run>
puts( Thread.new{ sleep }.kill.inspect )   #=> #<Thread:0x28cddc0 dead>
puts( Thread.new{ sleep }.inspect )        #=> #<Thread:0x28cdd48 sleep>
thread1 = Thread.new{ }
puts( thread1.status )                     #=> false
thread2 = Thread.new{ raise( "Exception raised!" ) }
puts( thread2 )                            #=> nil
```

Note that the status shown may differ according to the version of Ruby being used and also when the program is run at different times. This is because actions on threads may not occur instantly, and the timing of a change in status may vary with each execution. For example, sometimes you may see the status of a killed thread shown as "aborting" and at other times as "dead." The thread aborts before it dies, and its change in status may happen in milliseconds. Here is an example taken from the Ruby class library documentation. The documented status of each thread is shown in the comments:

thread_status2.rb
```
p  d.kill       #=> #<Thread:0x401b3678 aborting>
p  a.status     #=> nil
p  b.status     #=> "sleep"
```

```
p  c.status              #=> false
p  d.status              #=> "aborting"
p  Thread.current.status  #=> "run"
```

But when I run this code with Ruby 1.9, the status varies greatly, and it does not always match the status shown in the documented example shown earlier. At one moment, this is what I see:

```
#<Thread:0x401b3678 aborting>
"run"
"sleep"
false
false
"run"
```

But when I run it again, this is what I see:

```
#<Thread:0x401b3678 aborting>
"run"
"run"
"run"
false
"run"
```

Now look at this program:

thread_status3.rb
```
t = Thread.new{  }
p t
p t.kill
# sleep( 1 )      # try uncommenting this
puts( t.inspect )
```

Once again the output varies each time it is run. I often see the following, which shows that even after I have "killed" the thread, it may still be "aborting" when I test its status:

```
#<Thread:0x2be6420 run>
#<Thread:0x2be6420 aborting>
#<Thread:0x2be6420 aborting>
```

Now I force a time delay by calling sleep for one second:

```
sleep( 1 )
puts( t.inspect )
```

This time the thread has time to be terminated, and this is displayed:

```
#<Thread:0x2be6420 dead>
```

These timing issues are more likely to arise in Ruby 1.9 than in older versions. You need to be aware of them and, if necessary, check a thread's status repeatedly in order to verify that it is in the state expected at any given moment.

Ensuring That a Thread Executes

Let's return to the problem I had in the previous programs. Recall that I created two threads, but the program finished before either of them had a chance to run fully. I fixed this by inserting a fixed-length delay using the sleep method. Deliberately introducing gratuitous delays into your programs is not something you would want to do as a general rule. Fortunately, Ruby has a more civilized way of ensuring that a thread has time to execute. The join method forces the calling thread (for example, the *main* thread) to suspend its own execution (so it doesn't just terminate the program) until the thread that calls join has completed:

join.rb

```
words = ["hello", "world", "goodbye", "mars" ]
numbers = [1,2,3,4,5,6,7,8,9,10]

Thread.new{
    words.each{ |word| puts( word ) }
}.join

Thread.new{
    numbers.each{ |number| puts( number ) }
}.join
```

At first sight, this looks like progress since both threads get the time they need to execute and you haven't had to introduce any unnecessary delays. However, when you take a look at the output, you will see that the threads run in sequence—*the second thread starts to run after the first thread has finished.* This is why the output shows first all the words, displayed in the first Thread, and then all the numbers, displayed in the second Thread. But what you really want to do is get the two threads to run simultaneously, with Ruby switching from one to the next to give each thread a slice of the available processing time.

The next program, *threads3.rb*, shows one way of achieving this. It creates two threads, as before; however, this time it assigns each thread to a variable, namely, wordsThread and numbersThread:

threads3.rb

```
wordsThread = Thread.new{
    words.each{ |word| puts( word ) }
}
numbersThread = Thread.new{
    numbers.each{ |number| puts( number ) }
}
```

Now it puts these threads into an array and calls the each method to pass them into a block where they are received by the block variable, t, which simply calls the join method on each thread:

```
[wordsThread, numbersThread].each{ |t| t.join }
```

As you will see from the output, the two threads now run "in parallel," so their output is jumbled up, but there is no artificial delay, and the total execution time is negligible.

Thread Priorities

So far, I've given Ruby total freedom in slicing up the time between threads in any way it wants. But sometimes one thread is more important than the others. For example, if you are writing a file-copying program with one thread to do the actual copying and another thread to display the progress bar, it would make sense to give the file-copying thread most of the time.

NOTE   *There may be times when the currently executing thread specifically wants to give execution time to other threads. This is done by calling the Thread.pass method. However, this may not produce quite the results you expect. The pass method is discussed in more detail in "Digging Deeper" on page 278.*

Ruby lets you assign integer values to indicate the priority of each thread. In theory, threads with higher priorities are allocated more execution time than threads with lower priorities. In practice, things aren't that simple since other factors (such as the order in which threads are run) may affect the amount of time given to each thread. Moreover, in very short programs, the effects of varying the priorities may be impossible to determine. The little words-and-numbers thread example you've used up to now is far too short to show any clear differences. So, let's take a look at a slightly more labor-intensive program—one that runs three threads, each of which calls a method fifty times in order to compute the factorial of 50. For our purposes, it's not important to understand how the code calculates factorials. Bear in mind, though, that it uses the shorthand (ternary operator) *if..else* notation (< *Test Condition* > ? <*if true do this*> : <*else do this*>) explained in Chapter 6:

threads4.rb
```
def fac(n)
    n == 1 ? 1 : n * fac(n-1)
end

t1 = Thread.new{
    0.upto(50) {fac(50); print( "t1\n" )}
}

t2 = Thread.new{
    0.upto(50) {fac(50); print( "t2\n" )}
}
```

```
t3 = Thread.new{
    0.upto(50) {fac(50); print( "t3\n" )}
}
```

You can now set specific priorities for each thread:

```
t1.priority = 0
t2.priority = 0
t3.priority = 0
```

In this case, the priorities are the same for each thread, so, in principle, no thread will be given the biggest slice of the action, and the results from all three threads should appear in the usual jumble. This is indeed the case in Ruby 1.8, but be aware that thread priorities may not always produce the expected results in some versions of Ruby 1.9.

THREAD PRIORITY PROBLEMS IN RUBY 1.9

In Ruby 1.9, thread priorities do not always work as documented. Here is an example taken from the Ruby class library documentation:

priority_test.rb

```
count1 = count2 = 0
a = Thread.new do
        loop { count1 += 1 }
    end
a.priority = -1

b = Thread.new do
        loop { count2 += 1 }
    end

b.priority = -2
p sleep 1    #=> 1
p count1     #=> 622504
p count2     #=> 5832
```

In principle, count1 is incremented on a higher-priority thread (b) than count2 (on thread a), and it should, therefore, always result in a higher value number as indicated in the comments in this example. In practice (at least when running this program using Ruby 1.9.2 on Windows), count1 is sometimes higher and sometimes lower than count2. This behavior has been reported and documented, and its status as either a "bug" or a "feature" is open to debate. I personally regard it as undesirable and still hope that it will be remedied. However, you must be sure to verify the effect of thread priorities before using them in your own programs. Most of the discussion of thread priorities in this chapter assumes you are using a version of Ruby in which priorities work as documented.

Now, in *threads4.rb* try changing the priority of t3:

```
t3.priority = 1
```

This time when you run the code, t3 will (at least in Ruby 1.8) grab most of the time and execute (mostly) before the other threads. The other threads may get a look in at the outset because they are created with equal priorities and the priority is changed only after they have started running. When t3 has finished, t1 and t2 should share the time more or less equally.

So, let's suppose you want t1 and t2 to run first, sharing time more or less equally and running t3 only after those two threads have finished. Here's my first attempt; you may want to try it yourself:

```
t1.priority = 2
t2.priority = 2
t3.priority = 1
```

Hmm, the end result is not what I wanted! It seems that the threads are run in sequence with no time-slicing at all! Okay, just for the heck of it, let's try some negative numbers:

```
t1.priority = -1
t2.priority = -1
t3.priority = -2
```

Hurrah! That's more like it. This time (at least in Ruby 1.8), t1 and t2 run concurrently though you may also see t3 executing briefly before the thread priorities are set; then t3 runs. So, why do negative values work but positive values don't?

There is nothing special about negative values *per se*. However, you need to bear in mind that every process has at least one thread running—the *main* thread—and this too has a priority. Its priority happens to be 0.

The Main Thread Priority

You can easily verify the priority of the main thread:

main_thread.rb
```
puts( Thread.main.priority )        #=> 0
```

So, in the previous program (*threads4.rb*), if you set the priority of t1 to 2, it will "outrank" the main thread itself and will then be given all the execution time it needs until the next thread, t2, comes along, and so on. By setting the priorities lower than that of the main thread, you can force the three threads to compete only with themselves since the main thread will always outrank them. If you prefer working with positive numbers, you can specifically set the priority of the main thread to a higher value than all other threads:

```
Thread.main.priority=100
```

Ruby 1.9 may not respect all values assigned in this way. For example, when I display that the priority of a thread to 100 has been assigned, Ruby 1.9 shows 3, whereas Ruby 1.8 shows 100.

If you want t2 and t3 to have the same priority and t1 to have a lower one, you need to set the priorities for those three threads plus the main thread:

threads5.rb

```
Thread.main.priority = 200
t1.priority = 0
t2.priority = 1
t3.priority = 1
```

Once again, this assumes you are using a version of Ruby (such as Ruby 1.8) in which thread priorities are respected. If you look closely at the output, you may spot one tiny but undesirable side effect. It is possible (not *certain*, but *possible*) that you will see some output from the t1 thread right at the outset, just before t2 and t3 kick in and assert their priorities. This is the same problem noted earlier: Each of the threads tries to start running as soon as it is created, and t1 may get its own slice of the action before the priorities of the other threads are "upgraded." To prevent this, you can specifically suspend the thread at the time of creation using Thread.stop like this:

stop_run.rb

```
t1 = Thread.new{
   Thread.stop
   0.upto(50){print( "t1\n" )}
}
```

Now, when you want to start the thread running (in this case, after setting the thread priorities), you call its run method:

```
t1.run
```

Note that the use of some Thread methods may cause *deadlocks* in Ruby 1.9. A deadlock occurs when two or more threads are waiting for one another to release a resource. To avoid deadlocks, you may prefer to use mutexes, as I'll explain next.

Mutexes

There may be occasions when multiple threads each need to access some kind of global resource. This has the potential of producing erroneous results because the current state of the global resource may be modified by one thread and this modified value may be unpredictable when it is used by some other thread. For a simple example, look at this code:

no_mutex.rb

```
$i = 0

def addNum(aNum)
   aNum + 1
end
```

```
somethreads = (1..3).collect {
    Thread.new {
        1000000.times{ $i = addNum($i)  }
    }
}


somethreads.each{|t| t.join }
puts( $i )
```

My intention here is to create and run three threads, each of which increments the global variable, $i, 1 million times. I do this by enumerating from 1
to 3 and creating an array using the collect method (the map method is synonymous with collect so could also be used) from the results returned by the
block. This array of threads, somethreads, subsequently passes each thread, t,
into a block to be executed using join, as explained earlier. Each thread calls
the addNum method to increment the value of $i. The expected result of $i at the
end of this would (naturally) be 3 million. But, in fact, when I run this, the end
value of $i is 1,068,786 (though you may see a different result).

The explanation of this is that the three threads are, in effect, competing
for access to the global variable, $i. This means, at certain times, thread a
may get the current value of $i (let's suppose it happens to be 100), and
simultaneously thread b gets the current value of $i (still 100). Now, a incre-
ments the value it just got ($i becomes 101), and b increments the value *it*
just got, which was 100 (so $i becomes 101 once again). In other words, when
multiple threads simultaneously access a shared resource, some of them may
be working with out-of-date values, that is, values that do not take into account
any modifications that have been made by other threads. Over time, errors
resulting from these operations accumulate until you end up with results that
differ substantially from those you might have anticipated.

To deal with this problem, you need to ensure that when one thread
has access to a global resource, it blocks the access of other threads. This is
another way of saying that the access to global resources granted to multiple
threads should be "mutually exclusive." You can implement this using Ruby's
Mutex class, which uses a semaphore to indicate whether a resource is currently being accessed and provides the synchronize method to prevent access to
resources inside a block. Note that you must, in principle, require 'thread' to
use the Mutex class, but in some versions of Ruby this is provided automatically. Here is my rewritten code:

mutex.rb

```
require 'thread'

$i = 0
semaphore = Mutex.new

def addNum(aNum)
    aNum + 1
end
```

```
somethreads = (1..3).collect {
    Thread.new {
        semaphore.synchronize{
            1000000.times{ $i = addNum($i)  }
        }
    }
}

somethreads.each{|t| t.join }
puts( $i )
```

This time, the end result of $i is 3,000,000.

Finally, for a slightly more useful example of using threads, take a look at *file_find2.rb*. This sample program uses Ruby's Find class to traverse directories on disk. For a nonthreaded example, see *file_find.rb*. Compare this with the *file_info3.rb* program on page 222, which uses the Dir class.

This program sets two threads running. The first, t1, calls the processFiles method to find and display file information (you will need to edit the call to processFiles to pass to it a directory name on your system). The second thread, t2, simply prints out a message, and this thread runs while t1 is "alive" (that is, running or sleeping):

file_find2.rb

```
require 'find'
require 'thread'

$totalsize = 0
$dirsize = 0

semaphore = Mutex.new

def processFiles( baseDir )
    Find.find( baseDir ) { |path|
        $dirsize += $dirsize     # if a directory
      if (FileTest.directory?(path)) && (path != baseDir ) then

            print( "\n#{path} [#{$dirsize / 1024}K]" )
            $dirsize = 0
        else                     # if a file
            $filesize = File.size(path)
            print( "\n#{path} [#{$filesize} bytes]" )
            $dirsize += $filesize
            $totalsize += $filesize
        end
    }
end

t1 = Thread.new{
    semaphore.synchronize{
        processFiles( '..' ) # you may edit this directory name
    }
}
```

```
t2 = Thread.new{
    semaphore.synchronize{
        while t1.alive? do
            print( "\n\t\tProcessing..." )
            Thread.pass
        end
    }
}

t2.join

printf( "\nTotal: #{$totalsize} bytes, #{$totalsize/1024}K, %0.02fMB\n\n",
"#{$totalsize/1048576.0}" )
puts( "Total file size: #{$filesize}, Total directory size: #{$dirsize}" )
```

In a real application, you could adapt this technique to provide user feedback of some kind while some intensive process (such as directory walking) is taking place.

Fibers

Ruby 1.9 introduces a new class called a Fiber, which is a bit like a thread and a bit like a block. Fibers are intended for the implementation of "lightweight concurrency." This broadly means they operate like blocks (see Chapter 10) whose execution can be paused and restarted just as you can with threads. Unlike threads, however, the execution of fibers is not scheduled by the Ruby virtual machine; it has to be controlled explicitly by the programmer. Another difference between threads and fibers is that threads run automatically when they are created; fibers do not. To start a fiber, you must call its resume method. To yield control to code outside the fiber, you must call the yield method.

Let's look at some simple examples:

fiber_test.rb

```
f = Fiber.new do
    puts( "In fiber" )
    Fiber.yield( "yielding" )
    puts( "Still in fiber" )
    Fiber.yield( "yielding again" )
    puts( "But still in fiber" )
end

puts( "a" )
puts( f.resume )
puts( "b" )
puts( f.resume )
puts( "c" )
puts( f.resume )
puts( "d" )
puts( f.resume )    # dead fiber called
```

Here I create a new fiber, f, but don't immediately start it running. First I display "a", puts("a"), and then I start the fiber, f.resume. The fiber starts executing and displays the "In fiber" message. But then it calls yield with the "yielding" string. This suspends the execution of the fiber and allows the code outside the fiber to continue. The code that called f.resume now puts the string that's been yielded, so "yielding" is displayed. Another call to f.resume restarts the fiber where you left off, so "Still in fiber" is displayed, and so on. With each call to yield, execution returns to code outside the fiber. And, when that code calls f.resume, the remaining code in the fiber is executed. Once there is no more code left to be executed, the fiber terminates. When an inactive (or *dead*) fiber is called by f.resume, a FiberError occurs. This is the output from the program shown earlier:

```
a
In fiber
yielding
b
Still in fiber
c
But still in fiber
d
C:/bookofruby/ch17/fiber_test.rb:18:in `resume': dead fiber called
(FiberError)
from C:/bookofruby/ch17/fiber_test.rb:18:in `<main>'
```

You can avoid "dead fiber" errors by testing the state of a fiber using the alive? method. This returns true if the fiber is active and returns false if inactive. You must require 'fiber' in order to use this method:

fiber_alive.rb

```
require 'fiber'

if (f.alive?) then
    puts( f.resume )
else
    puts("Error: Call to dead fiber" )
end
```

The resume method accepts an arbitrary number of parameters. On the first call to resume, they are passed as block arguments. Otherwise, they become the return value of the call to yield. The following example is taken from the documentation in the Ruby class library:

fiber_test2.rb

```
fiber = Fiber.new do |first|
    second = Fiber.yield first + 2
end

puts fiber.resume 10      #=> 12
puts fiber.resume 14      #=> 14
puts fiber.resume 18      #=> dead fiber called (FiberError)
```

Here's a simple example illustrating the use of two fibers:

```
f = Fiber.new {
    | s |
    puts( "In Fiber #1 (a) : " + s )
    puts( "In Fiber #1 (b) : " + s )
    Fiber.yield
    puts( "In Fiber #1 (c) : " + s )
}

f2 = Fiber.new {
    | s |
    puts( "In Fiber #2 (a) : " + s )
    puts( "In Fiber #2 (b) : " + s )
    Fiber.yield
    puts( "In Fiber #2 (c) : " + s )
}

f.resume( "hello"  )
f2.resume( "hi" )
puts( "world" )
f2.resume
f.resume
```

This starts the first fiber, f, which runs until the call to yield. Then it starts the second fiber, f2, which runs until it too calls yield. Then the main program displays the string "world," and finally f2 and f are resumed. This is the output:

```
In Fiber #1 (a) : hello
In Fiber #1 (b) : hello
In Fiber #2 (a) : hi
In Fiber #2 (b) : hi
world
In Fiber #2 (c) : hi
In Fiber #1 (c) : hello
```

DIGGING DEEPER

Here you will learn how to pass execution from one thread to another. You will discover some things that the Ruby documentation doesn't tell you and some oddities about different versions of Ruby.

Passing Execution to Other Threads

Sometimes you might specifically want a certain thread to yield execution to any other threads that happen to be running. For example, if you have multiple threads doing steadily updated graphics operations or displaying various bits of "as it happens" statistical information, you may want to ensure that once one thread has drawn X number of pixels or displayed Y number of statistics, the other threads are guaranteed to get their chances to do something.

In theory, the `Thread.pass` method takes care of this. Ruby's source code documentation states that `Thread.pass` "invokes the thread scheduler to pass execution to another thread." This is the example provided by the Ruby documentation:

pass0.rb

```
a = Thread.new {   print "a"; Thread.pass;
                   print "b"; Thread.pass;
                   print "c" }
b = Thread.new {   print "x"; Thread.pass;
                   print "y"; Thread.pass;
                   print "z" }
a.join
b.join
```

According to the documentation, this code, when run, produces the output axbycz. And, sure enough, it does. In theory, then, this seems to show that by calling `Thread.pass` after each call to `print`, these threads pass execution to another thread, which is why the output from the two threads alternates.

Being of a suspicious turn of mind, I wondered what the effect would be with the calls to `Thread.pass` removed. Would the first thread hog all the time, yielding to the second thread only when it has finished? The best way to find out is to try it:

pass1.rb

```
a = Thread.new {   print "a";
                   print "b";
                   print "c" }
b = Thread.new {   print "x";
                   print "y";
                   print "z" }
a.join
b.join
```

If my theory is correct (that thread a will hog all the time until it's finished), this would be the expected output: abcdef. In fact (to my surprise!), the output actually produced was axbycz.

In other words, the result was the *same* with or without all those calls to Thread.pass. So what, if anything, is Thread.pass doing? And is the documentation wrong when it claims that the pass method invokes the thread scheduler to pass execution to another thread?

For a brief and cynical moment I confess that I toyed with the possibility that the documentation was simply incorrect and that Thread.pass didn't do anything at all. A look into Ruby's C-language source code soon dispelled my doubts; Thread.pass certainly does something, but its behavior is not quite as predictable as the Ruby documentation seems to suggest. Before explaining why this is, let's try an example of my own:

pass2.rb

```
s = 'start '
a = Thread.new { (1..10).each{
    s << 'a'
    Thread.pass
    }
}
b = Thread.new { (1..10).each{
    s << 'b'
    Thread.pass
    }
}

a.join
b.join
puts( "#{s} end" )
```

At first sight, this may look very similar to the previous example. It sets two threads running, but instead of printing out something repeatedly, these threads repeatedly add a character to a string—"a" being added by the a thread and "b" by the b thread. After each operation, Thread.pass passes execution to the other thread. At the end, the entire string is displayed. When run with Ruby 1.8, it comes as no surprise that the string contains an alternating sequence of "a" and "b" characters: abababababababababab. However, in Ruby 1.9, the characters do not alternate, and this is what I see: aaaaaaaaaabbbbbbbbbb. In my view, the pass method is not to be trusted with Ruby 1.9, and the remaining discussion applies to Ruby 1.8 only.

Now, remember that in the previous program, I obtained the same alternating output even when I removed the calls to Thread.pass. Based on that experience, I guess I should expect similar results if I delete Thread.pass in this program. Let's try it:

pass3.rb

```
s = 'start '
a = Thread.new { (1..10).each{
    s << 'a'
    }
}
```

```
b = Thread.new { (1..10).each{
    s << 'b'
    }
}

a.join
b.join
puts( "#{s} end" )
```

This time, this is the output: aaaaaaaaaabbbbbbbbbb.

In other words, this program shows the kind of differing behavior that I had originally anticipated in the first program (the one I copied out of Ruby's embedded documentation), which is to say that when the two threads are left to run under their own steam, the first thread, a, grabs all the time for itself and only when it's finished does the second thread, b, get a look in. But by explicitly adding calls to Thread.pass in Ruby 1.8, you can force each thread to pass execution to any other threads.

So, how can you explain this difference in behavior? In essence, *pass0.rb* and *pass3.rb* are doing the same things—running two threads and displaying strings from each. The only real difference is that, in *pass3.rb*, the strings are concatenated inside the threads rather than printed. This might not seem like a big deal, but it turns out that printing a string takes a bit more time than concatenating one. In effect, then, a call to print introduces a time delay. And as you found out earlier (when I deliberately introduced a delay using sleep), time delays have profound effects on threads.

If you still aren't convinced, try my rewritten version of *pass0.rb*, which I have creatively named *pass0_new.rb*. This simply replaces the prints with concatenations. Now if you comment and uncomment the calls to Thread.pass, you will indeed, in Ruby 1.8, see differing results:

pass0_new.rb
```
s = ""
a = Thread.new { s << "a"; Thread.pass;
    s << "b"; Thread.pass;
    s << "c" }

b = Thread.new { s << "x"; Thread.pass;
    s << "y"; Thread.pass;
    s << "z" }

a.join
b.join
puts( s )
```

With Thread.pass, Ruby 1.8 displays the following:

```
axbycz
```

Without Thread.pass, Ruby 1.8 displays the following:

```
abcxyz
```

In Ruby 1.9, the presence or absence of Thread.pass has no obvious effect. And, with or without it, this is displayed:

```
abcxyz
```

Incidentally, my tests were conducted on a PC running Windows. It is quite possible that different results will be seen on other operating systems. This is because the implementation of the Ruby scheduler, which controls the amount of time allocated to threads, is different on Windows and other operating systems.

As a final example, you may want to take a look at the *pass4.rb* program, which is intended for Ruby 1.8 only. This creates two threads and immediately suspends them (Thread.stop). In the body of each thread the thread's information, including its object_id is appended to an array, arr, and then Thread.pass is called. Finally, the two threads are run and joined, and the array, arr, is displayed. Try experimenting by uncommenting Thread.pass to verify its effect (pay close attention to the execution order of the threads as indicated by their object_id identifiers):

pass4.rb
```
arr = []
t1 = Thread.new{
    Thread.stop
    (1..10).each{
        arr << Thread.current.to_s
        Thread.pass
    }
}
t2 = Thread.new{
    Thread.stop
    (1..10).each{ |i|
        arr << Thread.current.to_s
        Thread.pass
    }
}
puts( "Starting threads..." )
t1.run
t2.run
t1.join
t2.join
puts( arr )
```

18

DEBUGGING AND TESTING

The development of any real-world application progresses in steps. Most of us would prefer to take more steps forward than backward. To minimize the backward steps—caused by coding errors or unforeseen side effects—you can take advantage of testing and debugging techniques. This chapter provides a brief overview of some of the most useful debugging tools available to Ruby programmers. Bear in mind, however, that if you are using a dedicated Ruby IDE, you may have more powerful visual debugging tools at your disposal. I will be discussing only the "standard" tools available to Ruby in this chapter.

IRB: Interactive Ruby

Sometimes you may just want to "try something" with Ruby. It is possible to do this using the standard Ruby interpreter: Enter ruby at the command prompt, and then enter your code one line at a time. However, this is far from being an ideal interactive environment. For one thing, the code you enter will be executed only when you enter an end-of-file character such as ^Z or ^D (that is, CTRL-Z on Windows or CTRL-D on some other operating systems). So, to do something as simple as displaying the value of 1 plus 1, you would enter the following sequence commands (remembering to enter whichever end-of-file character is required on your operating system).

```
ruby
1+1
^Z
```

Only once the end-of-file character (here ^Z) has been entered does Ruby execute the code and display the result:

```
2
```

For a better way to interact with Ruby, use the Interactive Ruby shell (IRB). To start IRB, go to a command prompt and enter the following:

```
irb
```

You should now see a prompt similar to the following:

```
irb(main):001:0>
```

Now you are ready to start entering some Ruby code. You can enter an expression over more than one line; as soon as the expression is complete, IRB will evaluate it and display the result. Try the following (pressing ENTER after the + on the first line):

```
x = ( 10 +
( 2 * 4 ) )
```

Finally, press ENTER after the closing parenthesis. Now IRB will evaluate the expression and show the result:

```
=> 18
```

You can now evaluate x. Enter this:

```
x
```

IRB shows this:

```
=> 18
```

So, up to this point, your entire IRB session should look like this:

```
irb(main):001:0> x = (10 +
irb(main):002:1* (2*4))
=> 18
irb(main):003:0> x
=> 18
irb(main):004:0>
```

Be careful, though. Try entering this:

```
x = (10
+ (2*4))
```

This time the result is as follows:

```
=> 8
```

This is, in fact, normal Ruby behavior. It is normal because a line break acts as a terminator, while the + operator, when it begins the new line, acts as a unary operator (that is, rather than adding together *two* values—one to its left and one to its right—it merely asserts that the *single* expression that follows the + is positive). You will find a fuller explanation of this in "Digging Deeper" on page 295.

For now, just be aware that when entering expressions one line at a time, the position of the line break is important! When using IRB, you can tell whether the interpreter considers that you have ended a statement. If you have done so, a prompt is displayed ending with > like this:

```
irb(main):013:1>
```

If a statement is complete and returns a result, a => prompt is displayed followed by the result. For example:

```
=> 18
```

If the statement is incomplete, the prompt ends with an asterisk:

```
irb(main):013:1*
```

To end an IRB session, enter the word quit or exit at the prompt. You can, if you want, load a Ruby program into IRB by passing to it the program name when you run IRB like this:

```
irb myprogram.rb
```

You may also invoke IRB with a variety of options to do things such as load a module (irb -r *[load-module]*) or display the IRB version number (irb -v). Many of the available IRB options are rather esoteric and are not likely to be required by most users. The full range of options may be listed by entering this at the command line:

```
irb --help
```

Although IRB may be useful for trying out some code, it does not provide all the features you need for debugging programs. Ruby does, however, provide a command-line debugger.

Debugging

The default Ruby debugger allows you to set breakpoints and watchpoints and evaluate variables while your programs execute. To run a program in the debugger, use the -r debug option (where -r means "require" and debug is the name of the debugging library) when you start the Ruby interpreter. For example, this is how you would debug a program called *debug_test.rb*:

```
ruby -r debug  debug_test.rb
```

Once the debugger has started, you can enter various commands to step through your code, set breakpoints to cause the execution to pause at specific lines, set watches to monitor the values of variables, and so on. The following are the available debugging commands:

b[reak] [file|class:]<line|method> and b[reak] [file|class:]<line|method>
    Sets breakpoint to some position

b[reak] [class.]<line|method>
    Sets breakpoint to some position

wat[ch] <expression>
    Sets watchpoint to some expression

cat[ch] <an Exception>
    Sets catchpoint to an exception

b[reak]
    Lists breakpoints

cat[ch]
    Shows catchpoint

del[ete][nnn]
    Deletes some or all breakpoints

disp[lay] <expression>
    Adds expression to display expression list

undisp[lay][nnn]
    Deletes one particular or all display expressions

c[ont]
>Runs until end or breakpoint

s[tep][nnn]
>Steps (into code) one line or to line nnn

n[ext][nnn]
>Goes over one line or until line nnn

w[here]
>Displays frames

f[rame]
>Is the alias for where

l[ist][(-|nn-mm)]
>Lists program, lists backward nn-mm, lists given lines

up[nn]
>Moves to higher frame

down[nn]
>Moves to lower frame

fin[ish]
>Returns to outer frame

tr[ace] (on|off)
>Sets trace mode of current thread

tr[ace] (on|off) all
>Sets trace mode of all threads

q[uit]
>Exits from debugger

v[ar] g[lobal]
>Shows global variables

v[ar] l[ocal]
>Shows local variables

v[ar] i[nstance] <object>
>Shows instance variables of object

v[ar] c[onst] <object>
>Shows constants of object

m[ethod] i[nstance] <obj>
>Shows methods of object

m[ethod] <class|module>
>Shows instance methods of class or module

th[read] l[ist]
>Lists all threads

th[read] c[ur[rent]]
>Shows current thread

th[read] [sw[itch]] <nnn>
>Switches thread context to nnn

th[read] stop <nnn>
    Stops thread nnn

th[read] resume <nnn>
    Resumes thread nnn

p expression
    Evaluates expression and prints its value

h[elp]
    Prints this help

<everything else>
    Evaluates

UBYGEMS? WHAT'S UBYGEMS?

In some cases, if you enter the command ruby -r debug, you may see an inscrutable message similar to the following:

```
c:/ruby/lib/ruby/site_ruby/1.8/ubygems.rb:4:require 'rubygems'
```

If this happens, when you then start debugging, you will find yourself trying to debug the file *ubygems.rb* rather than your program! This problem may occur when some software (for example, some customized Ruby installers) set the environment variable RUBYOPT=-rubygems. In most cases, this has the desirable effect of allowing your Ruby programs to use the Ruby Gems "packaging system," which helps install Ruby libraries. When you try to use the -r option, however, this is interpreted as -r ubygems, which is why an attempt is made to load the file *ubygems.rb*. Ruby conveniently (or possibly confusingly?) provides a file named *ubygems.rb* that does nothing apart from requiring *rubygems.rb*. There are two ways of dealing with this. You can remove RUBYOPT permanently, or you can disable it temporarily. If you choose to remove it permanently, however, you may encounter side effects when using Ruby Gems later. The way in which environment variables are added or removed varies according to your operating system. On Windows, you would need to click the Start menu (then Settings if using XP) and click Control Panel (then System and Maintenance if using Vista); then click System (on Vista, you should now click Advanced System Settings). In the System Properties dialog, select the Advanced tab. Next, click Environment Variables; finally, in the System Variables panel, find RUBYOPT and delete it. A safer alternative is to disable the variable at the command prompt prior to loading the debugger. To do this, enter the following:

```
set RUBYOPT=
```

This will disable the RUBYOPT environment variable for this command session only. You can verify this by entering the following:

```
set RUBYOPT
```

You should see the message:

```
Environment variable RUBYOPT not defined
```

However, open another command window and enter set RUBYOPT, and you will see that the environment variable here retains its default value.

Let's see how a few of these commands might be used in a real debugging session. Open a system prompt, and navigate to the directory containing the file *debug_test.rb*, which is supplied in the sample code for this chapter. Start the debugger by entering this:

```
ruby -r debug debug_test.rb
```

Now, let's try a few commands. In these examples, I've written [Enter] to show that you should press the ENTER key after each command. First let's see a code listing (here note that l is a lowercase *L* character):

```
l [Enter]
```

You should see this, which is a partial listing of the file *debug_test.rb*:

```
debug_test.rb:2:          class Thing
(rdb:1) l
[-3, 6] in debug_test.rb
   1      # Thing
=> 2      class Thing
   3
   4               attr_accessor( :name )
   5
   6               def initialize( aName )
(rdb:1)
```

NOTE *If you see a listing from a file called* ubygems.rb *at this point instead of your program, refer to "Ubygems? What's Ubygems?" on page 288 for ways of correcting this problem.*

The l you entered is the "list" command, which instructs the debugger to list the code in bite-sized chunks. The actual number of lines will vary with the code being debugged. Let's list some more:

```
l [Enter]
l [Enter]
```

Now list a specific number of lines. Enter the letter l followed by the digit 1, a hyphen, and 100:

```
l 1-100 [Enter]
```

Let's put a breakpoint on line 78:

```
b 78 [Enter]
```

The Ruby debugger should reply with this:

```
Set breakpoint 1 at debug_test.rb:78
```

You might also set one or more *watchpoints*. A watchpoint can be used to trigger a break on a simple variable (for example, entering `wat @t2` would break when the `@t2` object is created); or it may be set to match a specific value (for example, `i == 10`). Here I want to set a watchpoint that breaks when the `name` attribute of `@t4` is "wombat". Enter this:

```
wat @t4.name == "wombat" [Enter]
```

The debugger should confirm this:

```
Set watchpoint 2:@t4.name == "wombat"
```

Notice the watchpoint number is 2. You'll need that number if you subsequently decide to delete the watchpoint. Okay, so now let's continue (c) execution:

```
c [Enter]
```

The program will run until it hits the breakpoint. You will see a message similar to the following:

```
Breakpoint 1, toplevel at debug_test.rb:78
debug_test.rb:78:         puts("Game start" )
```

Here it shows the line number it's stopped on and the code on that line. Let's continue:

```
c [Enter]
```

This time it breaks here:

```
Watchpoint 2, toplevel at debug_test.rb:85
debug_test.rb:86:         @t5 = Treasure.new("ant", 2)
```

This is the line immediately following the successful evaluation of the watchpoint condition. Check that by listing the line number indicated:

```
l 86
```

The debugger shows a set of lines with the current line of execution (86) preceded by the => marker:

```
[81, 90] in debug_test.rb
   81      @t1 = Treasure.new("A sword", 800)
   82      @t4 = Treasure.new("potto", 500 )
   83      @t2 = Treasure.new("A dragon Horde", 550)
   84      @t3 = Treasure.new("An Elvish Ring", 3000)
   85      @t4 = Treasure.new("wombat", 10000)
```

```
=> 86      @t5 = Treasure.new("ant", 2)
   87      @t6 = Treasure.new("sproggit", 400)
   88
   89      #   ii) Rooms
   90      @room1 = Room.new("Crystal Grotto", [])
```

As you can see, line 86 contains the code that matches the watchpoint condition. Notice that execution did not stop after line 82, where @t4 was originally created, because the watchpoint condition was not met there (its name attribute was "potto" and not "wombat"). If you want to inspect the value of a variable when paused at a breakpoint or watchpoint, just enter its name. Try this:

```
@t4 [Enter]
```

The debugger will display the following:

```
#<Treasure:0x315617c @value=10000, @name="wombat">
```

You can similarly enter other expressions to be evaluated. Try this:

```
@t1.value [Enter]
```

This shows 800.
Or enter some arbitrary expression such as this:

```
10+4/2 [Enter]
```

This shows 12.
Now delete the watchpoint (recall that its number is 2):

```
del 2 [Enter]
```

And continue until the program exits:

```
c [Enter]
```

You can use many more commands to debug a program in this way, and you may want to experiment with those shown in the table given earlier. You can also view a list of commands during a debugging session by entering help or just h:

```
h [Enter]
```

To quit a debugging session, enter quit or q:

```
q [Enter]
```

Although the standard Ruby debugger has its uses, it is far from as simple or convenient to use as one of the graphical debuggers provided by integrated development environments. Moreover, it is quite slow. In my view, it is fine for debugging simple scripts but cannot be recommended for debugging large and complex programs.

Unit Testing

Unit testing is a postdebugging testing technique that lets you try bits of your program in order to verify that they work as expected. Some programmers use unit testing habitually in addition to or even instead of interactive debugging; other programmers use it rarely or never. Entire books have been written on the techniques and methodologies of unit testing, and I will only cover its fundamentals here.

The basic idea of unit testing is that you can write a number of "assertions" stating that certain results should be obtained as the consequence of certain actions. For example, you might assert that the return value of a specific method should be 100, that it should be a Boolean, or that it should be an instance of a specific class. If, when the test is run, the assertion proves to be correct, it passes the test; if it is incorrect, the test fails.

Here's an example, which will fail if the getVal method of the object, t, returns any value other than 100:

```
assert_equal(100, t.getVal)
```

But you can't just pepper your code with assertions of this sort. There are precise rules to the game. First you have to require the *test/unit* file. Then you need to derive a test class from the TestCase class, which is found in the Unit module, which is itself in the Test module:

```
class MyTest < Test::Unit::TestCase
```

Inside this class you can write one or more methods, each of which constitutes a test containing one or more assertions. The method names must begin with test (so methods called test1 or testMyProgram are okay, but a method called myTestMethod isn't). The following method contains a test that makes the single assertion that the return value of TestClass.new(100).getVal is 1,000:

```
def test2
    assert_equal(1000,TestClass.new(100).getVal)
end
```

And here is a complete (albeit simple) test suite in which I have defined a TestCase class called MyTest that tests the class, TestClass. Here (with a little imagination!), TestClass may be taken to represent a whole program that I want to test:

```
require 'test/unit'

class TestClass
    def initialize( aVal )
        @val = aVal * 10
    end

    def getVal
        return @val
    end
end

class MyTest < Test::Unit::TestCase
    def test1
        t = TestClass.new(10)
        assert_equal(100, t.getVal)
        assert_equal(101, t.getVal)
        assert(100 != t.getVal)
    end

    def test2
        assert_equal(1000,TestClass.new(100).getVal)
    end
end
```

This test suite contains two tests: test1 (which contains three assertions) and test2 (which contains one). To run the tests, you just need to run the program; you don't have to create an instance of MyClass. You will see a report of the results that states there were two tests, three assertions, and one failure:

```
1) Failure:
test1(MyTest) [C:/bookofruby/ch18/test1.rb:19]:
<101> expected but was
<100>.

2 tests, 3 assertions, 1 failures, 0 errors
```

In fact, I made *four* assertions. However, assertions following a failure are not evaluated in a given test. In test1, this assertion fails:

```
assert_equal(101, t.getVal)
```

Having failed, the next assertion is skipped. If I now correct this failed assertion (asserting 100 instead of 101), this next assertion will also be tested:

```
assert(100 != t.getVal)
```

But this too fails. This time, the report states that four assertions have been evaluated with one failure:

```
2 tests, 4 assertions, 1 failures, 0 errors, 0 skips
```

Of course, in a real-life situation, you should aim to write correct assertions, and when any failures are reported, it should be the failing code that is rewritten—not the assertion!

For a slightly more complex example of testing, see the *test2.rb* program (which requires a file called *buggy.rb*). This is a small adventure game that includes the following test methods:

test2.rb

```ruby
def test1
    @game.treasures.each{ |t|
        assert(t.value < 2000, "FAIL: #{t} t.value = #{t.value}" )
    }
end

def test2
    assert_kind_of( TestMod::Adventure::Map, @game.map)
    assert_kind_of( Array, @game.map)
end
```

Here the first method, test1, performs an assert test on an array of objects passed into a block, and it fails when a value attribute is *not* less than 2,000. The second method, test2, tests the class types of two objects using the assert_kind_of method. The second test in this method fails when @game.map is found to be of the type TestMod::Adventure::Map rather than Array as is asserted.

The code also contains two more methods named setup and teardown. When defined, methods with these names will be run before and after each test method. In other words, in *test2.rb*, the following methods will run in this order:

1. setup   2. test1   3. teardown
4. setup   5. test2   6. teardown

This gives you the opportunity of reinitializing any variables to specific values prior to running each test or, as in this case, re-creating objects to ensure that they are in a known state as in the following example:

```ruby
def setup
    @game = TestMod::Adventure.new
end

def teardown
    @game.endgame
end
```

DIGGING DEEPER

This section contains a summary of assertions for unit testing, explains why IRB may show different results for what appears to be the same code, and considers the merits of more advanced debugging tools.

Assertions Available When Unit Testing

The list of assertions shown next is provided for ease of reference. A full explanation of each assertion is beyond the scope of this book. You can find complete documentation of the testing libraries at *http://ruby-doc.org/stdlib/*. On this site, select the class listing for `Test::Unit::Assertions` in order to view the full documentation of the available assertions plus numerous code samples demonstrating their usage.

`assert(boolean, message=nil)`
> Asserts that boolean is not false or nil.

`assert_block(message="assert_block failed.") {|| ...}`
> The assertion upon which all other assertions are based. Passes if the block yields true.

`assert_equal(expected, actual, message=nil)`
> Passes if expected == actual.

`assert_in_delta(expected_float, actual_float, delta, message="")`
> Passes if expected_float and actual_float are equal within delta tolerance.

`assert_instance_of(klass, object, message="")`
> Passes if object .instance_of? klass.

`assert_kind_of(klass, object, message="")`
> Passes if object .kind_of? klass.

`assert_match(pattern, string, message="")`
> Passes if string =~ pattern.

`assert_nil(object, message="")`
> Passes if object is nil.

`assert_no_match(regexp, string, message="")`
> Passes if regexp !~ string.

`assert_not_equal(expected, actual, message="")`
> Passes if expected != actual.

`assert_not_nil(object, message="")`
> Passes if ! object .nil?.

`assert_not_same(expected, actual, message="")`
> Passes if ! actual .equal? expected.

```
assert_nothing_raised(*args) {|| ...}
```
Passes if block does not raise an exception.

```
assert_nothing_thrown(message="", &proc)
```
Passes if block does not throw anything.

```
assert_operator(object1, operator, object2, message="")
```
Compares the object1 with object2 using operator. Passes if object1.send(operator, object2) is true.

```
assert_raise(*args) {|| ...}
```
Passes if the block raises one of the given exceptions.

```
assert_raises(*args, &block)
```
Alias of assert_raise. (Deprecated in Ruby 1.9 and to be removed in 2.0.)

```
assert_respond_to(object, method, message="")
```
Passes if object .respond_to? method.

```
assert_same(expected, actual, message="")
```
Passes if actual .equal? expected (in other words, they are the same instance).

```
assert_send(send_array, message="")
```
Passes if the method send returns a true value.

```
assert_throws(expected_symbol, message="", &proc)
```
Passes if the block throws expected_symbol

```
build_message(head, template=nil, *arguments)
```
Builds a failure message; head is added before the template and *arguments replaces the question marks positionally in the template.

```
flunk(message="Flunked")
```
flunk always fails.

Line Breaks Are Significant

I said earlier that you need to take care when entering line breaks into the interactive Ruby console (IRB) since the position of line breaks may alter the meaning of your Ruby code. So, for example, the following:

linebreaks.rb

```
x = ( 10 +
( 2 * 4 ) )
```

assigns 18 to x, but the following:

```
x = (10
+ (2*4))
```

assigns 8 to x.

This is not merely a quirk of IRB. This is normal behavior of Ruby code even when entered into a text editor and executed by the Ruby interpreter. The second example just shown evaluates 10 on the first line, finds this to be a perfectly acceptable value, and promptly forgets about it; then it evaluates + (2*4), which it also finds to be an acceptable value (8), but it has no connection with the previous value (10), so 8 is returned and assigned to x.

If you want to tell Ruby to evaluate expressions split over multiple lines, ignoring the line breaks, you can use the line continuation character (\). This is what I've done here:

```
x = (10 \
+ (2*4) )
```

This time, x is assigned the value 18.

Graphical Debuggers

For serious debugging, I strongly recommend a graphical debugger. For example, the debugger in the Ruby In Steel IDE allows you to set breakpoints and watchpoints by clicking the margin of the editor.

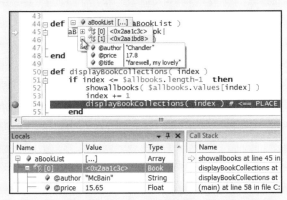

It lets you monitor the values of selected "watch variables" or all local variables in separate docked windows. It maintains a "callstack" of all method calls leading to the current point of execution and allows you to navigate "backward" through the callstack to view the changing values of variables. It also has "drill-down" expansion of variables to allow you to expand arrays and hashes and look inside complex objects. These capabilities go well beyond the features of the standard Ruby debugger. For information on Ruby IDEs, see Appendix D.

19

RUBY ON RAILS

Rails has become so closely connected with Ruby that it is now quite commonplace for people to talk about programming "in" Ruby on Rails as though "Ruby on Rails" were the name of the programming language.

In fact, Rails is a framework—a set of tools and code libraries—that can be used in cahoots with Ruby. It gives you the ability to develop database-driven websites that respond to user interaction. For example, users might enter and save data on one page and search for data on other pages. This makes Rails suitable for creating dynamic websites that generate web pages "on the fly" rather than loading up static, predesigned pages. Typical applications include collaborative sites such as online communities, multi-author books or wikis, shopping sites, discussion forums, and blogs.

I'll provide a hands-on guide to creating a blog shortly. First, though, let's take a closer look at the nitty-gritty details of the Rails framework.

NOTE *This chapter will give you a taste of developing in Ruby on Rails. Bear in mind, however, that Rails is a big and complex framework, and I will cover only the fundamental features. At the time of writing, Rails 3 is the latest version, but Rails 2 is still widely used; therefore, both versions are covered in this chapter.*

Installing Rails

Rails is not a standard part of Ruby, so you may need to install it as a separate operation. Note that Ruby and Rails ship as standard with some operating systems, such as Mac OS X. There is, however, no guarantee that these are the latest versions, and you may want to update the default installation manually.

Do It Yourself . . .

There are various ways in which Rails can be installed. The easiest way is to use an all-in-one installer (some alternatives are described in this chapter). However, you may also install Rails and the tools it requires one at a time. Rails may be installed using the Ruby Gems "package manager." As long as you are connected to the Internet, Ruby Gems will go online to find and install the latest version of Rails.

NOTE *For Ruby Gems documentation, go to* http://docs.rubygems.org/.

At the command prompt, enter the following:

```
gem install rails
```

If, instead of installing the latest version, you want to install a specific version of Rails, you should append `--version=` followed by the appropriate version number when entering the previous command. For example, to install Rails 2.3.8, enter the following:

```
gem install rails --version=2.3.8
```

Alternatively, you can download and install Rails from the Ruby on Rails website, *http://www.rubyonrails.org/*. Most Rails applications require a database, which you will need to install as a separate operation. Many people use either SQLite or the free MySQL database server. MySQL is the more powerful of the two systems and is used on many professional websites. However, many people find SQLite simpler to use for local development of Ruby applications. Installation of SQLite varies according to which operating system is being used. SQLite3 is pre-installed on Mac OS X Leopard.

Installation of SQLite3 can be notably tricky on Windows. You should begin by running this command at the command line:

```
gem install sqlite3-ruby
```

Pay close attention to the message that is displayed when this executes. This tells you which version of the SQLite3 DLL you need to install and the web address from which you can download it. This DLL is a requirement. Failure to install it will mean that SQLite3 will not be available for use with Rails. This message will state something like this:

```
You've installed the binary version of sqlite3-ruby.
It was built using SQLite3 version 3.7.3.
It's recommended to use the exact same version to avoid potential issues.

At the time of building this gem, the necessary DLL files where available
in the following download:

http://www.sqlite.org/sqlitedll-3_7_3.zip

You can put the sqlite3.dll available in this package in your Ruby bin
directory, for example C:\Ruby\bin
```

Be sure to follow the instructions, download the correct DLL, and copy it into the \bin directory beneath your Ruby installation.

Refer to the SQLite site for more information on SQLite: *http://www.sqlite .org/docs.html.* You can find installation help on MySQL in Appendix B of this book. Many other database servers can also be used including Microsoft SQL Server, PostgresSQL, and Oracle.

NOTE *If you plan to install or update Rails from scratch or if you need to update the version pre-installed with your operating system, you should refer to Rails Guides website at* http://guides.rubyonrails.org/getting_started.html. *These guides provide detailed OS-specific information relating to Rails 3. Several Rails wikis also provide information on supporting older versions of Rails—for example,* http://en.wikibooks.org/ wiki/Ruby_on_Rails.

Or Use an "All-in-One" Installer

Various all-in-one Ruby and Rails setup programs are available. These include the Bitnami RubyStack installers for Windows, Linux, and Mac: *http://www .bitnami.org/stack/rubystack/.* Windows users can also use the Rails installer from RubyForge: *http://www.rubyforge.org/frs/?group_id=167.* These installers provide their own installation guides.

Model-View-Controller

A Rails application is divided into three main areas: the Model, the View, and the Controller. Put simply, the Model is the data part—the database and any programmatic operations (such as calculations) that are done upon that data. The View is what the end user sees; in Rails terms, that generally means the web pages that appear in the browser. The Controller is the programming logic—the "glue" that joins the Model to the View.

The Model-View-Controller methodology is used in various forms by all kinds of programming languages and frameworks. It is more fully described in "Digging Deeper" on page 322. For the sake of brevity, I will henceforward call it MVC.

A First Ruby on Rails Application

Without more ado, let's start programming with Rails. I'll assume you have Rails installed, along with a web server. I happen to be using the WEBrick server, which is installed as standard with Rails, but you may use some other server such as Apache, LightTPD, or Mongrel. You can find more information on web servers in Appendix D.

NOTE   *A web server is a program that delivers data, such as web pages, using the Hypertext Transfer Protocol (HTTP). You don't need to understand how this works. You just need to be aware that you need a web server for use with Rails.*

This chapter assumes you are using only the "raw" Rails development tools—programs that are executed from the command line—plus, at the very least, a text editor and a web browser; as a consequence, you will find that you frequently have to enter commands at the system prompt. If you are using an integrated development environment for Rails, you will probably be able to accomplish these tasks much more easily using the tools provided by the IDE.

Unlike the source code examples supplied for the other chapters in this book, the sample code for the Ruby on Rails applications in this chapter is not complete and "ready to run." There are three reasons for this:

- Each Rails application comprises a great many files and folders, most of which are autogenerated by Rails, so it would be pointless to distribute them separately.

- I would also have to supply the data for each database, and you would have to import it prior to using it. Importing databases is often more difficult than creating your own.

- Not only is it simpler to create Rails applications yourself, but doing so will also help you understand how Rails works. I have, however, supplied some sample files—component parts of a complete application—with which you can compare your own code in case you run into problems.

Create a Rails Application

For the sake of simplicity, this first application will not use a database at all. This will let you explore the View and the Controller without having to worry about the complexities of the Model.

To begin, open a system prompt (on Windows, select the Start menu, and enter cmd into the Run or Search box). Navigate to a directory into which you intend to place your Rails applications. Let's assume this is *C:\railsapps*.

Check that Rails is installed and that its home directory is on the system path. To do this, enter the following:

```
rails
```

If all is well, you should now see a screenful of help about using the `rails` command. If you don't see this, there is a problem with your Rails installation that you need to fix before continuing. Refer to "Installing Rails" on page 300.

NOTE *When there are any differences in the commands or code for Rails 2 and Rails 3, these will be indicated in the text with the Rails version number—Rails 2 or Rails 3—in the margin next to the example.*

Assuming Rails is working, you can now create an application. Enter this:

Rails 3
```
rails new helloworld
```

Rails 2
```
rails helloworld
```

After a bit of whirring of your hard disk, you should see a list of the files that Rails has just created (the actual list is quite long, and some of the items created are different in Rails 2 and Rails 3):

```
create  app
create  app/controllers/application_controller.rb
create  app/helpers/application_helper.rb
create  app/mailers
create  app/models
create  app/views/layouts/application.html.erb
create  config
(etcetera)
```

Take a look at these files using your computer's file manager. Beneath the directory in which you ran the Rails command (*\helloworld*), you will see that several new directories have been created: *\app*, *\config*, *\db*, and so on. Some of these have subdirectories. The *\app* directory, for example, contains *\controllers*, *\helpers*, *\models*, and *\views*. The *\views* directory itself contains a subdirectory, *\layouts*.

The directory structure in a Rails application is far from random; the directories (or *folders*) and the names of the files they contain define the relationships between the various parts of the application. The idea behind this is that by adopting a well-defined file-and-folder structure, you can avoid the necessity of writing lots of configuration files to link the various bits of the application together. There is a simplified guide to the default directory structure of Rails in "Digging Deeper" on page 322.

Now, at the system prompt, change the directory to the top-level folder (\helloworld) of your newly generated Rails application. Assuming you are still in the C:\railsapps directory and you named the Rails application *helloworld*, as suggested earlier, you would (on Windows) enter this command to change to that directory:

```
cd helloworld
```

Now run the server. If (like me) you are using WEBrick, you should enter the following:

Rails 3
```
rails server
```

Rails 2
```
ruby script/server
```

Note that servers other than WEBrick may be started in different ways, and if the previous does not work, you will need to consult the server's documentation. You should now see something similar to the following:

```
=> Booting WEBrick...
=> Rails application started on http://0.0.0.0:3000
=> Ctrl-C to shutdown server; call with --help for options
[2006-11-20 13:46:01] INFO  WEBrick 1.3.1
[2006-11-20 13:46:01] INFO  ruby 1.8.4 (2005-12-24) [i386-mswin32]
[2006-11-20 13:46:01] INFO  WEBrick::HTTPServer#start: pid=4568 port=3000
```

PROBLEMS?

If, instead of seeing a message confirming that the server has started, you see error messages, check that you have entered the server command exactly as shown for the version of Rails being used, and check that it is run from within the appropriate directory: \helloworld.

If you still have problems, it is possible that the default port (3000) is already in use—for example, if you already have an Apache server installed on the same PC. In that case, try some other value such as 3003, placing this number after -p when you run the script:

Rails 3
```
rails server –p3003
```

Rails 2
```
ruby script/server –p3003
```

If you see error messages that include the text no such file to load -- sqlite3, be sure you have correctly installed SQLite3 as explained in "Installing Rails" on page 300. If you are attempting to use MySQL and the error message includes the text no such file to load–mysql, refer to Appendix B.

Now fire up a web browser. Enter the host name, followed by a colon and the port number, into its address bar. The host name should (normally) be *localhost*, and the port number should match the one used when starting the server, or else it defaults to 3000. Here is an example:

```
http://localhost:3000/
```

The browser should now display a page welcoming you aboard Rails. If not, verify that your server is running on the port specified in the URL.

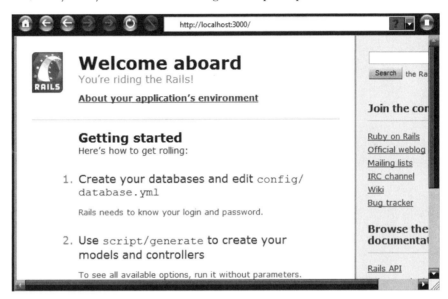

Create a Controller

As mentioned earlier, a Controller is where much of your Ruby code will live. It is the part of the application that sits between the View (what appears in the browser) and the Model (what happens to the data). Because this is a "Hello world" application, let's create a Controller to say "hello." In the spirit of originality, I'll call this the *SayHello* controller. Once again, you can create this by running a script at the system prompt. You will need to open another command window in the directory from which you previously ran the server script (for example, *C:\railsapps\helloworld*). You can't reuse your existing command window because the server is running in that one, and you would need to close it down to get back to the prompt—and that would stop your Rails application from working!

At the prompt, enter this (be sure to use the capitalization of SayHello as shown):

Rails 3

```
rails generate controller SayHello
```

Rails 2

```
ruby script/generate controller SayHello
```

After a few moments, you will be informed that various files and directories have been created, including the following:

```
app/views/say_hello
app/controllers/say_hello_controller.rb
test/functional/say_hello_controller_test.rb
app/helpers/say_hello_helper.rb
```

NOTE   *The generate controller script also creates the file* application_controller.rb *in Rails 3 or* application.rb *in Rails 2, which is the controller for the entire application, plus a folder,* /views/say_hello, *which you will make use of shortly.*

Notice how Rails has parsed the name SayHello into two lowercase words, say and hello, separated by an underscore, and it has used this name as the first part of the generated Ruby files such as say_hello_controller.rb. This is just one example of the "configuration by convention" approach that Rails uses.

Locate the controller file *say_hello_controller.rb*, which has been created in *\helloworld\app\controllers*. Open this file in a text editor. This empty method has been autogenerated:

```
class SayHelloController < ApplicationController
end
```

Inside this class you can write some code to be executed when a certain page is displayed. Edit the class definition to match the following:

```
class SayHelloController < ApplicationController
    def index
        render :text => "Hello world"
    end

    def bye
        render :text => "Bye bye"
    end
end
```

This now contains two methods, index and bye. Each method contains a single line of code. In spite of the fact that I have omitted parentheses (a parentheses-light style of coding is favored by many Rails developers), you can probably deduce that render is a method that takes a hash as an argument; the hash itself contains a key-value pair comprising a symbol and a string. For parentheses-lovers, the index method can be rewritten like this:

```
def index
   render( { :text => "Hello world" } )
end
```

And there you have your first real Rails application. To try it, you need to go back to the web browser and enter the full "address" of the two functions you just wrote. But first you may need to restart your server. Just press CTRL-C in the command window where the server is running. When the server exits, restart by entering the following:

Rails 3

```
rails server
```

Rails 2

```
ruby script/server
```

There's just one more thing you have to do in Rails 3. You need to tell it how to find a "route" specified by an address entered into web browser. This step is not required for Rails 2. In Rails 3, open the *routes.rb* file in your *helloworld\config* folder. Now edit it to match the following (or simply uncomment the line of code that you'll find at the bottom of the file):

```
match ':controller(/:action(/:id(.:format)))'
```

You are now ready to test the application. To do so, you just need to enter an address to access a controller method. The address takes the form of the host and port (the same as you entered previously—for example, *http://localhost:3000*), plus the name of the controller (*/say_hello*) and finally the name of a specific method (*/index* or */bye*). Try entering these, as shown next, into your browser's address field, once again ensuring that you are using the appropriate port number if it is not 3000:

```
http://localhost:3000/say_hello/index
http://localhost:3000/say_hello/bye
```

Your browser should display "Hello world" and "Bye bye" respectively for each address. If all is working at this point, you can bathe in the warm glow of having created your first Ruby on Rails application. If however, you are seeing MySQL database errors, read "Can't Find the Database?" on page 351 and fix the problem before continuing.

Incidentally, Rails uses the index method as a default so you can use the index view as your home page and omit that part of the URL when entering the address into the browser:

```
http://localhost:3000/say_hello
```

Anatomy of a Simple Rails Application

Before moving on, let's take a closer look at the class that you have created in this application. Rails has named the class by appending *Controller* to the name you specified when running the controller generator script (HelloWorld), and it has made it a descendant of the ApplicationController class:

```
class SayHelloController < ApplicationController
```

But what exactly is the ApplicationController class? You may recall that I mentioned that the generate `controller` script you ran earlier silently created a file called *application_controller.rb* (Rails 3) or *application.rb* (Rails 2) inside the */app/controllers* folder. This file is the application controller, and if you open it, you will see that it contains a class called as follows:

```
ApplicationController < ActionController::Base
```

So, the SayHelloController class descends from the ApplicationController class that itself descends from the Base class in the `ActionController` module. You can prove this by climbing back through the hierarchy and asking each class to display itself. This, incidentally, also gives you the chance to try doing some real Ruby programming in the SayHelloController class.

Just edit the contents of *say_hello_controller.rb* file to match the following (or copy and paste the code from the *sayhello1.rb* file in the code archive for this chapter):

sayhello1.rb

```
class SayHelloController < ApplicationController
    def showFamily( aClass, msg )
        if (aClass != nil) then
            msg += "<br />#{aClass}"
            showFamily( aClass.superclass, msg )
        else
            render :text => msg
        end
    end

    def index
        showFamily( self.class, "Class Hierarchy of self..." )
    end
end
```

To see the result, enter this address into your browser (once again, change the port number if necessary):

```
http://localhost:3000/say_hello
```

Your web browser should now display the following (in Rails 3):

```
Class Hierarchy of self...
SayHelloController
ApplicationController
ActionController::Base
ActionController::Metal
AbstractController::Base
Object
BasicObject
```

In Rails 2 it will display the following:

```
Class Hierarchy of self...
SayHelloController
ApplicationController
ActionController::Base
Object
```

Don't worry about the actual class ancestry; the internal implementation details of the Rails framework are not of immediate interest. The important thing to understand is that a controller is a real Ruby object that inherits behavior from the ApplicationController class and its ancestors. Any Rails controller class you write or that is autogenerated by running scripts can contain normal Ruby code, just like all the other classes you've written in previous chapters. Within a controller, you can use all the usual Ruby classes such as strings and hashes.

But bear in mind that the end result needs to be displayed in a web page. This has certain consequences. For example, instead of putting line-feeds ("\n") into strings, you should use HTML paragraph (<P>) or break (<br />) tags, and it is only permissible to call render once each time a page is displayed, which explains why I've constructed a string in the course of calling the method recursively and then passed this to the render method right at the end:

```
def showFamily( aClass, msg )
    if (aClass != nil) then
        msg += "<br />#{aClass}"
        showFamily( aClass.superclass, msg )
    else
        render :text => msg
    end
end
```

The Generate Controller Script Summarized

Before moving on, let's consolidate the fundamental details of running the Rails generate controller script and learn a few extra tricks you can use when creating views. Each time a new controller is generated, it creates a Ruby code file in the *app/controllers* directory, with a name matching the name you entered but all in lowercase, with any noninitial capitals that you specified being preceded by an underscore and *_controller* appended. So, if you entered *SayHello*, the controller file will be called *say_hello_controller.rb*. The controller will contain a class definition such as SayHelloController. You may subsequently add to this class some "view methods" such as index and bye. Alternatively, you may use the generate script to create one or more empty view methods automatically by including those view names when you execute the script.

For example, you could run this script:

Rails 3

```
rails generate controller SayHello index bye
```

Rails 2

```
ruby script/generate controller SayHello index bye
```

Rails will now create the file *say_hello_controller.rb*, containing this code:

```
class SayHelloController < ApplicationController
    def index
    end

    def bye
    end
end
```

Whether or not you specify views, a folder in the */views* directory is created with a name matching the controller (*views/say_hello*). In fact, the script also creates a few other files including some more Ruby files in the */helpers* folder, but in our simple application you can ignore these files.

If you specified view names when running the controller script, some files with matching names and the extension *.html.erb* will be added to the appropriate view folder. For instance, if you entered the following command:

```
ruby script/generate controller SayHello xxx
```

the */views/say_hello* directory should now contain a file called *xxx.html.erb*. If, on the other hand, you entered the following:

```
ruby script/generate controller Blather xxx bye snibbit
```

the *views/blather* directory should now contain three files: *xxx.html.erb*, *bye.html.erb*, and *snibbit.html.erb*.

Create a View

It would be possible to create an entire application by coding everything inside a Controller and doing all the formatting inside view methods. However, you would soon end up with some pretty ugly web pages. To apply more formatting, you need to create a View that more accurately defines the layout of a web page.

You can think of a View as an HTML page that will be displayed when someone logs onto a specific web address—in which case, the name of the View forms the final part of the address as in the previous examples where the */index* and */bye* parts of the URL took you to views that displayed data supplied by the index and bye methods in the Controller.

You can create HTML view "templates" that match these web addresses and the corresponding method names. Using an HTML (or plaintext) editor, create a file named *index.html.erb* in the *\app\views\say_hello* directory, if such a template does not already exist. Remember, as explained previously (in "The Generate Controller Script Summarized" on page 309), you can optionally autocreate one or more view templates when you initially generate the Controller.

Now that you have a view template, you can edit it in order to control the way data is displayed in the web page. That means you won't need to display plain, unformatted text using the render method in the Controller from now on. But, with the View being out of the Controller's control (so to speak), how can the Controller pass data to the View? In turns out that it can do this by assigning data to an instance variable.

Edit the code in *say_hello_controller.rb* (or delete it and paste in the code from the file *sayhello2.rb*, supplied in the source code archive) so that it matches the following:

sayhello2.rb

```
class SayHelloController < ApplicationController
    def showFamily( aClass, msg )
        if (aClass != nil) then
            msg += "<li>#{aClass}</li>"
            showFamily( aClass.superclass, msg )
        else
            return msg
        end
    end

    def index
        @class_hierarchy = "<ul>#{showFamily( self.class, "" )}</ul>"
    end
end
```

This version calls the showFamily() method in order to build up a string inside two HTML "unordered list" tags, <ul> and </ul>. Each time a class name is found, it is placed between two HTML "list item" tags, <li> and </li>. The complete string forms a valid HTML fragment, and the index method simply assigns this string a variable named @class_hierarchy.

HTML TAGS IN THE CONTROLLER?

Some Ruby on Rails developers object to having *any* HTML tags, no matter how trivial, included in the Controller code. In my opinion, if you intend to display the end results in a web page, it little matters where you put the odd <p>, <ul>, or <li> tag. Although the MVC paradigm encourages strong separation between the program code of the Controller and the layout definition of the View, you will inevitably have to make some compromises—at the very least by putting some program code into the View. Avoiding the use of HTML tags in the Controller is, largely, an aesthetic rather than a pragmatic objection. I personally have no very strong views on the subject, though (be warned!) other people do.

All you need to do now is to find some way of putting that HTML fragment into a fully formed HTML page. That's where the View comes in. Open the view file you just created, *index.html.erb*, in the *app/views/say_hello* folder. According to the Rails naming convention, this is the default view (the "index" page) that is partnered with the *say_hello_controller.rb* file. Since Rails works out relationships based on file, folder, class, and method names, you don't have to load or require any files by name or write any configuration details.

In the *index.html.erb* file, add this:

```
<h1>This is the Controller's Class Hierarchy</h1>
<%= @class_hierarchy %>
```

The first line is nothing more than plain HTML formatting that defines the text enclosed by the <h1></h1> tags as a heading. The next line is more interesting. It contains the variable @class_hierarchy. Look back at the index method in *say_hello_controller.rb*, and you'll see that this is the variable to which you assigned a string. Here in the View, @class_hierarchy is placed between two odd-looking delimiters: <%= and %>. These are special Rails tags. They are used to embed bits of Ruby that will be executed prior to displaying a web page in the browser. The page that is finally displayed will be a fully formed HTML page that includes any HTML fragments from the view template plus the results, after execution, of any embedded Ruby code. Try it now, by entering the page address into your browser:

```
http://localhost:3000/say_hello/
```

This should now display the heading "This is the Controller's Class Hierarchy" in big, bold letters followed by a list of classes each element of which is preceded by a dot. In Rails 2, this is what you'll see:

- SayHelloController
- ApplicationController
- ActionController::Base
- Object

However, in Rails 3, you seem to have a problem. Instead of a list, the HTML tags are rendered literally like this:

```
<ul><li>SayHelloController</li><li>ApplicationController</
li><li>ActionController::Base</li><li>ActionController::Metal</
li><li>AbstractController::Base</li><li>Object</li><li>BasicObject</li></ul>
```

This definitely is not what you want. The explanation for this is that the default treatment of HTML tags embedded in strings has changed between Rails 2 and Rails 3. In Rails 2, tags were passed through to the View unmodified. In Rails 3, substitution is done to ensure that HTML tags are displayed on the screen rather than rendered by the browser. For example, the <li> tag is changed to <li> where < and > are the HTML codes for angle brackets (< and >). To ensure that HTML tags are not substituted in this way, you need to use the raw method, passing to it a string argument. This is *index.html.erb* rewritten for Rails 3:

```
<h1>This is the Controller's Class Hierarchy</h1>
<%= raw( @class_hierarchy ) %>
```

Now when you log onto the address *http://localhost:3000/say_hello* in Rails 3, you should see class names shown as a bulleted list with no HTML tags displayed.

You could, if you want, remove all the HTML from the view file by creating the heading in the Controller and assigning the resulting string to another variable. You can do this by editing the index method in *say_hello_controller.rb* to this:

```
def index
    @heading = "<h1>This is the Controller's Class Hierarchy</h1>"
    @class_hierarchy = "<ul>#{showFamily( self.class, "" )}</ul>"
end
```

Then edit the view file (*/app/views/say_hello/index.html.erb*) to match the code shown next (or cut and paste the code from the sample file into *index.html.erb*) for use with Rails 3:

say_hello_rails3
.html.erb
```
<%= raw( @heading ) %>
<%= raw( @class_hierarchy ) %>
```

For Rails 2, use this code:

say_hello.html.erb
```
<%= @heading %>
<%= @class_hierarchy %>
```

If you do this, the end result, as displayed in the web page, will remain unchanged. All that's happened is that some formatting has been moved out of the view template and into the Controller.

Rails Tags

There are two variations on the Rails tags that you can place into Rails HTML Embedded Ruby (ERb) template files. The ones you've used so far include an equal sign in the opening delimiter: <%=.

These tags cause Rails not only to evaluate Ruby expressions but also to display the results in a web page. If you omit the equals sign from the opening delimiter, then the code will be evaluated, but the result will not be displayed: <%.

NOTE *ERb files contain a mix of HTML markup and Ruby code between tags such as <%= and %>. Rails processes these files before the final pages are displayed in the web browser, executing the embedded Ruby and constructing the HTML page as a result.*

If you want, you can place quite long pieces of code—your entire Ruby program even!—between <% and %> tags and then use <%= and %> when you want to display something in the web page. In fact, you could rewrite your application by omitting the Controller entirely and putting everything into the View. Try it by editing *app/views/say_hello/index.html.erb* to match the following (or copy and paste the code from the file *embed_ruby_rails2.html.erb* or *embed_ruby_rails3.html.erb* according to the Rails version being used):

embed_ruby_ rails3.rhtml

```
<% def showFamily( aClass, msg )
     if (aClass != nil) then
         msg += "<li>#{aClass}</li>"
         showFamily( aClass.superclass, msg )
     else
       return msg
     end
   end %>

<%= raw( "<ul>#{showFamily( self.class, "" )}</ul>" ) %>
```

In this particular case, the text displayed in the web page will be slightly different from before since it now shows the class hierarchy of the *view's* class, rather than that of the controller's class. As you will see, the view descends from the ActionView::Base class.

You can also divide a contiguous block of code by placing the individual lines between <% and %> tags instead of placing the entire block between a single pair. The advantage of doing this is that it lets you put standard HTML tags outside the individually delimited lines of Ruby code. You could, for instance, put this into a view:

```
<% arr = ['h','e','l','l','o',' ','w','o','r','l','d'] %>

<% # sort descending from upper value down to nil
reverse_sorted_arr = arr.sort{
    |a,b|
        b.to_s <=> a.to_s
    } %>

<% i = 1 %>
<ul>
<% reverse_sorted_arr.each{ |item| %>
<li><%= "Item [#{i}] = #{item}" %></li>
<% i += 1 %>
<% } %>
</ul>
```

Here, I've assigned an array of chars to the variable, arr, between one set of tags. I've written a block to reverse-sort the array and assigned the result to another variable between a second set of tags. Then I've assigned 1 to the variable, i; and finally I've written this method:

```
reverse_sorted_arr.each{ |item|
    "Item [#{i}] = #{item}"
    i += 1
}
```

But instead of enclosing the method between a single set of <% %> tags, I've enclosed each separate line within its own pair of tags. Why should I do this? Well, there are two reasons. First, I want the string in the middle of the block to be displayed on the web page, so I need to use the <%= tag there:

```
<%= "Item [#{i}] = #{item}" %>
```

And second, I want the whole set of strings to be displayed as an HTML list. So, I've placed the <ul> and </ul> tags before and after the Ruby code block, and I've placed the line of code that displays each array item inside <li> and </li> tags. Notice that these tags are *inside* the Ruby code block but *outside* the embedded Ruby tags on this particular line:

```
<li><%= "Item [#{i}] = #{item}" %></li>
```

So, by dividing up a contiguous block of Ruby code into separately delimited lines, I am no longer forced to construct strings to contain HTML tags. Instead, I have been able to do the useful trick of mixing HTML into the Ruby code itself. To be honest, I haven't really mixed it in at all—the Ruby code is still closed off inside the tags; what I've done is told Rails to mix in the HTML at specific points prior to displaying the page in a web browser.

Incidentally, you may find it interesting to compare the version of the application that puts all the embedded Ruby code into the view (*index.html.erb*) with the previous version in which the code was all put into the Controller (the version of *say_hello_controller.rb* supplied in the sample file *sayhello2.rb*) and only tiny bits of embedded Ruby (a couple of variables) were placed into the view:

```
<%= @heading %>
<%= @class_hierarchy %>
```

You will probably agree that the first version, in which the programming logic was put into the Controller rather than embedded into the View, is neater. On the whole, Ruby code belongs in Ruby code files, and HTML formatting belongs in HTML files. Although embedded Ruby provides an easy way of letting a View and a Controller communicate, it is generally better to keep embedded Ruby code short and simple and put more complex Ruby code into Ruby code files.

Let's Make a Blog!

For many people, the one thing that really "turned them on" to Ruby on Rails was the 20-minute demo given by Rails's creator, David Heinemeier Hansson, in which he showed how to create a simple weblog. That demo was originally done using Rails 1 and has since been updated (and changed somewhat) for Rails 2 and Rails 3. You can watch the latest demos online at *http://www.rubyonrails.com/screencasts/*.

A blog is a great way to show how easy it is to create a fairly complex application using Rails. In the remainder of this chapter, I'll explain how you can create a very simple blog application. I'll use a feature called *migrations*, which will cut out a lot of the hard work of creating the database structure of the Model.

Bear in mind that I have tried to keep the creation of this application as simple as possible. It is not an exact duplication of David Heinemeier Hansson's tutorial, and it has only a subset of the features of a fully functional blog (there are no user comments and no administration interface, for example). Once you have completed my blog application, you may want to study the screencast tutorials mentioned earlier. These will show you alternative ways of producing similar results, and they will also take you further toward the creation of a more complex blog.

NOTE *You can compare the code of your blog application with one I created. My code is supplied in the\blog subdirectory of the code accompanying this chapter. This blog application is not "ready to run," however, because it requires a database that you will have to create. You should create your own blog application by following the instructions given in the chapter. You may use the supplied code as a reference to check that the files you create match the ones I created.*

Open a command prompt in the directory in which you keep your Rails applications (for example, *C:\railsapps*), and execute a command to create an application called Blog:

Rails 3

```
rails new blog
```

Rails 2

```
rails blog
```

Create the Database

Now let's create a database. Here I am assuming you are using either the SQLite3 or MySQL database. As said earlier, SQLite3 is regarded as the standard database system for local development with Rails 3, and it is easier to set up and use. MySQL, on the other hand, is an industry-standard database that is more likely to be used for deployment on a website. If you are using SQLite3, you won't need to take any special actions to create the database—Rails does it for you. You can skip straight to "Scaffolding" on page 317. If you are using MySQL, you should follow the steps outlined in the next sections.

Creating a MySQL Database

If you are using MySQL, open a MySQL prompt by running the MySQL Command Line Client from the MySQL program group. When prompted, enter your MySQL password. Now you should see this prompt:

```
mysql>
```

Enter the following at the prompt (be sure to put the semicolon at the end):

```
create database blog_development;
```

MySQL should reply "Query OK" to confirm that the database has been created. Now ensure that your database configuration file for your Rails application contains the appropriate entries for the development database. If you are using some other database (not MySQL), your configuration entries must refer to that database.

Go to the folder in which Rails created your new blog application, and open the file *database.yml* in the \config\ subdirectory. Assuming you are using MySQL, enter *mysql* as the adapter, *localhost* as the host, your MySQL username (for example, *root*), and your password, if you have one. The database name should match the database you just created. Here is an example (where you would enter an actual password instead of *mypassword*):

```
development:
  adapter: mysql
  host: localhost
  username: root
  database: blog_development
  password: mypassword
```

NOTE   *If the server is running when you make changes to* database.yml, *you should restart the server afterward!*

It is common to have multiple configurations—for example, for development, test, and production. For the sake of simplicity, here you will create a development configuration only; you may comment out any other entries in *database.yml*.

Scaffolding

You are going to use a feature called *scaffolding* to create a model, views, and controllers all in one go. Scaffolding is a convenient way of getting a simple application up and running quickly. Move into the new \blog directory, and enter the following at the system prompt:

Rails 3
```
rails generate scaffold post title:string body:text created_at:datetime
```

Rails 2
```
ruby script/generate scaffold post title:string body:text created_at:datetime
```

This tells the scaffold generator to create a model comprising Ruby code to access a database table called *post* with three columns, *title*, *body*, and *created_at*, each of which has the data type (*string, text* and *datetime*) specified after the colon. To create the database structure based on this model, you need to run a "migration" to update the database table itself.

Migration

The scaffold script has created a database migration file for you. Navigate to the *\db\migrate* directory. You will see that this contains a numbered migration file whose name ends with *_create_posts.rb*. If you open this file, you can see how the table structure is represented in Ruby code:

```
def self.up
    create_table :posts do |t|
        t.string :title
        t.text :body
        t.datetime :created_at

        t.timestamps
    end
end
```

An application may, over time, gain numerous migrations, each of which contains information on a specific iteration of the Model—changes and additions made to the table structure of the database. Experienced Rails developers can use migrations selectively to activate different versions of the Model. Here, however, you will use this migration to create the initial structure of the database.

At the system prompt in your application's main directory (for example, */blog*), you can use the rake tool to run the migration. Enter this command:

```
rake db:migrate
```

After a few moments, you should see a message stating that the rake task has completed and that CreatePosts has been migrated.

Partials

Now let's create a new partial view template. A *partial* is a fragment of a web page template that Rails may insert, at runtime, into one or more complete web pages. If, for example, you plan to have the same data entry form in multiple pages on your site, you could create that form inside a partial template. The names of partial templates begin with an underscore.

Create a new file called *_post.html.erb* in your *app**views**posts*\ directory. Open this file, and edit its contents to match the following (or you may copy the *_post.html.erb* from the sample project in the source code archive):

_post.html.erb

```
<div>
<h2><%= link_to post.title, :action => 'show', :id => post %></h2>
<p><%= post.body %></p>
<p><small>
<%= post.created_at.to_s %>
</small></p>
</div>
```

Save your changes. Then open the file named *show.html.erb*. This file was automatically created by the scaffold script. Delete the following "boilerplate" code from the file:

```
<b>Title:</b>
<%=h @post.title %>
</p>

<p>
<b>Body:</b>
<%=h @post.body %>
</p>

<p>
<b>Created at:</b>
<%=h @post.created_at %>
</p>
```

And replace it with this:

```
<%= render :partial => "post", :object => @post %>
```

This tells Rails to render the _post partial template at this point. The code in *show.html.erb* should now look like this:

```
<%= render :partial => "post", :object => @post %>

<%= link_to 'Edit', edit_post_path(@post) %> |
<%= link_to 'Back', posts_path %>
```

Test It!

And that's it! Now you are ready to test your application. First, run the server. At the prompt in the *\blog* directory, enter this:

Rails 3
```
rails server
```

Rails 2
```
ruby script/server
```

NOTE *Recall that if you are not using the default port, 3000, you will need to specify the actual port number after -p as explained earlier in this chapter, for example:* `rails server -p3003`.

Go into your web browser, and enter the following address (again, use the actual port number if this is not 3000):

```
http://localhost:3000/posts
```

You should see your page with its index page active. This is what should appear:

Now click the New Post link. In the New Post page, enter a title and some body text. Then click **Create**.

The next page that displays is the Show page. This is defined by the combination of the *show.html.erb* view and the *_post.html.erb* partial. Now carry on entering posts and clicking the links to navigate through the various defined views.

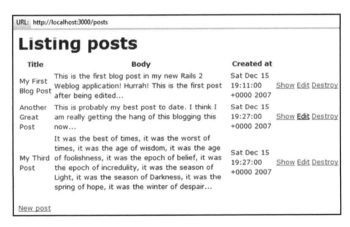

NOTE   *As mentioned earlier, this chapter assumes you are using Rails "in the raw," by entering all the necessary commands at the system prompt. Some IDEs provide a more integrated environment, which allows you to generate and code your application using built-in tools and utilities. You will find an overview of some Ruby and Rails IDEs in Appendix D.*

DIGGING DEEPER

The three letters "MVC" are fundamental to understanding how Rails works. Here I explain the underlying concepts. You will also learn about the Rails directory structure and alternative Ruby frameworks.

MVC

As explained earlier, Rails adopts the Model-View-Controller (MVC) paradigm. Put simply, these may be thought of as the database (Model), the display (View), and the programming logic (Controller).

Although these three component parts are, in theory, separate entities, there is, in practice, inevitably a degree of overlap. For instance, some calculations may be done in the Model with others done in the Controller; operations that affect the formatting of data could happen in the Controller or in the View. There are no hard-and-fast rules—just a general principle that, as much as possible, operations "close to the data" should happen in the Model, operations "close to the display" should happen in the View, and everything else should go into the Controller.

That's MVC in theory. Now let's see how it is implemented by Rails.

Model

The Model in Ruby on Rails is a combination of tables in a database—handled by a database server such as MySQL—and a matching set of Ruby classes to work upon those tables. For example, in a blog you might have a database containing a table called Posts. In that case, the Rails model would also contain a Ruby class named Post (notice that Rails works with plurals—the Posts table can contain many Post objects). The Ruby Post class would typically contain methods to find, save, or load individual Post records from the Posts database. This combination of database tables and corresponding Ruby classes comprises a Rails Model.

View

The View is pretty much what it sounds like—the visual representation of a Ruby on Rails application. It is (typically but not necessarily) created in the form of HTML templates with some Ruby code mixed in. In fact, other view types (for example, a graphical view made using Adobe's Flex or Microsoft's Silverlight) are possible, but the Rails default is HTML. These templates, which generally have the extension *.html.erb* (but may also use the extension *.rhtml* that was the Rails 1 default), are not loaded directly into a web browser—after all, web browsers haven't any way of running Ruby code. Instead, they are preprocessed by a separate tool that executes the Ruby code in order to interact with the Model (finding or editing data as necessary); then, as an end result, it creates a new HTML page whose basic layout is defined by an

ERb template but whose actual data (that is, the blog posts, shopping cart items, or whatever) are provided by the Model. This makes it possible to create highly dynamic web pages that change as a user interacts with them.

Controller

The Controller takes the form of Ruby code files that act as go-betweens that link the Model and the View. For example, in the web page (the View), a user might click a button to add a new post to a blog; using ordinary HTML, this button submits a value named Create. This causes a method named create, in a post "controller" (a file of Ruby code) to save the new blog entry (some text) that has been entered in the web page (the View) into the database (the data repository of the Model).

The Rails Folders

This is a simplified guide to the top-level folders generated by Rails, with a brief description of the files and folders they contain:

app	This contains the code specific to this application. Sub-folders may include *app\controllers*, *app\models*, *app\views*, *app\helpers*, and *app\mailers*.
config	This contains configuration files for the Rails environment, the routing map, the database, and other dependencies; database configuration is put into the file *database.yml*.
db	This contains the database schema in *schema.rb* and may contain code that works on the data in the database. If migrations have been applied, it will also contain migration files in the *\migrate* subdirectory.
doc	This may contain RDOC documentation (see Appendix A for more on RDOC).
lib	This may contain code libraries (that is, code that does not logically belong in *\controllers*, *\models*, or *\helpers*) for the application.
log	This may contain error logs.
public	This directory contains "static" files that may be used by the web server. It has subdirectories for *images*, *stylesheets*, and *javascripts*.
script	This contains scripts that Rails uses to perform various tasks such as generating certain file types and running the web server.
test	This may contain tests generated by Rails or specified by the user.
tmp	This contains temporary files used by Rails.
vendor	This may contain third-party libraries that do not form part of the default Rails installation.

Other Ruby Frameworks

Rails may be the most famous Ruby framework, but it certainly is not the only one. Others such as Ramaze and Sinatra also have a dedicated following. A framework called Merb was once seen as the closest competitor to Rails. However, in December 2008, the Rails and Merb teams announced they would be collaborating on the next iteration of Rails, and it was that collaboration that resulted in Rails 3.

If you are interested in exploring other Ruby frameworks, follow these links:

- Ramaze: *http://www.ramaze.net/*
- Sinatra: *http://www.sinatrarb.com/*
- Waves: *http://www.rocket.ly/waves*

Bear in mind that open source Ruby frameworks have a tendency to come and go, waxing and waning according to the enthusiasm or other commitments of the core developers. The Ramaze team maintains a list of Ruby frameworks on its home wiki: *http://wiki.ramaze.net/Home#other-frameworks.*

20

DYNAMIC PROGRAMMING

In the past 19 chapters, I've covered a huge range of features of the Ruby language. One thing I haven't covered in any detail is Ruby's dynamic programming capability.

If you have used only a nondynamic language (say one of the languages from the C or Pascal family), it is likely that dynamism in programming may take a little getting used to. Before going any further, I'll clarify what I mean by a *dynamic* language. The definition is, in fact, a bit vague, and not all languages that lay claim to being dynamic share all the same features. In a general sense, however, a language that provides some means by which programs may be modified at runtime can be considered to be dynamic. Another quality of a dynamic language is its ability to change the type of a given variable—something you have done countless times in the examples throughout this book.

A further distinction may also be made between a *dynamically typed* language such as Ruby and a *statically typed* language (one in which the type of a variable is predeclared and fixed) such as C, Java, or Pascal. In this chapter, I will concentrate on the self-modifying capabilities of Ruby.

NOTE *In formal computer science, the term* dynamic programming *is sometimes used to describe an analytic approach to solving complex problems. That is not the sense in which the term is used in this chapter.*

Self-Modifying Programs

In most compiled languages and many interpreted languages, writing programs and running programs are two completely distinct operations: The code you write is fixed, and it is beyond any possibility of further alteration by the time the program is run.

That is not the case with Ruby. A program—by which I mean *the Ruby code itself*—can be modified while the program is running. It is even possible to enter new Ruby code at runtime and execute the new code without restarting the program.

The ability to treat data as executable code is called *metaprogramming*. You've been doing metaprogramming, albeit of a rather simple sort, throughout this book. Every time you embed an expression inside a double-quoted string, you are doing metaprogramming. After all, the embedded expression is not really program code—it is a string—and yet Ruby clearly has to "turn it into" program code in order to be able to evaluate it.

Most of the time you will probably embed rather simple bits of code between the #{ and } delimiters in double-quoted strings. Often you might embed variable names, say, or mathematical expressions:

str_eval.rb
```
aStr = 'hello world'
puts( "#{aStr}" )
puts( "#{2*10}" )
```

But you aren't limited to such simple expressions. You could, if you wanted, embed just about anything into a double-quoted string. You could, in fact, write an entire program in a string. You don't even need to display the end result using print or puts. Just placing a double-quoted string into your program will cause Ruby to evaluate it:

```
"#{def x(s)
        puts(s.reverse)
    end;
(1..3).each{x(aStr)}}"
```

Even though the previous code fragment is a string, the Ruby interpreter will evaluate its embedded code and display the result, shown here:

```
dlrow olleh
dlrow olleh
dlrow olleh
```

Interesting as this may be, writing a whole program inside a string would probably be a pretty pointless endeavor. However, there are other occasions when this, and similar, features can be used much more productively. For example, you might use metaprogramming to explore artificial intelligence and "machine learning." In fact, any application that would benefit from having a program's behavior modified in response to user interaction is a prime candidate for metaprogramming.

NOTE   *Dynamic (metaprogramming) features are ubiquitous in Ruby. Consider, for example, attribute accessors: Passing a symbol (such as :aValue) to the* attr_accessor *method causes two methods (*aValue *and* aValue= *) to be created.*

eval

The eval method provides a simple way of evaluating a Ruby expression in a string. At first sight, eval may appear to do the same job as the #{ } delimiters in a double-quoted string. These two lines of code produce identical results:

eval.rb
```
puts( eval("1 + 2" ) )      #=> 3
puts( "#{1 + 2}" )          #=> 3
```

Sometimes, however, the results may not be what you are expecting. Look at the following, for instance:

eval_string.rb
```
exp = gets().chomp()     #<= User enters 2*4
puts( eval( exp ))       #=> 8
puts( "#{exp}" )         #=> 2*4
```

Let's suppose you enter 2 * 4, and this is assigned to exp. When you evaluate exp with eval, the result is 8, but when you evaluate exp in a double-quoted string, the result is "2*4". This is because anything read in by gets() is a string and "#{exp}" evaluates it *as a string* and not as an expression, whereas eval(exp) evaluates a string *as an expression*. To force evaluation inside a string, you could place eval in the string (though that, admittedly, might defeat the object of the exercise):

```
puts( "#{eval(exp)}" )
```

Here is another example. Try it, and follow the instructions when prompted:

```
print("Enter a string method name (e.g. reverse or upcase):")
                              # user enters: upcase
methodname = gets().chomp()
exp2 = "'Hello world'."<< methodname
puts( eval( exp2 ) )                 #=> HELLO WORLD
puts( "#{exp2}" )                    #=> 'Hello world'.upcase
puts( "#{eval(exp2)}" )              #=> HELLO WORLD
```

The eval method can evaluate strings spanning many lines, making it possible to execute an entire program embedded in a string:

```
eval( 'def aMethod( x )
    return( x * 2 )
end


num = 100
puts( "This is the result of the calculation:" )
puts( aMethod( num ))' )
```

Look carefully at the previous code. It contains just one executable expression, which is a call to the eval() method. Everything else, which at first sight *looks* like code, is in fact a single-quoted string that is passed as an argument to eval(). The eval() method "unpacks" the contents of the string and turns it into real Ruby code that is then executed. This is displayed:

```
This is the result of the calculation:
200
```

With all this eval cleverness, let's now see how easy it is to write a program that can itself write programs. Here it is:

```
input = ""
until input == "q"
    input = gets().chomp()
    if input != "q" then eval( input ) end
end
```

This may not look like much, and yet this little program lets you both create and execute Ruby code from a prompt. Try it. Run the program, and enter the two methods shown here one line at a time (but *don't hit* Q *to quit yet*—you'll be writing some more code in a moment):

```
def x(aStr); puts(aStr.upcase);end
def y(aStr); puts(aStr.reverse);end
```

Note that you have to enter each whole method on a single line since the program evaluates every line as it is entered. I'll explain how to get around that limitation later. Thanks to eval, each method is turned into real, workable Ruby code. You can prove this by entering the following:

```
x("hello world")
y("hello world")
```

Now, when you press ENTER after each line in the previous code, the expressions are evaluated, and they call the two methods, x() and y(), which you wrote a moment ago, resulting in this output:

```
HELLO WORLD
dlrow olleh
```

That's not bad for just five lines of code!

Special Types of eval

There are some variations on the eval theme in the form of the methods named instance_eval, module_eval, and class_eval. The instance_eval method can be called from a specific object, and it provides access to the instance variables of that object. It can be called either with a block or with a string:

instance_eval.rb
```
class MyClass
 def initialize
   @aVar = "Hello world"
 end
end

ob = MyClass.new
p( ob.instance_eval { @aVar } )          #=> "Hello world"
p( ob.instance_eval( "@aVar" ) )         #=> "Hello world"
```

The eval method, on the other hand, cannot be called from an object in this way because it is a private method of Object (whereas instance_eval is public):

```
p( ob.eval( "@aVar" ) )      # This won't work!
```

In fact, you could explicitly change the visibility of eval by sending its name (the symbol :eval) to the public method. Here I am adding eval as a public method of the Object class:

```
class Object
    public :eval
end
```

Indeed, bearing in mind that when you write "free-standing" code you are actually working within the scope of Object, simply entering the following code (without the Object class "wrapper") would have the same effect:

```
public :eval
```

Now you can use eval as a method of the ob variable:

```
p( ob.eval( "@aVar" ) )          #=> "Hello world"
```

NOTE   *Strictly speaking,* eval *is a method of the* Kernel *module that is mixed into the* Object *class. In fact, it is the* Kernel *module that provides most of the functions available as methods of Object.*

The modification of class definitions at runtime is sometimes called *monkey patching.* This may have a part to play in certain highly specialized types of programming, but as a general principle, gratuitous messing about with standard Ruby classes is definitely *not* recommended. Changing the visibility of methods and adding new behavior to base classes are excellent ways of creating inscrutable code dependencies (in which, for example, your own programs work because you happen to know how you've changed a base class, but your colleagues' programs don't work because they don't know how the classes have been changed).

The module_eval and class_eval methods operate on modules and classes rather than on objects. For example, the code shown next adds the xyz method to the X module (here xyz is defined in a block and added as an instance method of the receiver by define_method, which is a method of the Module class), and it adds the abc method to the Y class:

module_eval.rb
```
module X
end

class Y
    @@x = 10
    include X
end

X::module_eval{ define_method(:xyz){ puts("hello" ) } }
Y::class_eval{ define_method(:abc){ puts("hello, hello" ) } }
```

NOTE   *When accessing class and module methods, you can use the scope resolution operator* :: *or a single dot. The scope resolution operator is obligatory when accessing constants and optional when accessing methods.*

So, now an object that is an instance of Y will have access to both the abc method of the Y class and the xyz method of the X module that has been mixed into the Y class:

```
ob = Y.new
ob.xyz        #=> hello
ob.abc        #=> hello, hello
```

In spite of their names, module_eval and class_eval are functionally identical, and each can be used with either a module or a class:

```
X::class_eval{ define_method(:xyz2){ puts("hello again" ) } } }
Y::module_eval{ define_method(:abc2){ puts("hello, hello again") }}
```

You can also add methods into Ruby's standard classes in the same way:

```
String::class_eval{ define_method(:bye){ puts("goodbye" ) } }
"Hello".bye        #=> goodbye
```

Adding Variables and Methods

You can also use the module_eval and class_eval methods to retrieve the values of class variables (but bear in mind that the more you do this, the more your code becomes dependent on the implementation details of a class, thereby compromising encapsulation):

```
Y.class_eval( "@@x" )
```

In fact, class_eval can evaluate expressions of arbitrary complexity. You could, for example, use it to add new methods to a class by evaluating a string:

```
ob = X.new
X.class_eval( 'def hi;puts("hello");end' )
ob.hi        #=> hello
```

Returning to the earlier example of adding and retrieving class variables from *outside* a class (using class_eval), it turns out that there are also methods designed to do this from *inside* a class. The methods are called class_variable_get (this takes a symbol argument representing the variable name, and it returns the variable's value) and class_variable_set (this takes a symbol argument representing a variable name and a second argument that is the value to be assigned to the variable).

Here is an example of these methods in use:

classvar_getset.rb
```ruby
class X
    def self.addvar( aSymbol, aValue )
        class_variable_set( aSymbol, aValue )
    end

    def self.getvar( aSymbol )
        return class_variable_get( aSymbol )
    end
end

X.addvar( :@@newvar, 2000 )
puts( X.getvar( :@@newvar ) )    #=> 2000
```

To obtain a list of class variable names as an array of strings, use the class_variables method:

```ruby
p( X.class_variables )    #=> ["@@abc", "@@newvar"]
```

You can also add instance variables to classes and objects after they have been created using instance_variable_set:

dynamic.rb
```ruby
ob = X.new
ob.instance_variable_set("@aname", "Bert")
```

By combining this with the ability to add methods, the bold (or maybe reckless?) programmer can completely alter the internals of a class "from the outside." Here I have implemented this in the form of a method called addMethod in class X, which uses the send method to create the new method m using define_method with the method body, defined by &block:

```ruby
def addMethod( m, &block )
    self.class.send( :define_method, m , &block )
end
```

NOTE   *The send method invokes the method identified by the first argument (a symbol), passing to it any arguments specified.*

Now, an X object can call addMethod to insert a new method into the X class:

```ruby
ob.addMethod( :xyz ) { puts("My name is #{@aname}") }
```

Although this method is called from a specific instance of the class (here ob), it affects the class itself, so the newly defined method will also be available to any subsequent instances (here ob2) created from the X class:

```ruby
ob2 = X.new
ob2.instance_variable_set("@aname", "Mary")
ob2.xyz
```

If you don't care about the encapsulation of data in your objects (my definition of *encapsulation* assumes the hiding of internal data, though some people have less rigorous definitions), you can also retrieve the value of instance variables using the instance_variable_get method:

```
ob2.instance_variable_get( :@aname )
```

You can similarly *set* and *get* constants:

```
X::const_set( :NUM, 500 )
puts( X::const_get( :NUM ) )
```

Because const_get returns the value of a constant, you could use this method to get the value of a class name, which is itself a constant, and then append the new method to create a new object from that class. This could even give you a way of creating objects at runtime by prompting the user to enter class names and method names. Try this by running this program:

dynamic2.rb

```
class X
    def y
        puts( "ymethod" )
    end
end

print( "Enter a class name: " )           #<= Enter: X
cname = gets().chomp
ob = Object.const_get(cname).new
p( ob )                                    #=> #<X:0x2bafdc0>
print( "Enter a method to be called: " )   #<= Enter: y
mname = gets().chomp
ob.method(mname).call                      #=> ymethod
```

Creating Classes at Runtime

So far, you have modified classes and created new objects from existing classes. But how would you go about creating a completely new class at runtime? Well, just as you can use const_get to access an existing class, you can use const_set to create a new class. Here's an example of how to prompt the user for the name of a new class before creating that class, adding a method (myname) to it, creating an instance (x) of that class, and calling its myname method:

create_class.rb

```
puts("What shall we call this class? ")
className = gets.strip().capitalize()
Object.const_set(className,Class.new)
puts("I'll give it a method called 'myname'" )
className = Object.const_get(className)
className::module_eval{ define_method(:myname){
        puts("The name of my class is '#{self.class}'" ) }
    }
```

```
x = className.new
x.myname
```

If you run this program and enter Xxx when prompted for the name of a new class, the code will use const_set to create the constant Xxx as a new class; then module_eval is called on this class, and define_method is used to create a method whose name matches the symbol :myname and whose contents are given by the code in the curly brace–delimited block; here this happens to be a single puts statement that displays the class name.

Run this code, and enter Xxx when prompted. An object, x, is created from the Xxx class; its myname() method is called; and, sure enough, it displays the class name:

```
The name of my class is 'Xxx'
```

Bindings

The eval method may take an optional "binding" argument that, if provided, causes the evaluation to be done within a specific scope or "context." It probably won't come as any surprise to discover that, in Ruby, a binding is an object that is an instance of the Binding class. You can return a binding using the binding method. The documentation of eval in the Ruby class library provides this example:

binding.rb

```
def getBinding(str)
    return binding()
end
str = "hello"
puts( eval( "str + ' Fred'" ) )              #=> "hello Fred"
puts( eval( "str + ' Fred'", getBinding("bye") ) ) #=> "bye Fred"
```

Simple as it may look, this example may take a bit of thinking about in order to understand what's going on. Essentially, the first call to puts evaluates str in the current scope where it has a "hello" value. The second call to puts evaluates str in the scope of the getBinding() method where it has a "bye" value. In this example, str happens to be passed as an argument, but this is not a requirement. In the rewritten version here, I've made str a local variable inside getBinding(). The effect is the same:

binding2.rb

```
def getBinding()
    str = "bye"
    return binding()
end
str = "hello"
puts( eval( "str + ' Fred'" )   )            #=> "hello Fred"
puts( eval( "str + ' Fred'", getBinding() ) )    #=> "bye Fred"
puts( eval( "str + ' Fred'" )   )            #=> "hello Fred"
```

Note that binding is a private method of Kernel. The getBinding method is able to call binding within the current context and return the current value of str. At the time of the first call to eval, the context is the *main* object, and the value of the local variable, str, is used; in the second call, the context moves inside the getBinding method, and the local value of str is now that of the str argument or variable within that method. The context may also be defined by a class. In *binding3.rb*, you can see that the values of the instance variable @mystr varies according to the class. So, what happens when you eval those variables with different bindings?

binding3.rb

```
class MyClass
   @@x = " x"
   def initialize(s)
      @mystr = s
   end
   def getBinding
      return binding()
   end
end

class MyOtherClass
   @@x = " y"
   def initialize(s)
      @mystr = s
   end
   def getBinding
      return binding()
   end
end

@mystr = self.inspect
@@x = " some other value"

ob1 = MyClass.new("ob1 string")
ob2 = MyClass.new("ob2 string")
ob3 = MyOtherClass.new("ob3 string")

puts(eval("@mystr << @@x", ob1.getBinding))
puts(eval("@mystr << @@x", ob2.getBinding))
puts(eval("@mystr << @@x", ob3.getBinding))
puts(eval("@mystr << @@x", binding))
```

In Ruby 1.8, you see the following output, showing that the bindings for both the instance variable, @mystr, and the class variable, @@x, are applied:

```
ob1 string x
ob2 string x
ob3 string y
main some other value
```

But in Ruby 1.9, only the binding of the instance variable is applied; the class variable in the current (*main*) context is always used:

```
ob1 string some other value
ob2 string some other value
ob3 string some other value
main some other value
```

Does this mean class variables in given bindings are ignored? Let's try an experiment. Just comment out the assignment to @@x in the main context:

```
# @@x = " some other value"
```

Now run the program again. This time, Ruby 1.9 displays this:

```
ob1 string x
ob2 string x
ob3 string y
...uninitialized class variable @@x in Object (NameError)
```

Clearly, Ruby 1.9 *does* evaluate class variables within a binding. However, it gives preference to class variables, if they exist, in the *current* binding. You need to be aware of this difference if you are migrating Ruby 1.8 programs to Ruby 1.9 or newer.

send

You can use the send method to call a method with the same name as the specified symbol:

send1.rb

```
name = "Fred"
puts( name.send( :reverse ) )    #=> derF
puts( name.send( :upcase ) )     #=> FRED
```

Although the send method is documented as requiring a symbol argument, you can also use a string argument. Or, for consistency, you could use to_sym to transform the string to a symbol and then call the method with the same name as that symbol:

```
name = MyString.new( gets() )
methodname = gets().chomp.to_sym #<= to_sym is not strictly necessary
name.send(methodname)
```

Here is a working example of using send to execute a named method entered at runtime:

send2.rb

```
class MyString < String
    def initialize( aStr )
        super aStr
    end

    def show
        puts self
    end

    def rev
        puts self.reverse
    end
end

print("Enter your name: ")           #<= Enter: Fred
name = MyString.new( gets() )
print("Enter a method name: " )      #<= Enter: rev
methodname = gets().chomp.to_sym
puts( name.send(methodname) )        #=> derF
```

Removing Methods

Recall you created a new method earlier (*dynamic.rb*) using send to call define_method and passed to it the name, m, of the method to be created plus a block, &block, containing the code of the new method:

dynamic.rb

```
def addMethod( m, &block )
    self.class.send( :define_method, m , &block )
end
```

In addition to creating new methods, sometimes you may want to remove existing methods. You can do this using remove_method within the scope of a given class. This removes the method specified by a symbol from a specific class:

rem_methods1.rb

```
puts( "hello".reverse )  #=> olleh
class String
    remove_method( :reverse )
end
puts( "hello".reverse )  #=> undefined method error!
```

If a method with the same name is defined for an ancestor of that class, the ancestor class method is *not* removed:

```
class Y
    def somemethod
        puts("Y's somemethod")
    end
end

class Z < Y
    def somemethod
        puts("Z's somemethod")
    end
end

zob = Z.new
zob.somemethod                    #=> Z's somemethod
class Z
    remove_method( :somemethod )  # Remove somemethod from Z class
end

zob.somemethod                    #=> Y's somemethod
```

In this example, somemethod is removed from the Z class, so when zob.somemethod is subsequently called on a Z object, Ruby executes the first method with that name in the *ancestor* classes of Z. Here, Y is the ancestor of Z, so its somemethod method is used.

The undef_method, by contrast, prevents the specified class from responding to a method call even if a method with the same name is defined in one of its ancestors. The following example uses the same Y and Z classes used in the previous example. The only difference is that this time somemethod is *undefined* using undef_method rather than merely *removed* from the current class using remove_method:

```
zob = Z.new
zob.somemethod                    #=> Z's somemethod

class Z
    undef_method( :somemethod )   #=> undefine somemethod
end

zob.somemethod                    #=> undefined method error
```

Handling Missing Methods

When Ruby tries to execute an undefined method (or, in object-oriented terms, when an object is sent a message that it cannot handle), the error causes the program to exit. You may prefer your program to recover from such an error. You can do this by writing a method named `method_missing`, with an argument to which the missing method's name is assigned. This will execute when a nonexistent method is called:

nomethod1.rb

```
def method_missing( methodname )
    puts( "Sorry, #{methodname} does not exist" )
end
xxx           #=> Sorry, xxx does not exist
```

The `method_missing` method can also take a list of incoming arguments (*args) after the missing method name:

nomethod2.rb

```
def method_missing( methodname, *args )
        puts( "Class #{self.class} does not understand:
                        #{methodname}( #{args.inspect} )" )
end
```

Assuming the previous `method_missing` method were written into a class called X, you could now attempt to call any method on an X object, whether or not that method exists and whether or not it is passed any arguments. If, for example, you were to attempt to call a nonexistent method called aaa, first with no arguments and then with three integer arguments, the `method_missing` method would respond to the invalid method call and display an appropriate error message:

```
ob = X.new
ob.aaa               #=> Class X does not understand: aaa( [] )
ob.aaa( 1,2,3 )   #=> Class X does not understand: aaa( [1, 2, 3] )
```

The `method_missing` method could even create an undefined method dynamically so that a call to a nonexistent method automatically brings that method into existence:

```
def method_missing( methodname, *args )
        self.class.send( :define_method, methodname,
            lambda{ |*args| puts( args.inspect) } )
end
```

Remember that the `lambda` method turns a block (here the code between curly brackets) into a Proc object. This is explained in Chapter 10. The code is then able to pass this object as an argument to `send`, defining a new method with the same name as the `methodname` argument passed to `method_missing`. The effect is that when an unknown method is called on a Z object, a method with that name is created. Run the *nomethod2.rb* program, which contains this code:

```
ob3 = Z.new
ob3.ddd( 1,2,3)
ob3.ddd( 4,5,6 )
```

This gives the following output:

```
Class Z does not understand: ddd( [1, 2, 3] )
Now creating method ddd( )
[4, 5, 6]
```

Writing Programs at Runtime

Finally, let's return to the program you looked at earlier: *eval4.rb*. This, you may recall, prompts the user to enter strings to define code at runtime, evaluates those strings, and creates new runnable methods from them.

One drawback of that program was that it insists that each method be entered on a single line. It is, in fact, pretty simple to write a program that allows the user to enter methods spanning many lines. Here, for example, is a program that evaluates all the code entered up until a blank line is entered:

writeprog.rb

```
program = ""
input = ""
line = ""
until line.strip() == "q"
    print( "?- " )
    line = gets()
    case( line.strip() )
    when ''
        puts( "Evaluating..." )
        eval( input )
        program += input
        input = ""
    when '1'
        puts( "Program Listing..." )
        puts( program )
    else
        input += line
    end
end
```

You can try this by entering whole methods followed by blank lines, like this (just enter the code, of course, not the comments):

```
def a(s)           # <= press Enter after each line
return s.reverse   # <= press enter (and so on...)
end

                   # <- Enter a blank line here to eval these two methods
def b(s)
return a(s).upcase
end

                   # <- Enter a blank line here to eval these two methods
puts( a("hello" ) )
```

```
                              # <- Enter a blank line to eval
                              #=> olleh
puts( b("goodbye" ) )
                              # <- Enter a blank line to eval
                              #=> EYBDOOG
```

After each line entered, a prompt (?-) appears except when the program is in the process of evaluating code, in which case it displays "Evaluating," or when it shows the result of an evaluation, such as olleh.

If you enter the text exactly as indicated earlier, this is what you should see:

```
Write a program interactively.
Enter a blank line to evaluate.
Enter 'q' to quit.
?- def a(s)
?- return s.reverse
?- end
?-
Evaluating...
?- def b(s)
?- return a(s).upcase
?- end
?-
Evaluating...
?- puts(a("hello"))
?-
Evaluating...
olleh
?- b("goodbye")
?-
Evaluating...
EYBDOOG
```

This program is still very simple. It doesn't even have any basic error recovery let alone fancy stuff such as file saving and loading. Even so, this small example demonstrates just how easy it is to write self-modifying programs in Ruby.

Exploring Further

Using the techniques outlined in this chapter, you could create anything from a natural-language parser that can be taught rules of grammar to an adventure game that can learn new puzzles.

In this book I've covered a lot of ground—from "hello world" to dynamic programming. You've explored most of the important and powerful features of the Ruby language. The rest is up to you.

This is where the adventure really begins.

DIGGING DEEPER

There may be times when you want to make sure that your Ruby objects cannot be modified in the ways described in this chapter. Here you will learn how to do this.

Freezing Objects

With all these ways of modifying objects at your disposal, you may be concerned that objects are at risk of being modified unintentionally. In fact, you can specifically fix the state of an object by "freezing" it using the freeze method, which you first encountered in Chapter 12. Once frozen, the data contained by an object cannot be modified, and if an attempt is made to do so, a TypeError exception will be raised. Take care when freezing an object, however, because, once frozen, it cannot be "unfrozen."

freeze.rb

```
s = "Hello"
s << " world"
s.freeze
s << " !!!"   # Error: "can't modify frozen string"
```

You can specifically check whether an object is frozen using the frozen? method:

```
a = [1,2,3]
a.freeze
if !(a.frozen?) then
    a << [4,5,6]
end
```

Be aware that although the data of a frozen object cannot be modified, the class from which it is defined can be modified. Let's suppose you have a class X that contains the method addMethod, which can create new methods with the name given by the symbol m:

cant_freeze.rb

```
def addMethod( m, &block )
    self.class.send( :define_method, m , &block )
end
```

Now, if you have an object, ob, created from the M class, then it is perfectly legitimate to call addMethod to add a new method to class M:

```
ob.freeze
ob.addMethod( :abc ) { puts("This is the abc method") }
```

If you want to prevent a frozen object from modifying its class, you could, of course, test its state using the frozen? method:

```
if not( ob.frozen? ) then
  ob.addMethod(:def){puts("'def' is not a good name for a method")}
end
```

You can also freeze the class itself (remember, a class is also an object):

freeze_class.rb

```
X.freeze
if not( X.frozen? ) then
  ob.addMethod(:def){puts("'def' is not a good name for a method")}
end
```

A

DOCUMENTING RUBY WITH RDOC

 RDoc is the name given to a Ruby source code documentation format and tool. The RDoc tool, which comes standard with Ruby, can process Ruby code files and Ruby's C-code class library in order to extract documentation and format it so that it can be displayed in, for example, a web browser. You can explicitly add RDoc documentation to your own code in the form of source code comments. The RDoc tool can also extract elements of the source code to provide the names of classes, modules, and methods, along with the names of any arguments required by methods.

It is easy to document your own code in a way that is accessible to the RDoc processor. Either you write a block of ordinary single-line comments before the code being documented (such as a class or method) or you write an embedded multiline comment delimited by =begin rdoc and =end. Note that rdoc must follow =begin; otherwise, the RDoc processor will ignore the comment block:

```
=begin rdoc
This is an RDoc comment
=end
```

This example, using single-line comments, is taken from the RDoc documentation:

```
# Determine the letters in a word or phrase
#
# * all letters are converted to lowercase
# * anything not a letter is stripped out
# * the letters are converted into an array
# * the array is sorted
# * the letters are joined back into a string
def letters_of(text)
    text.downcase.delete('^a-z').split('').sort.join
end
```

Here the * characters instruct RDoc to format items as a bulleted list, producing output similar to the following:

```
letters_of(text)
Determine the letters in a word or phrase
    • all letters are converted to lowercase
    • anything not a letter is stripped out
    • the letters are converted into an array
    • the array is sorted
    • the letters are joined back into a string
```

When you are ready to generate the documentation, you just need to run the RDoc processor from the command prompt. To generate documentation for a single file, enter **rdoc** followed by the name of the file:

```
rdoc rdoc1.rb
```

To generate documentation for multiple files, enter the filenames separated by spaces after the rdoc command:

```
rdoc rdoc1.rb rdoc2.rb rdoc3.rb
```

The RDoc tool will create a nicely formatted HTML file (*index.html*) with three panes at the top and a fourth, larger pane at the bottom. The three top panes display the names of the files, classes, and methods, while the bottom pane displays the documentation.

The HTML contains hyperlinks so that you can click class and method names to navigate to the associated documentation. The documentation is placed into its own subdirectory, \doc, along with a number of required HTML files and a style sheet to apply formatting.

You can add extra formatting to your RDoc comments by placing formatting characters around single words or by placing tags around multiple words. Use * and * for bold, _ and _ for italic, and + and + for a monospaced, "typewriter" font. The equivalent tags for longer pieces of text are <b> and </b> for bold, <em> and </em> for italic, and <tt> and </tt> for typewriter.

If you want to exclude comments, or parts of a comment, from the RDoc documentation, you can place it between #-- and #++ comment markers, like this:

```
#--
# This comment won't appear
# in the documentation
#++
# But this one will
```

Special instructions are also available, enclosed between pairs of colons. For instance, if you want to add a title to be displayed in the browser bar, use :title: like this:

```
#:title: My Fabulous RDoc Document
```

Many more options are available with RDoc to enable you to format documentation in a variety of ways and output in alternative formats to HTML. If you really want to master RDoc, be sure to read the complete documentation, available online at *http://rdoc.sourceforge.net/doc/index.html.*

B

INSTALLING MYSQL FOR RUBY ON RAILS

If you are working with Rails, you will need to install a database. Although quite a few choices are available to you, one of the most widely used is MySQL. If you've never used MySQL before, you may find some of the setup options confusing. Here, I'll try to guide you through the process to avoid potential problems. The MySQL main site is at *http://www.mysql.com/*, where you can navigate to the download page for various versions.

NOTE   *This appendix is based on an installation of MySQL 5.0 under Windows. There may be differences when installing other versions on other operating systems. Refer to the MySQL site for additional guidance.*

Downloading MySQL

I will assume you will be using the free edition of MySQL. This is available for download from *http://dev.mysql.com/downloads/*. The current version, at the time of writing, is MySQL 5 Community Server. The name and version number will, of course, change over time. Download whichever is the current (not an upcoming, alpha, or beta) release. Choose the specific version recommended for your operating system (there may be different versions for Win32 and Win64, for example).

You will need to locate the installer for your operating system. For Windows, you can download either the complete MySQL package or, if available, the smaller Windows Essentials package. The complete package contains extra tools for database developers, but these are not required for simple Rails development. For most people, therefore, the smaller Windows Essentials download file is the one to get. You may be asked to select a mirror site, and you may also be shown a questionnaire, which you can fill out if you want.

Installing MySQL

Once the download has completed, run the program by selecting **Open** or **Run** in the download dialog if this is still visible or by double-clicking the installation file via, for example, the Windows Explorer.

NOTE *During the installation of MySQL, some advertising screens may appear. Click the buttons to move through the screens. Some security warnings may also prompt you to verify your intention to install the software. When prompted, you should click the necessary options to continue with the installation.*

The first page of the Setup Wizard will now appear. Click the **Next** button. You can either leave the Typical setup option selected if you are happy to install the software into the default MySQL directory—on Windows that's beneath *C:\Program Files*. If you want to install to some other directory, however, select **Custom**. Then click **Next**. Click **Change** to change the directory.

When you are ready to move on, click **Next**.

You will see the screen stating "Ready To Install the Program." Verify that the destination folder is correct, and then click the **Install** button.

Depending on the version of MySQL, you may now be shown some promotional screens, or you may be prompted to create a new MySQL account, which will let you receive news of changes and updates. These are not an essential part of the software installation, and you can click the Next or Skip button to move on through the installation.

The Wizard Completed dialog now appears.

Click the **Finish** button.

Configuring MySQL

In fact, this isn't the end of the installation after all. With some installers, a new screen pops up welcoming you to the MySQL Server Instance Configuration Wizard. If this does not occur, you will need to load this yourself. On Windows, click the **Start** menu, and then navigate through your program groups to **MySQL ▸ MySQL Server 5.0** (or whichever version number you are using) **▸ MySQL Server Instance Config Wizard**. Click **Next**.

Assuming that this is the first time you have installed MySQL on this machine, you can select **Standard Configuration** (if you are upgrading from an older version of MySQL, you need to select Detailed Configuration, but that is beyond the scope of this simple setup guide). Click **Next**. In the next dialog, leave the default options selected (that is, Install As Windows Service, Service Name = 'MySQL', and Launch the MySQL Server automatically). Then click **Next**.

On the next screen, leave Modify Security Settings checked, and enter the same password (of your choice) into the first two text fields. You will need this password later, so remember it or write it down in a secure location. If you need to access MySQL from another computer, you can check "Enable root access from remote machines." Then click **Next**.

NOTE   *The default MySQL username is "root." The password is the one you just entered. You will need both of these items of information later when creating Rails applications.*

The next screen just gives you some information about the tasks that are about to be performed. Click the **Execute** button.

If you have previously installed or configured MySQL, you may see an error message that tells you to skip the installation. You can click **Retry** to see whether you can bypass this problem. If not, click **Skip**, and then restart the MySQL configuration process, selecting Reconfigure Instance and Standard Instance when prompted.

When everything is installed, click **Finish**.

And that's it!

Can't Find the Database?

When using MySQL with Rails, even following a successful installation of MySQL, Rails may display an error message similar to the following when you try to run your application:

```
no such file to load -- mysql
```

Some versions of Rails (Rails 2.2 and newer) require that the MySQL gem be installed as a separate operation. To do this, enter the following at the system prompt:

```
gem install mysql
```

Another problem may arise on Windows. When you run your application, it is possible that you will see an error message similar to this:

```
The specified module could not be found.
c:/ruby/lib/ruby/gems/1.8/gems/mysql-2.7.3-x86-mswin32/ext/mysql.so
```

If you encounter this problem, you should be able to fix it by making a copy of a file called *libmySQL.dll* from your MySQL binary directory (for example, *C:\Program Files\MySQL\MySQL Server 5.0\bin*) into the Ruby binary directory (for example, *C:\ruby\bin*). Restart your application (shut down and restart the server), and then try running it again.

FURTHER READING

 This appendix contains some of the most useful reading material about Ruby and Rails.

Books

There are many books on Ruby and Rails. In my opinion, the following are among the most useful.

> *Programming Ruby: The Pragmatic Programmer's Guide*
> by Dave Thomas, with Chad Fowler and Andy Hunt ($49.95)
> ISBN: 978-0-9745-1405-5 (second edition)
> ISBN: 978-1-9343-5608-1 (third edition)
> Pragmatic: *http://www.pragmaticprogrammer.com/titles/ruby/index.html*
> A vast guide to the Ruby language and libraries, the so-called Pickaxe

book is generally considered to be an essential Ruby reference. It's not a light read, though, and not (in my view) the best first book on Ruby. All the same, you may need it sooner or later. The second edition covers Ruby 1.8; the third edition covers Ruby 1.9.

Beginning Ruby: From Novice to Professional
by Peter Cooper ($39.99)
ISBN: 978-1-5905-9766-8 (first edition)
ISBN: 978-1-4302-2363-4 (second edition)
Apress: *http://www.apress.com/*

The book provides a gentle introduction to Ruby programming. The explanations are clear, and the code examples are useful. The second edition covers some aspects of Ruby 1.9 but not in much detail. If you already have some programming experience and want an accessible introduction to the world of Ruby, this would be a good book.

The Ruby Way
by Hal Fulton ($39.99)
ISBN: 978-0-6723-2884-8
Addison-Wesley: *http://www.awprofessional.com/ruby/*

This is a solid, in-depth book on aspects of Ruby programming. In the introductory section, the author states that because of its relative lack of tutorial material, "You probably won't learn Ruby from this book." He describes it more as a "sort of 'inverted reference.' Rather than looking up the name of a method or a class, you will look things up by function or purpose." Personally, I think he underestimates the tutorial value of *The Ruby Way*. The author does, however, assume you are already reasonably adept at programming.

The Well-Grounded Rubyist
by David A. Black ($44.99)
ISBN: 978-1-9339-8865-8 (softbound print book, includes free ebook)
Manning: *http://www.manning.com/black2/*

This is, in large part, an adaptation of David Black's previous book, *Ruby for Rails*, though this time the author concentrates on the Ruby language rather than the Rails framework. It covers Ruby 1.8 and 1.9 but is rather vague on the precise differences between the two versions. It's a decent introductory book for fairly experienced programmers.

Agile Web Development with Rails
by Sam Ruby, Dave Thomas, and David Heinemeier Hansson ($43.95)
ISBN: 978-1-93435-616-6 (third edition)
ISBN: 978-1-93435-654-8 (fourth edition)
Pragmatic: *http://pragprog.com/titles/rails4/agile-web-development-with-rails/*

This is the "must-have" book on Rails. Several Ruby programming books might compete for the claim to being essential, but I know of no other Rails book that comes anywhere close to rivaling *Agile Web Development with Rails* for its comprehensive coverage of its subject. The third edition covers Rails 2. The fourth edition covers Rails 3.

Ebooks

If you prefer to read books on your computer screen, here are some good choices—and they are all free.

Learn to Program
The first edition of Chris Pine's book provides a gentle introduction to Ruby.
http://www.pine.fm/LearnToProgram/

Programming Ruby: The Pragmatic Programmer's Guide
This is the first edition of the well-known "Pickaxe" book.
http://www.ruby-doc.org/docs/ProgrammingRuby/

The Little Book of Ruby
This is the baby brother to the book you are currently reading.
http://www.sapphiresteel.com/The-Little-Book-Of-Ruby/

Websites

There are innumerable websites devoted to Ruby, Rails, and related technologies. Here are a few to start exploring.

Ruby language site
http://www.ruby-lang.org/

Ruby documentation site
http://www.ruby-doc.org/

Ruby 1.8 class library reference (online)
http://www.ruby-doc.org/ruby-1.8/index.html

Ruby 1.9 class library reference (online)
http://www.ruby-doc.org/ruby-1.9/index.html

Ruby class library reference (to download)
http://www.ruby-doc.org/downloads/

Ruby on Rails
http://www.rubyonrails.org/

Ruby Inside (information/blog)
http://www.rubyinside.com/

My blog
http://www.sapphiresteel.com/Blog/

D

RUBY AND RAILS
DEVELOPMENT SOFTWARE

 To program Ruby, you will need a Ruby interpreter and an editor or IDE. This appendix lists the primary sources of Ruby and Rails development tools.

IDEs and Editors

Some Ruby programmers like to use simple text editors and run programs from the command line; others like a fully integrated IDE with built-in debugging. Here are some possibilities.

3rdRail
http://www.embarcadero.com/products/3rdrail/
This is a commercial Rails-centric IDE for Eclipse. It currently supports Rails 1.*x* and 2.*x* only.

Aptana RadRails
http://www.aptana.com/products/radrails/
This is a free Rails-centric IDE for Eclipse.

NetBeans
http://www.netbeans.org/ruby/
This is a free Ruby IDE for NetBeans. The future development of Ruby support in NetBeans has now been discontinued.

Ruby In Steel
http://www.sapphiresteel.com/
This is a commercial Ruby and Rails IDE for Visual Studio.

RubyMine
http://www.jetbrains.com/ruby/
This is a commercial Ruby IDE with emphasis on Rails.

TextMate
http://www.macromates.com/
This is a Ruby editor for Mac OS X.

Web Servers

Here are some popular web servers for use with Ruby on Rails.

WEBrick
http://raa.ruby-lang.org/project/webrick/

LightTPD
http://www.lighttpd.net/

Mongrel
http://www.rubygems.org/gems/mongrel/

Nginx
http://www.nginx.org/

Apache
http://www.apache.org/

Databases

If you are using Rails, you will need a database. Often SQLite 3 may be used for local development, while one of the others might be used for deployment.

MySQL
http://www.mysql.com/

SQLite
http://www.sqlite.org/

PostgreSQL
http://www.postgresql.org/

SQL Server Express
http://www.microsoft.com/sql/editions/express/

Ruby Implementations

At the time of writing, versions of both Ruby 1.8 and 1.9 are available, and version 2.0 is promised for some future date. Currently Ruby 1.8.6, 1.8.7, and 1.9.2 are probably the most widely used versions of Ruby. JRuby also has a pretty strong user base. Several other Ruby interpreters, compilers, and virtual machines are available or are in development. Here is a short list of websites that will provide more information on (and downloads of) implementations of Ruby.

Ruby
The "standard" Ruby implementation
http://www.ruby-lang.org/en/downloads/

JRuby
Ruby for Java
http://www.jruby.org/

IronRuby
An implementation of Ruby for .NET
http://www.ironruby.net/

Rubinius
Compiler/virtual machine for Ruby (written largely in Ruby)
http://www.rubini.us/

MagLev
Fast Ruby implementation (in development)
http://maglev.gemstone.com/

INDEX

assert_same, 296

assert_send, 296

assert_thrown, 296

assignment operator (=), 6

assignments, 135–136

    multiple, 133

    parallel, 133

associative arrays. *See* hashes

assoc operator (=>), 141

asterisk (*), 251–252, 260

at sign (@), 23, 100

attr_accessor, 21, 327

attributes, 20–23

attr_reader, 20, 182

attr_writer, 20, 182

B

\B, 260

\b, 260

backquotes. *See* strings

backtrace, 150. *See also* exceptions

BasicObject, 29, 106, 142

=begin, 4

begin..end, 73, 152

=begin rdoc, 345–346

bindings, 334–336

block_given?, 171

block parameters, 70, 157, 168,
       170, 179

blocks, 70, 155–156. *See also* fibers

    {}, 70, 161

    call, 162

    creating methods from, 332, 337

    creating objects from, 162

    do..end, 70, 158

    and for loops, 180

    and instance variables, 176–177

    and iterating arrays, 159–161

    as iterators, 172–174

    and line breaks, 156–157

    and local variables, 177–180

    nested, 165

    parameters, 70, 157, 168,
        170, 179

    passing as named arguments,
        165–170

    precedence, 170–171

    returning from methods,
        175–176

    Ruby 1.9, 155

    scope of, 168, 177

    sorting with, 54

blogs, 316–321

books, on Ruby, 353–354

Boolean operators, 85–86, 93–94

    negation, 86

    precedence, 93

    side effects, 94

break, 75, 90, 158–159

breaking code over a line, 297. *See
    also* line breaks

breakpoints, 289. *See also* debugging

build_message, 296

bytes, reading, 247

C

call, 187

camel case, xviii

capitalization. *See* strings

caret (^), 251, 260. *See also* regular
    expressions

case sensitivity, 2

case statements, 89

    return values, 92

    selectors, 91

catch, 94–96, 152–153

character codes. *See* strings

chomp, 42

chop, 42

classes, 6

    descending from Object, 106

    vs. modules, 192, 205

    as objects, 104

    open, 30

    partial, 30–31

    singleton, 108

class_eval, 329–331

class hierarchy, 15–16

class methods, 97, 98, 122. *See also*
    methods

class_variable_get, 331–333

class variables, 23, 99

class_variables, 332

class_variable_set, 331–333

do, 69, 156
documenting Ruby. *See* RDoc
do..end, 156, 158. *See also* blocks
dollar sign ($), 251–252, 260. *See also* regular expressions; variables
downto, 70–71
dynamic programming, 188, 325
    adding methods, 337
    adding methods to classes, 332
    creating classes at runtime, 333
    creating objects at runtime, 333
    and embedded evaluation, 326
    eval, 327
    freezing objects, 342
    monkey patching, 330
    removing methods, 337
    self-modifying programs, 326, 328
    writing programs at runtime, 340

E

each, 68, 79, 159, 234
    vs. for, 68
    and yield, 81
ebooks, on Ruby, 355
editors, Ruby, 357–358
Eiffel, xviii, 6
else, 145. *See also* exceptions
Embedded Ruby (ERb), 313, 314
encapsulation, 8, 128
    breaking, 131, 333
end, 5
=end, 4, 345–346
ensure, 145. *See also* exceptions
Enumerable, 76–81, 206
    collect, 76
    include?, 76
    including in a class, 79
    max, 76
    min, 76, 78
    overriding methods, 80
equal?, 135, 136, 183
equality, testing for, 136
equal-to operator (==), 56, 136
ERb (Embedded Ruby), 313, 314
Errno, 146–147. *See also* exceptions

eval, 186, 327. *See also* dynamic programming
example programs, xix
exception hierarchy, 142
exceptions, 140
    and $!, 141
    associating with variable name, 141
    backtrace, 150
    begin..end, omitting, 152
    creating custom messages for, 150–151
    custom, raising, 151
    displaying as strings, 148
    else, 145–146
    ensure, 144
    Errno constants, 147
    multiple, 142
    NoMethodError, 142
    raise, 149
    rescue, 140
    retry, 148
    RuntimeError, 150
    subclassing, 151
    TypeError, 142, 342
    ZeroDivisionError, 141
exclamation mark (!)
    at end of methods, 131
    as not operator, 85, 86, 93
extend, 210

F

%f, 43
fibers
    alive?, 276
    and blocks, 275
    dead, 276
    FiberError, 276
    parameters, 276
    resume, 275
    and threads, 275
    yield, 275
File methods, 98
files
    backing up, 219
    closing, 214–216
    copying, 217

super, 18, 23, 27, 104
superclasses, 17–18, 25–30
symbols, 20, 181
  defined, 181, 190
  and dynamic programming, 188
  evaluating, 186
  and regular expressions, 261
  scope of, 184
  sorting, 190
  vs. strings, 182
  uniqueness of, 182
  usefulness of, 188–189
  and variables, 186

T

teardown, 294. *See also* unit testing
TestCase, 292. *See also* unit testing
TextMate, 358
then, 4–5
threads, 263
  creating, 264
  deadlocks, 272
  ensuring execution of, 268–269
  and fibers, 275
  green, 265
  and join method, 268
  main, 266, 271
  mutexes, 272–275
  native, 265
  and pass method, 269, 278–281
  and preemptive multitasking, 265
  priorities, 269
    problems, 270
    setting, 270
  running, 264–265
  scheduling, 281
  and sleep method, 268
  statuses, 266–268
  and stop method, 272, 281
  synchronizing, 273
  time-slicing, 265
throw, 94–96, 152–153
times, 156, 178
to_a, 44, 255
to_f, 3, 216
to_s, 13, 22, 148
to_yaml, 228

U

ubygems.rb, 288
undef_method, 338
unit testing, 292
  assertions available, 295–296
  setup, 294
  teardown, 294
  TestCase, 292
unless modifiers, 88–89
unless tests, 88
until loops, 74–75. *See also* loops
upto, 70–71

V

variables
  class, 23
  class instance, 102
  class methods, 99
  global, 5, 184
  instance, 7, 100
  local, 5
  in modules, 195
  static, 99
vectors, 64–65
vertical pipe (|), 260
View, 310–313, 322–323

W

\W, 260
\w, 260
%W, 46, 49
%w, 49
Waves, 324
WEBrick, 302
  running, 304
  website, 358
web servers, 302, 358
websites, on Ruby, 355
when, 89–91, 92
while loops, 72–74
while modifiers, 72–73, 89
word counter, 258

X

%x, 36, 43

Y

The Book of Ruby is set in New Baskerville, TheSansMono Condensed, Futura, and Dogma.

This book was printed and bound by Transcontinental, Inc. at Transcontinental Gagné in Louiseville, Quebec, Canada. The paper is Domtar Husky 60# Smooth, which is certified by the Forest Stewardship Council (FSC). The book has an Otabind binding, which allows it to lie flat when open.

The Electronic Frontier Foundation (EFF) is the leading organization defending civil liberties in the digital world. We defend free speech on the Internet, fight illegal surveillance, promote the rights of innovators to develop new digital technologies, and work to ensure that the rights and freedoms we enjoy are enhanced — rather than eroded — as our use of technology grows.

PRIVACY   EFF has sued telecom giant AT&T for giving the NSA unfettered access to the private communications of millions of their customers. eff.org/nsa

FREE SPEECH   EFF's Coders' Rights Project is defending the rights of programmers and security researchers to publish their findings without fear of legal challenges. eff.org/freespeech

INNOVATION   EFF's Patent Busting Project challenges overbroad patents that threaten technological innovation. eff.org/patent

FAIR USE   EFF is fighting prohibitive standards that would take away your right to receive and use over-the-air television broadcasts any way you choose. eff.org/IP/fairuse

TRANSPARENCY   EFF has developed the Switzerland Network Testing Tool to give individuals the tools to test for covert traffic filtering. eff.org/transparency

INTERNATIONAL   EFF is working to ensure that international treaties do not restrict our free speech, privacy or digital consumer rights. eff.org/global

EFF.ORG
ELECTRONIC FRONTIER FOUNDATION
Protecting Rights and Promoting Freedom on the Electronic Frontier

EFF is a member-supported organization. Join Now! www.eff.org/support

ABOUT THE AUTHOR

Huw Collingbourne is the technology director at SapphireSteel Software (*http://www.sapphiresteel .com/*), developers of the "Ruby In Steel" Ruby and Rails IDE for Visual Studio and the "Amethyst" IDE for the Adobe Flash Platform. Huw has been a programmer for more than 30 years. He is a well-known technology writer in the UK and has written numerous opinion and programming columns (including tutorials on C#, Delphi, Java, Smalltalk, and Ruby) for a number of computer magazines, such as *Computer*  *Shopper, Flash & Flex Developer's Magazine, PC Pro*, and *PC Plus*. He is the author of the free ebook *The Little Book of Ruby* and is the editor of the online computing magazine *Bitwise* (*http://www.bitwisemag.com/*).

In the 1980s he was a pop music journalist and interviewed most of the New Romantic stars, such as Duran Duran, Spandau Ballet, Adam Ant, Boy George, and Depeche Mode. He is now writing a series of New Romantic murder mysteries.

At various times Huw has been a magazine publisher, editor, and TV broadcaster. He has an MA in English from the University of Cambridge and holds a 2nd dan black belt in aikido. The aikido comes in useful when trying (usually unsuccessfully) to keep his Pyrenean Mountain Dogs under some semblance of control.